UNDERSTANDING
CONTEMPORARY
INDIA

UNDERSTANDING
Introductions to the States and Regions of the Contemporary World
Donald L. Gordon, series editor

Understanding Contemporary Africa, 3rd edition
edited by April A. Gordon and Donald L. Gordon

Understanding the Contemporary Caribbean
edited by Richard S. Hillman and Thomas J. D'Agostino

Understanding Contemporary China, 2nd edition
edited by Robert E. Gamer

Understanding Contemporary India
edited by Sumit Ganguly and Neil DeVotta

Understanding Contemporary Latin America, 2nd edition
edited by Richard S. Hillman

Understanding the Contemporary Middle East
edited by Deborah J. Gerner

UNDERSTANDING
CONTEMPORARY
INDIA

edited by
Sumit Ganguly and
Neil DeVotta

LYNNE
RIENNER
PUBLISHERS

BOULDER
LONDON

Published in the United States of America in 2003 by
Lynne Rienner Publishers, Inc.
1800 30th Street, Boulder, Colorado 80301
www.rienner.com

and in the United Kingdom by
Lynne Rienner Publishers, Inc.
3 Henrietta Street, Covent Garden, London WC2E 8LU

Library of Congress Cataloging-in-Publication Data
Understanding contemporary India / edited by Sumit Ganguly and Neil DeVotta.
    p.   cm — (Understanding)
  ISBN 1-55587-982-9 (hc. : alk. paper)
  ISBN 1-55587-958-6 (pbk. : alk. paper)
  1. India.   I. Ganguly, Sumit.   II. DeVotta, Neil.   III. Understanding (Boulder, Colo.)
DS407.U47 2002
954.05—dc21

                                      2002075167

British Cataloguing in Publication Data
A Cataloguing in Publication record for this book
is available from the British Library.

Printed and bound in the United States of America

The paper used in this publication meets the requirements
of the American National Standard for Permanence of
Paper for Printed Library Materials Z39.48-1984.

5 4 3 2

Dedicated to
Robert L. Hardgrave, Jr.,
mentor, friend, and colleague

Contents

Illustrations

■ **Maps**

■ **Figures**

■ **Tables**

■ Photographs

Preface

This book represents efforts by a dozen scholars to share their expertise on India. Many policymakers and academics correctly see India playing a significant role on the global stage in the twenty-first century. *Understanding Contemporary India* is a good place to begin to appreciate this exceedingly fascinating, complex country. The chapters that follow are designed to acquaint students with India's geography, history, nationalist movement, politics, international relations, economy, society, religions, environmental challenges, and arts and literature. The book is not meant to be the most authoritative statement on India—the country's unrivaled diversity and complexity make such an endeavor impossible in a single volume. Yet, given that there is no comparable work on India geared toward introducing the country across a range of issues, *Understanding Contemporary India* is both unique and necessary.

India's ethnic and cultural diversity is well matched by its geographical diversity, and Chapter 2, by Ashok Dutt, seeks to map India's major geographical features. Indeed, Indian civilization was influenced by its geography so much that ancient Indian literature characterized India as the world in itself. Indians, like peoples elsewhere, have for millenniums sought to negotiate their country's climate and topography. Appreciating Indians' relationship to the land is crucial because it explains the mundane challenges many Indians face as they try to eke out a living from their lands, even as it helps us to understand better how the country's variegated cultures are related to the opportunities and constraints stemming from the country's topographical and geographical features.

In Chapter 3, Manu Bhagavan deals with India's rich historical heritage and its influence on the present. Indians crave modernity, even as they almost fanatically embrace their ancient heritage. This sense of rootedness to a magnificent past is so acute that foreigners sometimes complain that Indians, despite their many social and economic woes and the clear lack of amenities Westerners enjoy, can sometimes appear condescending, even arrogant, on cultural and historical matters. Bhagavan's chapter, which captures India's early history and covers the period up to the emergence of the Indian nationalist movement, clarifies India's rich and eventful history and indicates why Indians can effectively weave their past into the present.

Picking up from where Manu Bhagavan leaves off, Pratap Bhanu Mehta focuses on the Indian nationalist movement in Chapter 4. Britain's association with India immensely benefited the former, but it also introduced the Indians to new technologies, Western learning, and that soon-to-be indispensable lingua franca, the English language. Most important, the British helped mold a sense of national identity that eventually evicted them from India, even as it helped consolidate the Indian union. The most galvanizing figure in this nationalist movement was, of course, Mohandas Gandhi. But there were others who preceded Gandhi, and many important figures who conducted the struggle along with Gandhi. There were also certain significant episodes that helped cement an "Indian consciousness," even as they led to the subcontinent's dismemberment. These protagonists who fought for independence, the events they were influenced by, and the events they themselves influenced are analyzed by Mehta. His chapter supports the contention that nationalism is a modern construct. In conjunction with Chapter 3, it also makes clear how a nation's history provides ample fodder for those elites seeking to generate a nationalist movement: a glorious past helps leaders to appropriate various symbolisms and evoke a grandeur that may not be present if the nation concerned is of a recent pedigree. A country as ancient as India is thus equipped with ample history to legitimize its claims of nationhood, and that is more or less what ensued, especially after Indian soldiers in the British army revolted in 1857. The 1857 revolt, which the British conveniently branded a mutiny, led the British and Indians to resort to grotesque violence against each other. British and Indian relations would never be the same thereafter. But this unfortunate event also cultivated a reactive nationalism that led to India's independence in 1947, and Mehta's chapter provides the requisite details in this regard.

In Chapter 5, Shalendra Sharma discusses India's democratic government structure. If India's nationalist leaders like Jawaharlal Nehru were responsible for ensuring the country's unity through the nationwide Congress Party, recent events have made regional parties a major force in Indian politics. This change has led to coalition governments at the center and weakened the political stability Indians had taken for granted. As Sharma aptly notes, these and numerous other challenges notwithstanding, India continues its remarkable experiment with democracy. Sharma's detailed chapter captures recent political dynamics while introducing India's government structure and providing a useful understanding of democracy in India.

International relations are the subject of Chapter 6 by Sumit Ganguly. Modern India was born amid the bloodshed of the subcontinent's partition and fought four wars—three with Pakistan and one with China—during its first twenty-five years as a sovereign country. India preferred to be nonaligned during the Cold War, but it still sought recognition as a regional power. The country's disputes with Pakistan and China also forced it to turn to the former Soviet Union for security and diplomatic support. The country's international relations were consequently based on its regional security concerns and ambitions, which often led to tensions with other South Asian countries and the United States, as Ganguly explains. The Cold War's end portends new opportunities for India-U.S. relations, but it leaves intact India's concerns regarding Pakistan and China.

In Chapter 7, John Adams covers India's increasingly important and vibrant economy. Occasionally drawing apt comparisons between Indians and North Americans, Adams discusses the Indian village economy as well as the growth in commercial and industrial industries. India began opening up its markets more fully in 1992, and there is little doubt that this country of more than 1 billion people will play a major trading role in the twenty-first century. Yet, as Adams notes, India's exports "constitute less than 1 percent of the world's total," and its potential for being an economic powerhouse in the global arena will depend on how the country deals with problems relating to education and poverty and maintains a political environment conducive to increased foreign investment.

Chapter 8, by Barbara Crossette, focuses on one of India's most marginalized groups: its women. Like much else in India, however, the country's women represent a paradox; for although many millions of women, especially at the village level, are forced to subsist in grueling fashion, India also harbors other millions who engage in every conceivable occupation and represent a growing, progressive cohort of its population. This trend was and is evidenced by former prime minister Indira Gandhi, the current Congress Party leader Sonia Gandhi, and numerous other women party leaders at the state level. As Crossette indicates, India's full potential, however, will never be attained until the country fully liberates its women through education and a sense of economic and social independence that has hitherto only been accessible to the country's middle and upper classes.

In Chapter 9, Holly Sims deals with India's population, urbanization, and the environment. Although population growth and the concomitant demand for resources will determine political stability and economic viability in many of the world's countries, it is especially true for India. Indeed, how India tames its population growth, deals with the megacities that are in the process of springing up, and controls pollution and its environment will heavily affect intraethnic as well as intrastate relations. Sims's chapter captures well India's attempts to shrink its population bulge and also highlights the various challenges it faces in these areas.

Chapter 10, by Ainslie Embree, explores religion in India, home to Hindus, Muslims, Christians, Buddhists, Sikhs, Jains, and a number of other smaller groups that include Zoroastrians and Jews. With religion affecting politics and social and economic interactions at the most fundamental level, India, despite advertising itself as a secular state, is very much a religio-centric state. As Embree notes, India represents a truly religiously pluralistic society not simply because it harbors numerous groups espousing varied religious beliefs, "but because of the very large numbers of people in the different religious groups and their presence in India for hundreds of years." Embree discusses India's major religions and how politicians have manipulated religious sentiments to create communalism.

Vibha Pinglé covers India's caste identities and their resultant social inequalities in Chapter 11. Although the caste system is a Hindu construct and most insidiously affects Hindu society, Pinglé also elaborates on how the country's minorities relate to the caste system. India's caste system, although never static, has been challenged by increasing democratization and education, political contingencies, and the ongoing phenomenon of globalization. Pinglé's chapter succinctly captures the fascinating dynamic that has consequently ensued.

In Chapter 12, Ananda Lal reports on the arts in India. It is hardly contentious to claim that no country in the world has contributed to the arts in as many languages as has India. Thus, Salman Rushdie's comment that India's best literature has been produced in English is easily disregarded because there is, as Lal indicates, perhaps no one alive who can comment authoritatively on all the literature a Babel such as India has produced. Although the West is well aware of Indians writing in English, Lal's chapter introduces the reader to many of the most revered Indian artists who have contributed to the country's commendable multilingual artistic heritage.

Finally, in Chapter 13, Sumit Ganguly and Neil DeVotta summarize the challenges and opportunities facing India domestically and internationally and in doing so return to the issues dealt with here and in the Introduction.

—Sumit Ganguly,
Neil DeVotta

1

Introduction

Sumit Ganguly and Neil DeVotta

India is both a marvel and a paradox. The world's largest democracy, it is a mind-boggling polyethnic society numbering more than 1 billion people. It is one of the world's oldest civilizations and has produced four major religions—Hinduism, Buddhism, Jainism, and Sikhism. It is a mostly agrarian, poverty-stricken country, even though it is a world leader in information technology and space exploration. It is the birthplace of Mohandas Gandhi and the influence for various nonviolent crusades, even as the country ever more confidently brandishes its nuclear capabilities. And it is a young state that is constantly seeking to negotiate the present and future, even as it almost fanatically holds on to a glorious past.

India's constant dance with the past and present is nicely illustrated by the coded message that was sent out in 1974 to signal that the country had successfully tested its first nuclear device. The message, "the Buddha is smiling," referred to Buddha's reaction to a war between his kinsmen and disciples from two principalities. A dejected Buddha is supposed to have said that complete peace was unlikely until all the world's countries were equally mighty. If the code was meant to indicate that Buddha was now smiling because India had achieved a degree of parity in the nuclear realm, it also showed how Indians could connect a modern, revolutionary achievement (with potentially destructive consequences) to something said to have happened 2,500 years ago.

When India gained independence in 1947, its ethnic, caste, and religious conflicts, its security considerations, and its poverty, illiter-

and other social woes caused many experts to predict that the country was bound to disintegrate. India, however, has proven these doomsayers wrong—as it continues to provide fodder to those who want to believe that the country cannot sustain itself in the long run.

India's democracy must rank as its greatest postindependence achievement. In contrast to the situation in many western societies, where low voter turnout is the norm among ethnic minorities, the less educated, and the working class, India's "poor, the underclass, [and] the uneducated . . . tend to vote not less but more than others" (Gill 1998: 166). The country has held thirteen parliamentary elections since 1952; the most recent, in September and October 1999, encompassed 900,000 polling stations, more than 4.5 million election staffers, and an electorate of more than 600 million. Indeed, the idea of the democratic contest and respect for the electoral verdict are so entrenched in India that the country's election commissioner felt it appropriate to advise his U.S. counterparts following the latter's November 2000 election fiasco in Florida. India's vibrant democracy also contrasts with that of other South Asian states, where democracy has been jettisoned in favor of authoritarianism or has been compromised by illiberal and exclusivist practices.

India's strong democracy has resulted from compromise and accommodation with its diverse regional, ethnic, and caste groups. Indeed, at a time when we see widespread ethnic conflict, caused in part by various governments' unwillingness to allow increased autonomy to ethnic groups, India is arguably the only country in the world that is creating ethnoregional states that diminish ethnic tensions. The number of states in the Indian union is twenty-eight (three new states were created in 2000). The government realized early on that states demarcated along ethnolinguistic lines could serve to compartmentalize friction and prevent ethnic unrest from spreading across state boundaries. In the main, this strategy has worked and has led to the decision to continue to create new states. The approach has not been a cure-all for ethnic relations in India, but given the country's extraordinary diversity and complexity, such accommodation along ethnic and regional lines is a major reason that the Indian union is in a stronger position today than it was at independence.

This argument in no way suggests that Indians are able to take their boundaries or unity for granted: the country's borders and national identity continue to be challenged on a daily basis. With regard to borders, the Chinese, who inflicted a humiliating loss on the Indians during the 1962 Sino-Indian war, continue to claim territory in the country's northeast, while rebel groups in the same region militarily challenge the state and its security forces. The country's most costly conflict is taking place in the state of Kashmir, where militants, some of whom are sponsored by the Pakistani government, are engaged in a savage war against India. Pakistan, which was created together with India when the British partitioned the subcontinent in 1947 along principally religious lines, claims that Kashmir—India's only majority Muslim state—is in fact Pakistani territory. India's belief that Kashmir belongs within its sovereign borders, its determination not to give in to its rival, and its realization that giving up territory could create a precedent for other independence-seeking movements within the country has forced it into a debilitating conflict.

The Hindu-Muslim religious divide, which existed prior to independence and was intensified by the subcontinent's partition, also can be seen in the efforts of Hindu extremists who seek to discard India's secular status and instead make it a culturally Hindu country. The most atrocious act of this kind was committed in December 1992, when some 200,000 extremists tore down the sixteenth-century mosque at Ayodhya, claiming that it was built on the exact spot where the Hindu god Rama was born. The subsequent rioting between Hindus and Muslims, the terrible anti-Sikh riots in November 1984 (after Prime Minister Indira Gandhi was assassinated by her Sikh bodyguards to avenge her decision to invade the Sikh Golden Temple in Amritsar), and the March–April 2002 riots in the state of Gujarat signify the tenuous nature of ethnic relations in India.

Ethnic divisions and attempts to dismember the country are not the only challenges facing India. A relatively weak bureaucracy coupled with widespread corruption, especially at the state and local levels, also challenges the country's ability to govern efficiently and to improve its citizens' standard of living. In addition, India's burgeoning population makes the task even more difficult. At independence, India's population stood at 340 million. Just over fifty years later, that figure had reached 1 billion—two and a half times the population of the European Union (EU). Extending the comparison, 343,000 people were born in the European Union in the year 2000; India added that many people during the first week of 2000. When those who had immigrated to Europe were included, the EU states added approximately 1.2 million people in 2000; India added that many people during the first three weeks of that year. At this rate of growth, the country's population could rise to 1.5 billion by 2050. For a country that already has a poor record when it comes to the environment, with millions deprived of clean air and water, such a staggering increase over a fifty-year span will inevitably pose severe challenges to future governments.

This population bulge raises some fundamental questions: Despite having eradicated famines (though still dealing with significant malnutrition problems), how successfully will India be able to feed its millions? To what extent will such a population increase create unrest within and between states, as millions crave more resources or migrate to areas with relatively more resources? To what extent will the already woeful sanitary conditions in the country become worse, and what more dangerous conditions will such growth introduce? Fifty years ago, some experts looked at population trends in India and preached doom and gloom. Today, not only is India self-sufficient in food production, but life expectancy in the past twenty years alone has risen from 55.0 years in 1980 to 62.6 years in 1999; and there is evidence that the use of high-yielding seeds and other developments will allow such progress to be maintained. That noted, only time will tell if the country can consolidate such gains or if future growth estimates are unsustainable.

From an economic standpoint, India has made significant strides since the country began selectively opening its markets in 1991. Although the foreign investment that has since poured into the country is much lower than the amounts invested in China, for example, there is no denying that the relatively open market policies that successive governments have pursued have led to an expansion of the middle class (which was claimed to be the world's largest even before the reforms) and have placed the country on a trajectory to become a major player in the global marketplace. Certain nationalist groups oppose foreign involvement in the country's economy because they see it as compromising India's cultural identity, and their opposition has no doubt complicated the dynamic between foreign investors and their Indian counterparts. Nevertheless, it is clear that India's political and business elites are keen on participating in the global economy. Consequently, although domestic constraints may inhibit India from embracing economic reforms as fast and as fully as the International Monetary Fund and its western friends may like, few if any doubt the country's resolve to become a part of the burgeoning international free-trading regime.

Also in the realm of international relations, the end of the Cold War and the demise of the Soviet Union caused India to reevaluate its security alignments. Heavily dependent on the Soviet Union for diplomatic and military assistance during the Cold War—despite the rhetoric about India being a nonaligned power—the country now enjoys better relations with the United States and even China. It also continues to have healthy relations with Russia and other former Soviet states.

Relations between the United States and India (and, for that matter, between most western countries and India) were frayed in May 1998, when the latter conducted five nuclear tests. (Until that point, India had conducted only one test, in 1974.) Although all concerned had suspected that India and Pakistan possessed nuclear weapons, the May 1998 tests, which Pakistan reciprocated, led to economic sanctions against India. They also forced the world, and especially the recognized nuclear powers, to grapple with how to deal with the new reality. Those opposing India's decision to acquire nuclear weapons argue that it is immoral for a country with so much poverty to expend its scarce resources on such destructive technology. Others, however, argue that the country has no choice but to create the best possible deterrent capabilities against its enemies and that doing so means acquiring nuclear weapons. Although China's relatively advanced nuclear capabilities and its support for Pakistan's nuclear program clearly have been a factor in India's development of a nuclear arsenal, India's determination to be recognized as a regional superpower and a global power has no doubt also influenced its decision to enter the so-called nuclear club. This desire to be considered a global power, coupled with the fact that nearly one in every six persons in the world is an Indian, explains why the country calls repeatedly for a permanent Security Council seat in the United Nations. Whatever other consequences may stem from India's decision to build a nuclear arsenal, it has forced the world to pay even more serious attention to the marvel and the paradox that is India.

■ Bibliography

Gill, M. S. 1998. "India: Running the World's Biggest Elections." *Journal of Democracy* 9, no. 1: 166.

2

India:
A Geographic Preface

Ashok K. Dutt

India is a land of extraordinary diversity—and geography has been one of the principal contributors to its variety and its destiny. Its ancient civilizations have evolved into their modern forms shaped by wide coastal plains, the world's loftiest mountain ranges, and many different—and extreme—climates. With a population of more than 1 billion in the year 2000 and an area covering 1,284,375 square miles/ 3,288,000 square kilometers, India shares what is called the Indian subcontinent (also known as South Asia) with Pakistan, Bangladesh, Nepal, Bhutan, and Sri Lanka (see Map 2.1).

Its largest physiographic region is called the Deccan Plateau, at the northwestern edge of which are the oldest mountains of South Asia, the Aravalli Range, formed 600–700 million years ago (see Map 2.2). The northwestern part of the plateau is also home to an extensive area of volcanic-based soil ("black cotton soil"), making it the country's most important cotton-producing area. The earliest cotton mills were established here, and many of the region's cities—such as Ahmadabad, Nagpur, Mumbai (Bombay), and Sholapur—remain the country's main cotton textile centers. The rugged terrain in the Deccan Plateau, its lack of north-south river valleys, and the east-west alignment of its Vindhya and Satpura mountain ranges were a significant barrier to conquests from the north in the historic past. On only a few occasions was the plateau entirely conquered by the powerful north Indian kings.

When people think of India, they typically think of the Himalayas, home to twenty of the highest peaks of the world. This series of paral-

7

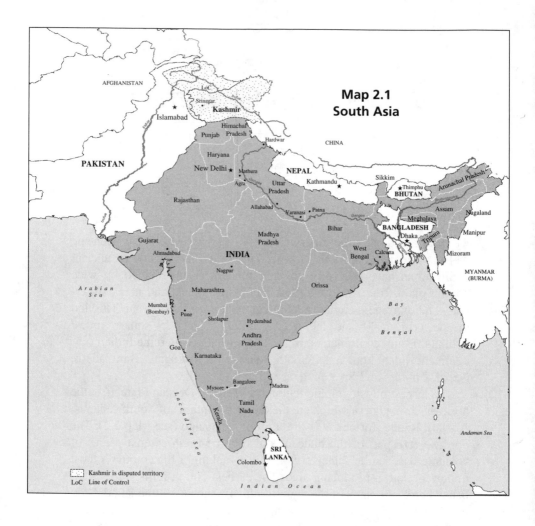

Map 2.1
South Asia

AFGHANISTAN

LoC

Srinagar

Kashmir

Islamabad

Himachal Pradesh

Punjab

Hardwar

CHINA

Haryana

PAKISTAN

New Delhi

Mathura

NEPAL

Sikkim

Arunachal Pradesh

Agra

Kathmandu

Thimphu

Uttar Pradesh

BHUTAN

Rajasthan

Allahabad

Varanasi

Patna

Assam

Nagaland

Ganges

Bihar

BANGLADESH

Meghalaya

Gujarat

Madhya Pradesh

Dhaka

Manipur

Ahmadabad

INDIA

West Bengal

Calcutta

Tripura

Mizoram

Nagpur

MYANMAR (BURMA)

Arabian Sea

Maharashtra

Orissa

Bay of Bengal

Mumbai (Bombay)

Pune

Sholapur

Hyderabad

Goa

Andhra Pradesh

Karnataka

Laccadive Sea

Mysore

Bangalore

Madras

Kerala

Tamil Nadu

Andaman Sea

SRI LANKA

Colombo

Indian Ocean

Kashmir is disputed territory

LoC   Line of Control

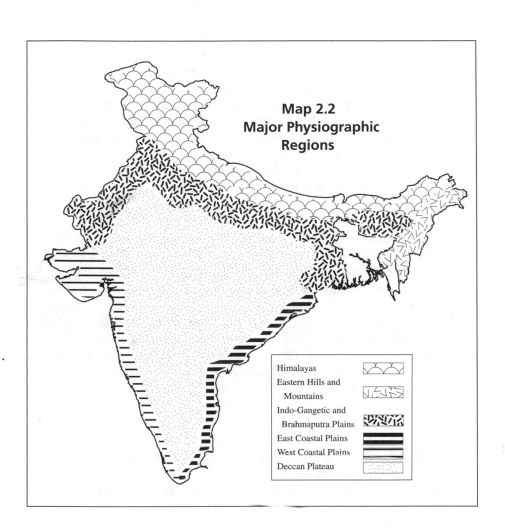

**Map 2.2
Major Physiographic
Regions**

Himalayas	
Eastern Hills and Mountains	
Indo-Gangetic and Brahmaputra Plains	
East Coastal Plains	
West Coastal Plains	
Deccan Plateau	

lel mountain ranges extends nearly 1,500 miles/2,400 kilometers across the northern edge of the country, crisscrossed by long valleys, wide plateaus, rivers, and glaciers. Though the major part of the Himalayas is located in India, a small part lies in Pakistan, and sections of the central and eastern parts are in Nepal and Bhutan. (Mount Everest, the world's highest peak at 29,029 feet/8,848 meters, is in Nepal.)

The Himalayas have proved a blessing in many ways. Air movements caused by the mountains bring the water-laden summer monsoon winds from the Indian Ocean, Arabian Sea, and the Bay of Bengal to the Deccan Plateau and the northern plains, and with them comes the rainfall on which Indian agriculture depends. The lofty east-west mountain system prevents the cold central Asian winds from invading the northern plains during winter, saving India from the frigid cold fronts that plague its neighbors to the north. And the mountains have provided a barrier against foreign invasions and large population movements from the north.

It is also true that the Himalayas, together with the Bay of Bengal in the southeast, the Arabian Sea in the southwest, and the thick forests and rugged terrain of the eastern Assam-Burma ranges, left only the northwestern corridor mountain passes open to continuous human migrations in the past. Nevertheless, through the centuries, trade networks linking India with China and the Mediterranean, invasions by groups of central Asian origin, and British imperialism—to mention only a very few of many factors—resulted in a land of plurality. The story of how India developed into a country of so many political, cultural, religious, and ethnic groups is told in the next chapter, "The Historical Context."

*   *   *

Three main river systems originate in the Himalayas: the Indus and its five tributaries in the northwest, the Brahmaputra in the northeast, and the Ganges (Ganga) and its tributaries in the center. The rich Indus-Ganges plain was the main area of early development on the subcontinent. The productivity of its land and its convenient east-west accessibility—it is possible to travel along the wide plain for more than 1,500 miles/2,413 kilometers without encountering a mountain barrier—made it the seat of political power for many early rulers. Through the centuries, capitals were established in Patna (Pathaliputra), Mathura, Agra, and Delhi—and New Delhi (adjacent to the original city) is the capital of modern India.

The Ganges River, originating in the Great Himalayas of northern Uttar Pradesh, is the most sacred of India's rivers, particularly for the Hindus. According to the Hindu religion, bathing in the Ganges washes away one's sins. There are several pilgrimage places along the river, such as at Hardwar, where the river emerges from the mountains, and Allahabad, where the Ganges and the Yamuna Rivers join. In both Hardwar and Allahabad, millions congregate for the festival of Kumbha Mela. In January–February 2001, the festival of Mahakhumbha Mela, held every twelve years in Allahabad, attracted 100 million pilgrims and visitors. Further eastward, at Varanasi, Hindus have established their most sacred place. For more than 3 miles along the banks of the Ganges at Varanasi, there are continuous ghats (wide steps descending to the river) with numerous temples and bathing areas.

*   *   *

Indian farmers have lived with unpredictable weather since they first cultivated the land more than 5,000 years ago, variously confronting drought and floods. Much of the country experiences a typical monsoon climate, with rainy summers and dry winters: the rains begin in May and last until October, and July and August are the rainiest

The ghats along the Ganges River in Varanasi

months. But the average rainfall across the country varies dramatically, from 7 inches/178 millimeters in the Rajasthan desert, to 26 inches/666 millimeters in Pune, to 71 inches/1,805 millimeters only 100 miles/161 kilometers away in Mumbai, to nearly 400 inches/more than 10,000 millimeters in Mausynram, south of the Assam Hills. Farmers await the onset of the monsoons to sow their rice, maize, and other rainy-season crops. But the rains are unpredictable. They can start early or be delayed by several weeks, and their duration is erratic: it may rain constantly for a week and then not rain again for several weeks. Such extreme conditions frequently resulted in famines in the past. Now, with the existence of railroad networks (first established in the mid–nineteenth century) and other modern means of transportation, grains can be moved from regions with surplus to areas of need. But the dread of drought and floods is so ingrained that an element of fatalism continues to exist: "The monsoon rains which give life as well take it, are uncontrollable and, therefore, it is believed that fate alone ultimately decides the well-being of the people" (Dutt and Geib 1987: 15). The drought-prone areas of India are shown in Map 2.3.

The arid landscape of Rajasthan

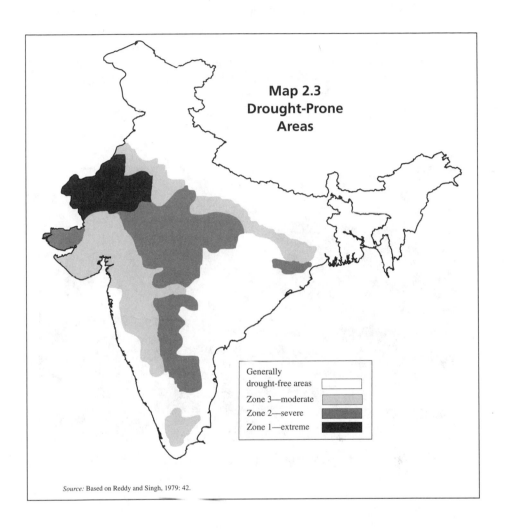

**Map 2.3
Drought-Prone
Areas**

Generally
drought-free areas

Zone 3—moderate

Zone 2—severe

Zone 1—extreme

Source: Based on Reddy and Singh, 1979: 42.

*   *   *

From the alpine lakes of Kashmir to the tropical beaches of Goa, from the deserts of Rajasthan to the lush forests of Karnataka, India encompasses every landscape imaginable. Its peoples have harnessed many of its features to improve their lives—for example, some rivers have been redirected in order to prevent flooding, and others have been dammed for irrigation purposes—but the challenge of sustaining the environment while supporting the development of 1 billion people remains an enormous one. That challenge is discussed fully in Chapter 9.

Lush fields on the way from Chennai to Kodaikanal in Tamil Nadu

■ Note

The author thanks Allen G. Noble, distinguished emeritus professor at the University of Akron, for reading and commenting on the manuscript for this chapter. He also thanks Mayuri Das, graduate assistant in the Department of Geography and Planning at the University of Akron, for help in preparing numerous versions of the manuscript.

■ Bibliography

Dasgupta, Shiba P. 1982. *National Atlas of India.* Vol. 2. Calcutta: National Atlas and Thematic Atlas Organization, Government of India.

Deshpande, Chandra Shekhar. 1992. *India: A Regional Interpretation.* New Delhi: Indian Council of Social Research and Northern Book Center.

Dutt, Ashok K., and Margaret Geib. 1987. *Atlas of South Asia.* Boulder: Westview Press.

Gregory, S. 1989. "The Changing Frequency of Drought in India, 1871–1985." *Geographical Journal* 55, no. 3: 322–334.

Reddy, Nalagatla Bala Krishna, and V. R. Singh. 1979. "Delimitation of Drought-Prone Areas of India: A Geographical Approach." In *Drought-Prone Areas of India*, Nalagatla Bala Krishna Reddy, ed. Tirupathi: Sri Venkateswara University.

3

The Historical Context

Manu Bhagavan

The purpose of this book is to convey an understanding of contemporary India.[1] To this end, most of the book is dedicated to issues that concern the functioning of modern South Asia, but it is important to recognize that all such issues have a connection to the past.

For instance, in May 1998, India and Pakistan exploded nuclear bombs and announced their entry into the world's select club of openly declared nuclear powers. Although the initial aftermath of the detonations was filled with pledges from both countries that they intended to use their weapons only for the purposes of defense and deterrence, it was not long before both turned to serious saber rattling, threatening each other with nuclear annihilation. Since they both possessed atomic capability, their boasts centered on their payload delivery systems, that is, their missiles. India went on about its Prithvi missile, and Pakistan celebrated its Ghauri missile. The names of these weapons correspond to those of two kings, one Hindu and one Muslim, who met in battle in the late twelfth century just northwest of Delhi.[2] That battle, although it had little to do with religion, has been reinterpreted and mythologized by many in both Pakistan and India as the start of a legendary conflict between Hindus and Muslims, a conflict that still rages on today. What I seek to illustrate with this example is the way in which history and its interpretation lie at the center of many modern debates and events. It is therefore important to begin this survey of contemporary India with a grounding in the history of the subcontinent.

Of course, it is not possible to cover in a few pages the totality of the subcontinent's roughly 4,600 years of history.[3] Thus, what follows is an examination of selected events, considered in the context of the larger themes that run through India's past.

■ Ancient India

According to the latest research, India's first major civilization emerged around 2600 B.C.E., shortly after the establishment of the Sumerian and Babylonian cultures in Mesopotamia and the Old Kingdom in Egypt. This Indian civilization grew along the Indus River valley (in parts of the Punjab and Sind in modern-day Pakistan) and had several major urban centers, the most well known being the cities of Mohenjo-Daro and Harappa; it is popularly known today as either the Indus River Valley or Harappan civilization.[4] The Indus civilization, agrarian and peaceful, was also the center of a flourishing trade network. It was not marked by any large art forms (there are no traces of large sculpture, for example, though it is possible that such items might have been constructed from perishable material), but it was rich in resources, with gold found abundantly in the Indus River valley itself and wood and lapis lazuli—plentiful in the Himalayas and the Arabian/Persian Gulf areas, respectively—brought in through trade networks. The Indus cities had an advanced sense of civic planning, with remarkable drainage systems, bath areas, and water tanks. Houses were built of sun-dried mud brick or baked brick. Copper and bronze were used to make a variety of tools, mirrors, and pots, and bone and ivory became tools, jewelry, gaming pieces, and furniture inlay. Silver and gold were used to craft utensils and various kinds of ornaments.

Although each of these things is striking in and of itself, it is the existence of a number of seals carved with various human and animal images and an unknown script that has most excited and baffled scholars of Harappan culture. Perhaps the most famous of these seals is that of a human male with a great horned headdress seated on a raised dais in the center of a number of animals. Although the significance of this figure or that of any of the other seals is difficult to ascertain, some have suggested that the man in the center of the seal is a "proto-Shiva," or a primitive caricature of one of the major, modern Hindu deities. Most scholars, however, believe that a direct correlation between the seated male and Shiva is unlikely, though it is possible that elements of this figure were combined with images from other cultures and civilizations to contribute to the development of the modern-day concept of Shiva. All of this is speculation and will probably remain so until new discoveries, such as the deciphering of the Indus script, shed more light on the matter.

The Harappan civilization began to regionalize around 1900 B.C.E., an event that eventually resulted in the dissipation of the urban-centered culture of the region. The end of this urbanized Indus culture led many scholars to believe that it had somehow been wiped out. The "fact" that a massive wave of nomadic peoples from central Asia (the Aryans) entered the area from the northwest at the same time lent credibility to this theory, and the myth of the Aryan invasion of India was born. Today, there is consensus that there was no invasion and that Harappan culture gradually decentralized on its own. There is also general agreement that a group of people who called themselves *arya* (literally, "noble" or "honorable") and were distinguished by their language, later known as Sanskrit, migrated into the subcontinent from the northwest at some point after the Harappan civilization ended. Archaeologists and linguistic historians disagree over the exact timing and nature of this migration, with some arguing that it coincided with the "posturban" phase of the Indus civilization and others arguing that there was no overlap. What is clear, however, is that it was the Aryans who established Vedic culture in India, the substance of which became the foundation of "Hinduism."[5]

The Aryans moved eastward, eventually inhabiting much of northern India and becoming the dominant people of the region. Although they saw themselves as superior to indigenous groups, there was a good deal of interaction between the two peoples (Olivelle 1998: xxvii). The rub lies in the extent to which non-Aryan beliefs and traditions influenced or joined with the "original" Aryan system(s), if at all, to produce the body of Vedic literature (*Samhitas, Brahmanas, Aranyakas,* and *Upanishads*) that has come down to us. Recent research suggests that there was indeed a good deal of influence.

In addition to the contribution of its literature, Vedic culture had one other major historical effect on Indian society: it resulted in the foundation of what we today call the caste system (see Chapter 11).[6]

The rise of the first major empire on the subcontinent occurred in the middle of the fourth century B.C.E. Mahapadma Nanda had extended the control of the kingdom of Magadha (centered to the east of the Gangetic plain) to include most of northern India and pockets of eastern and central India.[7] The creation of a large, centralized political structure should not be interpreted as the first change in some sort of stagnant, tradition-driven society; to the contrary, the previous 1,000 years had witnessed great philosophical and theological upheaval. A variety of new, controversial, and sometimes conflicting ideas contributed to the evolution of Hindu traditions and to the subsequent foundation of both Buddhism and Jainism. In this context, the establishment of empire in the fourth century B.C.E. reflected the workings of a dynamic society—an important fact to keep in mind to counter modern misperceptions of India as a civilization unchanged "since antiquity."

Mahapadma Nanda was succeeded by his eight sons, all of whom proved to be less competent rulers than he. While the Nandas were squabbling over succession, Alexander the Great had defeated King Darius III of Persia, occupied Kabul, and begun a march into the Punjab. He was forced to stop at the Beas River for fear of a mutiny among his troops, though his brief entry into India had lasting repercussions. Greek records indicate that an Indian named Sandrocottus sided with Alexander and tried to convince him to cross the Beas River and advance on the kingdom of Magadha. Scholars have inferred that "Sandrocottus" refers to a figure known in Indian records as Chandragupta Maurya. A legend surrounding Chandragupta suggests that the Nandas saw the Mauryas as potential rivals and killed the entire clan. As the legend goes, Chandragupta's quick wit helped him to escape. Soon thereafter, he overthrew the Nandas and claimed their capital of Pataliputra, acceding to the throne of Magadha sometime between 324 and 313 B.C.E. He drove out the Greek garrisons left behind following Alexander's retreat and defeated Greek troops again in 305, when Alexander's general, Seleucus Nicator, marched once more on northwestern India. The agreement that ended the conflict between the Indians and the Greeks included some sort of marital alliance. The exact nature of the arrangement is unclear, but some scholars believe that the successors of Chandragupta were part Greek.

Around 268 B.C.E., Chandragupta's grandson Ashoka succeeded to the Mauryan throne. By this time, the boundaries of the Mauryan Empire had reached their peak, encompassing vast portions of south, central, western, and eastern India and virtually all of northern India. Ashoka became disillusioned with warfare after a particularly bloody battle against the eastern state of Kalinga and thereafter became famous for his tolerance and liberalism. He converted to Buddhism (and is celebrated in the Buddhist tradition for his devotion), but he was open to and supportive of many of the other beliefs of the time.

Ashoka is perhaps best remembered for the monuments he had built and the carved pillars he had inscribed with Buddhist teachings. Notably, it is the three-lioned capital of one of those pillars that is used today as the official seal of India. Ashoka died in about 232 B.C.E., marking the beginning of a rapid end to the Mauryan Empire and a 500-year interlude before the rise of the next great centralized authority on the subcontinent.

During these five centuries, trade networks were established that materially and culturally linked India with China and the Mediterranean. Politically, a number of smaller ruling alliances emerged, most notably the Indo-Greeks; the Shakas, a nomadic tribe from east-central Asia; and the Kushanas, another group of central Asian origin that created an empire reaching from central Asia to the Indo-Gangetic plain. These latter two groups governed using large coalitions of local rulers, a pattern quite distinct from the formal, centralized authority of the Mauryas; this form of rule served as the blueprint for many future regional Indian empires. In addition, this period saw great changes in Indian art, the production of the Hindu *Dharmashastra,* or law books, and the widespread adoption of Sanskrit as a literary language. In other words, as before, India was an ever-changing, ever-growing society.

In 320 C.E., Chandra Gupta emerged to rule over an area that generally included the kingdoms of Magadha and Kosala; his reign heralded the beginning of the Gupta Empire. The reigns of Chandra Gupta and those of his successors were marked by constant skirmishes with the Shakas, a conflict that only came to an end in 388 C.E. when Chandra Gupta II, the new king, led his forces to a resounding victory (see Map 3.1).

Several inscriptions indicate that Chandra Gupta II was also referred to as Vikramaditya, a fact that has led many to link him with the mythic king of the same name. Vikramaditya, it is said, was told by the god Prayag that it was his destiny to reestablish the glory of Ayodhya, which was the old capital city of Kosala and the birthplace of the god-king Rama. Vikramaditya was instructed to follow Mata Gajendra, a cow whose milk would flow incessantly at the site of Rama's birth. The king obliged the god and set about his task, designating as Ayodhya the precise site where the milk began to flow, and constructing a marvelous temple there dedicated to Rama.

Whether Chandra Gupta II was "the" Vikramaditya is, of course, debatable. A variety of sources refer to Chandra Gupta II's grandson, Skanda Gupta, as Vikramaditya, and a number of later kings also bore

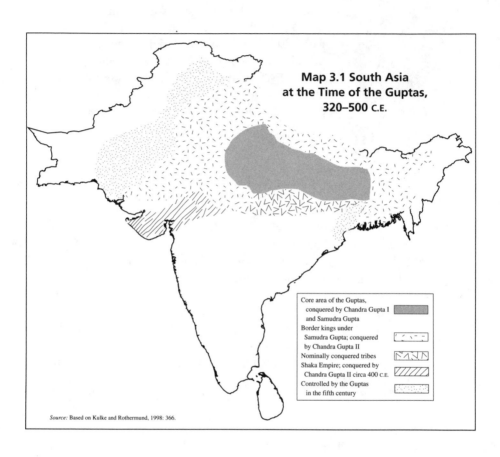

Map 3.1 South Asia at the Time of the Guptas, 320–500 C.E.

Core area of the Guptas, conquered by Chandra Gupta I and Samudra Gupta

Border kings under Samudra Gupta; conquered by Chandra Gupta II

Nominally conquered tribes

Shaka Empire; conquered by Chandra Gupta II circa 400 C.E.

Controlled by the Guptas in the fifth century

Source: Based on Kulke and Rothermund, 1998: 366.

this name. Regardless of the particulars, however, the legend narrated above has played an important role in modern Indian politics. The existence of a historical figure bearing the name of this divine king has allowed some modern-day politicians and revisionist historians to argue that the legend itself is true, at least inasmuch as a fabulous temple was constructed at the site of Rama's birthplace. Using a variety of Hindu religious sources, they claim to have pinpointed the exact location of the birthplace as the site of a mosque built in the sixteenth century and dedicated to Babur, the first Mughal emperor. Hindu nationalists concluded that the temple had been destroyed by Muslims—an egregious assault on the "Hindu nation." We shall return to this controversy a bit later, but the important thing for now is to recognize that this issue has been used to rally a conservative Hindu movement in India and abroad and is at the heart of much of the religious tension in contemporary South Asia.

Chandra Gupta II's time was documented by a Chinese traveler named Fa-Hsien, who came to India in search of authentic copies of Buddhist scriptures. Fa-Hsien's observations indicate that India at this time was generally a peaceful and safe society where Buddhism and Hinduism flourished. Perhaps most notably, Chandra Gupta II's reign was recognized for its "Nine Jewels," an array of distinguished artists who graced his court. Most prominent of this group was Kalidasa, the poet who wrote a number of masterpieces, among them the play *Shakuntala* and the epic *Raghuvamsa*, a retelling of the story of Rama that blended divine myths with the exploits of various Guptas.

Following the death of Chandra Gupta II in 415, the Gupta Empire was ruled by his son, Kumara Gupta, and then his grandson, Skanda Gupta. The reigns of both were religiously tolerant and relatively peaceful, though the latter part of Kumara Gupta's reign and most of Skanda Gupta's were marked with some conflict with the Hunas.[8] Skanda Gupta's successors, who became mired in controversies over who should rule, suffered a number of military setbacks at the Hunas' hands, and the influence of the Guptas came to an end.

In 606 C.E., Harsha established an empire centered in the city of Kanauj. He ruled for the following forty-one years, restoring some of the former glory of the Guptas. A patron of the arts and a philosopher, he was fond of pomp and ceremony, but he also tended to the needs of the peasants. His reign was described by Huan Tsang, another Chinese traveler who, like Fa-Hsien, had come to India in search of Buddhist manuscripts. The differences between the accounts of Fa-Hsien and Huan Tsang are remarkable, with the latter commenting on the decline of Buddhism and the rise of crime. Harsha controlled all of north India, but his was an authority held together mostly by the sheer force of his personality, and the empire quickly faded upon his death.

While all of this was going on in north India, a massive and complex transmission of culture, language, and philosophy was occurring from north to south. Brahmans (members of the priestly Hindu caste) played a major role in this process of transmission, migrating to the south to spread their knowledge and their beliefs. Buddhism and Jainism, however, were also highly influential.

Politically, the south was the home of numerous regional empires and conflicts. It is difficult to deal with any one southern kingdom outside the context of the others or to call one more important than the other. Still, it is necessary to mention the contribution of the Cholas, who rose to prominence in the late tenth century. The Chola kingdom reached its apex under the leadership of its greatest king, Rajendra, in the early eleventh century. Because of a trade dispute, Rajendra launched a naval campaign that resulted in India acquiring its first overseas empire, with control extending into parts of modern-day Malaysia and Indonesia.[9]

Following the decline of the Cholas in the early twelfth century, a variety of new regional powers emerged—the Hoysalas, centered in Mysore, the Kakatiyas, centered in modern-day Andhra Pradesh, and the Yadavas, centered in Devagiri—that would remain dominant until the early fourteenth century. It was at this time that several concurrent circumstances came together to again alter the Indian landscape.

■ Medieval India

The dawn of the medieval age of India marks the beginning of what is perhaps the most contested and most misunderstood period of South Asian history. One common misinterpretation of this period involves the notion that it began with an Arab "conquest" of Sind (in what is now southeastern Pakistan) in 712 C.E., a story that suggests many misconceptions about the initial Muslim interaction with the subcontinent. In fact, Arab Muslims had established trading posts along the subcontinent's southwestern coast by the end of the seventh century. A variety of military campaigns did take place in Sind, but these were not different from the military activity that typically accompanied the interregional migration of peoples in other parts of the subcontinent.

Around 1000 C.E., the ruler of the Ghaznavid kingdom (in modern Afghanistan), Mahmud, began a series of raids into northwestern India. During these raids, he looted a number of places, including a variety of religious sites, the most notable being the legendary grand Hindu temple of Somnath. Modern research has revealed that the primary factor driving Mahmud was a need to acquire wealth to fund his expansionist campaigns westward into central Asia. This conclusion is supported by the fact that, although he continued his campaigns in India for more than twenty years, he did not attempt to incorporate any new Indian territory into his empire until 1020, when he left a governor behind in Lahore (in what is now Pakistan). The Somnath expedition was his final foray into India, and when it ended in 1026, Mahmud spent the rest of his life concentrating on his military campaigns in central Asia.

The issue of temple desecration is one that has been greatly misunderstood. It was common for rulers (of any faith) to patronize local religious establishments in an effort to legitimize their own rule. When rulers from different regions attempted to expand their spheres of influence, they often plundered temples, not only to fund their military campaigns (Hindu temples in particular were renowned for their lavish displays and ornate edifices), but also to strike at the symbols of leadership of their local opponents.[10]

In the late twelfth century, Muhammad Ghuri took charge of Ghazni and in 1175 began a series of raids into India. His aim, unlike Mahmud's, was to acquire territory. It was during one of these raids in the Punjab in the winter of 1190–1191 that he encountered Prithviraj Chauhan, ruler of Delhi and Ajmer and leader of a confederacy of local rulers put together to halt Ghuri's expansion. Prithviraj emerged as the victor, forcing Muhammad Ghuri to return to his base in Afghanistan. Regrouping, Ghuri attacked again one year later, with the Ghurid forces emerging as the victors this time.

What happened to Prithviraj thereafter is a bit unclear. A number of myths have arisen around him, suggesting that he and a loyal servant killed their Afghan captors and then killed themselves in a heroic effort to protect their honor. Other accounts suggest that Prithviraj was eventually put to death for treason, though his son was made governor of Ajmer. Several of Prithviraj's coins have been found with the word *amir* printed in Sanskrit, and some scholars have taken this to mean that he had at some point accepted the Ghurid authority.

Although there are conflicting interpretations of what happened and historians by and large admit the limits of their knowledge on this topic, the story has taken on a life of its own, becoming (as noted at the

The Lingaraj temple in Bhubaneswar, Orissa, built around 1100, is one of the most splendid of the many erected for the worship of Shiva. It is still a center of pilgrimage and devotion today.

Ainslie T. Embree

beginning of this chapter), a rhetorical pawn in the nuclear chess match between India and Pakistan. The most disturbing thing about this situation is the rigid certainty with which both sides interpret the story for their own political purposes.

Muhammad Ghuri returned to Afghanistan following his victories, but he left behind one of his slaves, Qutb-ud-din Aibak, as his viceroy in India.[11] Ghuri was assassinated in 1206, and Aibak subsequently became the sultan of Delhi, the first major independent Muslim ruler of north India. The Delhi Sultanate remained a significant political force on the subcontinent until the sixteenth century. Aibak, who was freed from slavery in 1208, was felled by a *buskhazi* accident in 1211.[12] He was succeeded by his son, whom the court nobles quickly replaced with Aibak's son-in-law, Shams-ud-din Iltutmish, who firmly established the authority of Delhi.

Iltutmish's reign was concurrent with that of the Mongol leader Genghis Khan. The Mongols, for the most part, were occupied with activity in central and western Asia and did not really involve themselves much with the subcontinent, though they did make a foray or two into the Punjab. More significantly, Mongol activity disrupted cultural activities in Baghdad, and as a result, huge numbers of scholars, poets, and artists migrated from Baghdad to the subcontinent, the one region that they felt was free of Mongol interference. This massive influx of talent into India brought with it a period of dynamic cultural change.

During his tenure in office, Iltutmish called a meeting of religious scholars, at which he argued that "Hindus"—meaning non-Muslim people under the authority of Delhi—were the majority community of the kingdom and should therefore be given, as a community, access to the privileged positions of administration and authority. It was in this way, he argued successfully, that the stability and legitimacy of the Delhi Sultanate could be maintained.

Iltutmish was succeeded by his daughter, Raziya, in 1236. Though she was capable at both military matters and statecraft, she fell victim to palace intrigue three years after her assumption of the throne. Despite her short reign, Sultana Raziya has acquired legendary status, with her courage, skill, and gender all contributing to her mythology.[13]

Raziya's fall was masterminded by the military oligarchy and aristocracy known as "the Forty." Her successor, Balban, was originally a member of this group, but upon taking the throne, he set about the task of eliminating the Forty and consolidating the authority and administration of Delhi. Balban, like Iltutmish and Aibak, had been a slave at one time, and for this reason we refer to this lineage as the Slave Dynasty.

Balban's death marked the transition of the Delhi Sultanate from the Slave Dynasty to the Khalji Dynasty. This process was subsequently repeated three more times, as the Tughlaqs, Sayyids, and Lodis each became the ruling family in Delhi. The period of the Delhi Sultanate was one of great intellectual, artistic, and philosophical rigor, with the sultanate's rulers patronizing some of the world's most renowned artists, Amir Khusrao being a prominent example. Some of India's most well known architecture also resulted from sultanate sponsorship, notably Delhi's Qutb Minar and Hauz Khas.

The sultanate was hardly a single, monolithic entity. Its boundaries, in fact, were continually shifting, as territory was added to or lost from the periphery. These challenges to Delhi's authority involved a varied

Ainslie T. Embree

One of the many tombs in Lodi Gardens, Delhi,
of a member of the Lodi Dynasty (1451–1526)

mix of inter- and intraregional issues, economic disagreements, and religious disputes. Significantly, the constant fluctuation and negotiation of power was a driving engine of cultural growth, as regional kingdoms patronized a variety of local talent, generating new forms of artistic and architectural expression.

A common myth in many histories of this period is that one such regional breakaway occurred in the early fourteenth century during the reign of the Tughlags. According to these accounts, a local southern prince named Harihara was captured by sultanate forces, whereupon he converted to Islam and became a member of the conquering force. He then returned to the south, unified the region, reconverted to Hinduism, and declared himself the independent ruler of the region. It was in this way that the famed empire of Vijayanagar was born.

Recent research has suggested that Harihara was in fact a vassal of the local Hoysala king. Around 1336, he took over the throne and made a number of regional alliances, but only after the last Hoysala king had died and only with support from some of the surviving members of the Hoysala royal family. The capital of this new kingdom was near the old Hoysala stomping grounds of Hampi, a newly constructed city known as Vijayanagar, or "city of victory." In an effort to help legitimize their rule, Harihara and his descendants became patrons of identifiably religious (Hindu) art and architecture.

The empire of Vijayanagar continued to grow and flourish for nearly two hundred years, ultimately comprising most of south India. It reached its peak in the early sixteenth century under the leadership of Krishna Deva Raya, celebrated for his patronage of massive Hindu temple complexes throughout the kingdom. Krishna Deva Raya oversaw a period of economic growth and expansion, generated in large measure by a burgeoning trade with the Portuguese, based in Goa, and with various other kingdoms throughout the subcontinent.

An easy mistake that a number of scholars have made is to contrast the religious aspects of the great kingdoms of this period and to set Vijayanagar's "Hinduness" in opposition to other regions' "Muslimness." This kind of characterization is misleading and misguided, overlooking the intrareligious tensions that existed and failing to accurately evaluate the importance that other factors, such as economics, may have played in forcing politicians and military personnel to turn to religion as a means of mobilizing support. Moreover, there was a great deal of cultural and technological exchange between Vijayanagar and the "Muslim" kingdoms, a fact that further blurred the distinctions between them. Lastly, "Hindu versus Muslim" characterizations generally ignore the development of the bhakti and Sufi traditions, devotional and mystical elements in both religions that tended to have more in common with each other than with any strict scriptural code.[14]

■ Mughal India

The medieval period of the subcontinent's history drew to a close in 1526, when Babur, a descendant of the Mongol Genghis Khan and the Turk Timur (or Tamerlane), engaged Ibrahim Lodi, the last sultan of Delhi, at the Battle of Panipat. Babur was the decisive victor of this battle, in part because of his forces' superior use of cavalry and artillery. As a result, Babur assumed control of the Indian capital, becoming the founder of a dynasty that would continue to hold virtually uninterrupted sway for the next 300 years.

Babur's reign has taken on enormous importance in contemporary India. As we saw in the discussion of Chandra Gupta II, a controversy has erupted regarding the construction of a temple at the site of Rama's birth in Ayodhya. The controversy has its origins in the nineteenth century, but it has been an issue of particular political prominence since the

1980s. A mosque dedicated to Babur, the Babri-Masjid (Mosque of Babur), built by one of his generals, Mir Baqi, stood at the precise location that Hindu activists claimed as the birthplace of Rama. Together with the legend of Vikramaditya and the common misperceptions of temple pillaging discussed earlier in this chapter, the existence of the mosque led many to argue that Rama's temple had been destroyed by Muslims and that this situation needed to be rectified by eliminating the mosque and reconstructing the temple. Violence erupted around this issue in the early 1990s, the worst since the partition of India and Pakistan. The mosque was destroyed in December 1992, although there is no archaeological or historical evidence that suggests that any temple existed at this location during Babur's time. Again, the main point here is the role that history, real and imagined, plays in affecting the present.

Babur was succeeded by his son, Humayun, who was immediately challenged by a local Afghan chief named Sher Shah Suri. Humayun was defeated in battle by Sher Shah in 1540 and was forced to flee to the protection of the shah of Persia. Sher Shah, who ruled until 1545 (followed by his son Islam Shah), is credited with constructing the administrative framework that would be the foundation of later Mughal rule. His principal reform was in the area of taxation, but he also created an extensive system of toll-free roads, complete with managed scenery and lodging for travelers, with local villagers held responsible for safety. The result was a prospering trade that again helped to fill Delhi's coffers.

Nevertheless, Humayun retook Delhi in 1555, and when he died in January 1556, he left the empire to his son, Akbar. Regarded as the greatest Mughal emperor, Akbar immediately vanquished the Suri forces at the Second Battle of Panipat in 1556.

Highly influenced by Sufi tradition, Akbar eventually created his own personal spiritual path, the Din-e-Ilahi (divine faith). At its peak, the Din-e-Ilahi had only eighteen members, virtually all of them Akbar's closest friends and courtiers. But it is important for what it represents: Akbar's wide-ranging interest in and passion for philosophical and theological exploration. Also notable was the diversity of Akbar's court, which included Turks, Afghans, Persians, and various regional peoples, with Persian used as the court language.

Prince Salim, named for the Sufi saint Shaikh Salim Chishti, succeeded his father to the throne in 1605, whereupon he took the name Jahangir. Almost immediately, Jahangir faced a challenge from one of his sons, and his attempt to put down the rebellion brought him into conflict with Guru Arjan, leader of the Sikhs.[15] Because Arjan had aided Jahangir's rebellious son, he was put to death, which began a long, bitter conflict between the Sikhs and the Mughal government.

Jahangir was married to Nur Jahan, a politically active and powerful woman who directed that vast sums of money be spent on charities and, in particular, the needs of destitute women. It was her niece, Mumtaz Mahal, who became the wife of Jahangir's son, Shah Jahan, and the inspiration for the Taj Mahal. The reign of Jahangir and Nur Jahan was the Mughal Age of Splendor, for they lavishly patronized art and architecture.

The grandeur of Jahangir's time continued into the reign of Shah Jahan. An example of the opulence of this period can be found in the description of Shah Jahan's Peacock Throne. It was bejeweled from top to bottom, encrusted with sapphires, rubies, and emeralds. Two peacocks stood watch over a garden of jewels studded with rubies, diamonds, emeralds, and pearls. A parrot cut from a single emerald stood between the peacocks (Davies 1989).

The creation of the Taj is, of course, the achievement for which Shah Jahan is best known. But his vision helped drain the Mughal treasury, already under strain from the years of lavish spending. This began to have some minor effects during the reign of Shah Jahan's successor and took a harsher toll thereafter.

Lynne Rienner

The Taj Mahal

Shah Jahan's heir apparent was his scholarly son Dara Shikoh, whose Persian translation of the *Upanishads* (Hindu mystical writings) later served as the basis for the English version that influenced Ralph Waldo Emerson and the Transcendentalists. Dara Shikoh also studied Sufism and Hindu Vedantism and concluded, as many had before him, that there was lots of common ground between the two philosophies.

For all his talents at scholarship and theology, Dara Shikoh was relatively uninitiated in the ways of politics. He was attacked by his brother Aurangzeb, captured, and put to death. Aurangzeb formally ascended the throne in 1659. In Aurangzeb's view, his predecessors had not been faithful enough to the views espoused by the ulema, the Muslim religious scholarly community. Aurangzeb struggled his whole life to live up to what he perceived to be the ideals of a good Muslim. He appointed a police force in all major cities to enforce Islamic law and to ban such activities as drinking, gambling, and prostitution. He forbade narcotics and banned sati, the practice of immolating widows on the funeral pyres of their husbands. He also got rid of all taxes he thought were not specifically authorized by Islamic law. This last move was very popular with the people but was a staggering blow to the already weak treasury. In the midst of these dramatic changes, Aurangzeb also extended the borders of the Mughal Empire to their farthest reach, encompassing virtually the entire subcontinent.

The combination of financial strain, overextended forces, and dictated Muslim orthodoxy led to various authority struggles, with pockets of resistance appearing on the periphery as well as in the heart of Mughal territory. The Sikhs, at odds with the Mughals since the time of Guru Arjan, were particularly fierce in their resistance, eventually establishing as markers of their faith and identity the visual characteristics—the *kes* (uncut hair), *kanga* (wooden comb), *kirpan* (sword), *kara* (steel bangle), and *kachera* (short breeches)—by which they are distinguished today.

The Mughals also faced a threat from Shivaji, a leader based in the Deccan Plateau, in modern-day Maharashtra, who had taken advantage of economic dissatisfaction and a backlash against orthodoxy to create a powerful military base of operations. Shivaji had already gained legendary status for resisting the forces of Bijapur, a local kingdom in which his father had served as a military officer. As the story goes, a general from the Bijapuri army had requested a meeting to call for a truce, and only he and Shivaji were to attend. As a sign of their impending friendship, the two men embraced. The general then drew a dagger and attempted to kill Shivaji, who, suspecting a trap, had come wearing tiger claws attached to his fingers. Shivaji evaded the dagger and gutted the general, giving rise to theories about a "divine mission" and "invincibility." Shivaji declared himself maharaja (king) of the western portion of India in 1674. His kingdom would serve as the basis for the Maratha Empire, one of the great eighteenth-century powers.

Shivaji himself has been appropriated by a number of political groups in contemporary India. Hindu conservatives name him as a source of inspiration for their movement, casting him as a patriot who stood against Muslim invaders. The Mumbai-based Shiv Sena, for example, one of the most activist of Hindu nationalist organizations, takes its name and symbols from the myths and legends surrounding Shivaji. In contrast, the historical king incorporated people of many faiths, including Islam, into his administration and entered into a number of alliances with so-called Muslim kingdoms.

The period following Aurangzeb's death in 1707 has often been mislabeled a period of decline. In truth, it was more a period of decentralization, as regional powers and entities began to take advantage of the weaknesses in Mughal central authority. Merchants also grew in power during this time. It is important to recognize, though, that the Mughals themselves, although greatly reduced in stature, remained in power for another 150 years.

■ The Emergence of British India

The British had been in India since the time of Akbar. Originally attracted by tales of a dazzling Orient, they established the British East India Company in 1601 as a commercial venture meant to take advantage of the wealth and riches of India. There were several branches of the company in the subcontinent, but they were primarily centered in the northeastern region of Bengal.

By the eighteenth century, India had become a site of great interest to several of the emerging expansionist powers of Europe, with England and France vying for supremacy. The rivalry between these powers fed paranoia, and they expended a great many resources fortifying their establishments in India. Although some regional authorities were displeased with such activity, others, happy with the assistance they were receiving from the British East India Company, did not seem to mind.

In 1756, the nawab of Bengal, a regional ruler who had emerged from the decentralization of Mughal authority, asked the British to halt their fortifications in Calcutta. They refused, and he attacked and routed them. The treatment of British prisoners following this incident gave rise to the myth of the Black Hole of Calcutta, in which it was claimed that hundreds of British captives were killed by suffocation in their cells. Tales of the Black Hole were exaggerated, allowing the British to demonize Indians, paint them as backward and uncivilized, and, in the process, galvanize British support for a military response.

Robert Clive, who had been based in Madras, responded in 1757 at the Battle of Plassey, which he won thanks to the financial support of a number of Bengali banking families and the military aid of a traitor within the nawab's forces.[16] It was followed by the Battle of Buxar in 1764, in which the British defeated the combined forces of the regional northeastern powers and the Mughal emperor. The twin victories at Plassey and Buxar marked the emergence of the British as one of the great powers on the subcontinent. They spent the rest of the eighteenth century fighting the other major kingdoms.

Though there were hundreds of small principalities, several major centers of influence besides those under the British and the Mughals had emerged by this time, notably the Sikh kingdom in the northwest, the Maratha Empire in the west, and the kingdoms of Hyderabad and Mysore in the center and south. The Marathas soon fell to internal dissent. The British had waged several wars against Mysore but had lost or stalemated each conflict, in part because of the military genius of Mysore's successive rulers, Haidar Ali and Tipu Sultan. Eventually, however, taking advantage of regional disputes and fears, the British convinced Hyderabad to enter into a treaty with the British East India Company, and together they defeated Tipu at his home base in Srirangapatnam (just outside of modern Mysore) in 1799. The Hyderabadi treaty became the prototype for all future agreements between the British and local rulers.

The Sikhs, led by Ranjit Singh, remained the last major holdout (though their location on the periphery of the subcontinent in the northwestern corner meant that the defeat of Tipu was really the beginning of British supremacy in India). But after Ranjit Singh died in 1839, the British took advantage of internal disputes and gradually took over the area. Charles Napier's capture of Sind (southeastern Pakistan) in 1842 led to the myth of his famous one-word communiqué, "Peccavi," Latin for "I have sinned."[17]

The British spent the first part of the nineteenth century consolidating their power and trying to find a philosophical stand that would explain and warrant their presence in India. Anglicist, Orientalist, and

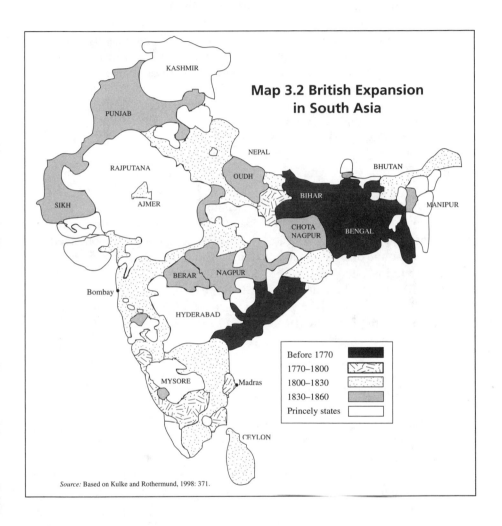

Map 3.2 British Expansion in South Asia

KASHMIR

PUNJAB

RAJPUTANA

SIKH

AJMER

NEPAL

OUDH

BIHAR

BHUTAN

MANIPUR

CHOTA NAGPUR

BENGAL

BERAR

NAGPUR

Bombay

HYDERABAD

MYSORE

Madras

CEYLON

Before 1770	
1770–1800	
1800–1830	
1830–1860	
Princely states	

Source: Based on Kulke and Rothermund, 1998: 371.

Utilitarian interpretations and explanations all initially influenced British actions, though the "Minute on Education" produced by Thomas Babington Macaulay in 1835 marked the onset of outright racist, patronizing, and discriminatory policies. The "Minute" specifically urged the creation of an educated elite of "Brown Englishmen" to serve as go-betweens from British masters to the Indian masses. Many Indian elites were all too happy to take their place in the British system, and their collaboration helped secure and stabilize colonialism. Various other Indian intellectuals responded to English criticisms with a series of reform movements designed to redefine, renegotiate, or reinvigorate Indian customs and practices.

From 1848 to 1856, the new governor-general, Lord Dalhousie, pursued the doctrine of lapse, under which the British assumed direct control over native territory if local rulers were guilty of "misrule" or if they had no legitimate heir. The actual application of this policy was haphazard, as the British frequently changed the definitions of "misrule" and "legitimate heir" and in some instances leveled false charges against rulers. Their callousness in this and other regards combined with economic disparity to anger various groups of people across class, caste, religious, and regional lines. These tensions eventually exploded in the first major show of resistance to British domination, the revolt of 1857. The British were the victors in this conflict, but the dam had been broken, and the next few decades would see the emergence of India's nationalist movement.

■ Conclusion

The subcontinent's long and diverse history reveals a dynamic, ever-growing society. The complexities and nuances of this history extend into the present day, the past serving both active and passive roles in the modern subcontinent. An awareness of these roles, then, is fundamental to our understanding of contemporary India.

Today's nationalist organizations, for example, have based their exclusionist ideologies and rhetoric on imagined notions of an ideal past. Hindu nationalists believe that India is and always has been a Hindu homeland, one that has been under assault for centuries, particularly by Muslims. Muslim nationalists argue that Muslims have always constituted a separate and distinct community, one that had once witnessed a golden age but has since declined. Each philosophy feeds off and into the other, creating a circular logic that justifies and sustains both.

It is interesting to note here that the constructed notions of *nation* and *community* on which these ideologies are based did not exist during the period of history surveyed in this chapter. India as it is presently defined, in other words, is a relatively new concept. Historically, this region was home to multiple political, cultural, religious, and ethnic groupings and forms of government, with boundaries of authority that were constantly changing and being renegotiated. South Asia, in short, was a land of plurality.

Indeed, modern India's popular slogan, "Unity in Diversity," seems to recognize plurality, both historical and contemporary, as a source of strength and national character. Yet, current-day nationalisms claim otherwise, denying both the historical existence of this multiplicity and any positive values that might be attributed to it.

Recent research has revealed that nationalism in South Asia in fact derives from the very process it was designed to negate: colonialism. The two share a dialectic relationship, that is, an interdependent, at times contentious, relationship. With Indian independence in 1947, when colonialism ceased to exist in its overt, structured, bureaucratic form, nationalism was left without its complementary other. Postcolonial nationalism was therefore predetermined to break down, to *fragment,* along the divisions in society that colonialism had created. It is in this way that communalism, the creation of communities on ethnic or religious lines to the exclusion of other groups, took center stage, replacing colonialism in a new dialectic relationship with nationalism.[18] The British imperial project and the Indian nationalist movement, then, are crititcal to our understanding of contemporary India and are dealt with in the next chapter.

■ Notes

1. I would like to thank Syed Akbar Hyder, Gail Minault, and Cynthia Talbot for their comments and criticisms regarding this chapter.

2. Interestingly, India's Prithvi missile originally referred to "earth," the literal translation of *prithvi,* and was a follow-up to its Agni, or "fire," missile (*agni* and *prithvi* are both important words and concepts in the Hindu tradition). The meaning of the Prithvi missile was popularly reinterpreted as a reference to the twelfth-century battle only after Pakistan introduced its Ghauri missile.

3. If we take the first Neolithic settlements as our point of origin, we would be dealing with nearly 8,000 years of history.

4. Other major cities include Dholavira, Rakhigarhi, and Ganweriwala. Several sites have also been discovered along the banks of a river that many now argue was the legendary Saraswati River.

5. There is considerable debate as to what exactly "Hinduism" is and whether such a label can even be properly used to refer to such a wide range of belief systems and traditions. Many scholars have argued that it is more appropriate to refer to a body of philosophies and rituals that make up "the Hindu tradition," and this argument is of considerable relevance, given current attempts by certain religious groups to codify and narrowly define "the real Hindu way of life." For more on the history and nature of Hinduism, see Chapter 10 of this book. Also see Flood 1999.

6. The term *caste* is Portuguese in origin and became popular only after the Europeans began to interact with India.

7. The process of state formation during this early classical period was accompanied by the reappearance of urban centers.

8. Some link the Hunas with the Huns, but others argue that the Hunas were descended from migrants from the Iranian area.

9. India had a major impact on the societies of Southeast Asia that went beyond military conquest. Trade and the migration of Brahmans, Buddhists, and Jains all contributed to a massive transmission of culture. Islam was also transmitted to Southeast Asia via trade routes linking the region with India.

10. For more information on temple desecration, see Eaton 2000: 94–132.

11. The terms *slavery* and *slaves* carry different connotations here than those that arise from discussions of slavery in the Americas. Ghuri's slaves, who came from all over central Asia, were usually members of defeated ruling families. The treatment of slaves was also quite different, witnessed by the fact that many of Ghuri's most trusted generals were slaves. The fact that a slave was appointed first as viceroy and then as sultan is further proof of this point.

12. A predecessor to polo.

13. Issues surrounding the lives and status of women are some of the most important yet underplayed and understudied parts of South Asian history. As in most of the rest of the world, women were denied full, open participation in the patriarchal political sphere, yet they remained highly influential in politics and other areas of public and private, as well as religious, life. Any understanding of either historical or contemporary India is simply not possible without a thorough analysis of women's many roles. And an accurate understanding of this endeavor must deal directly not only with the material achievements of specific women but also with the history of gendered practices, a topic that broaches the issues of discrimination and sexuality. (For further details on the roles of women throughout South Asian history, see Ramusack 1999: 15–76.)

14. Both the bhakti movement, emerging from the Hindu tradition, and Sufism, rooted in Islam, focus on love and devotion as paths to God. The bhakti and Sufi traditions at times had a symbiotic relationship in the subcontinent, each influencing the other and both opening the doors of religious participation to otherwise underrepresented groups, particularly women.

15. The Sikh religion, which emerged in the time of the Lodis as a strand of devotional mysticism, represented a synthesis of elements from the Hindu and Muslim traditions. There were ten successive spiritual leaders, or gurus, of the Sikhs. Guru Arjan was the fifth.

16. These families had been contesting the authority of the nawab for some time and saw their support for the British as a convenient means to an end.

17. Napier never actually sent such a message. For details, see Doniger 1999: 940–960.

18. For further details on these arguments, please see Chatterjee 1993a and 1993b.

■ **Bibliography**

Basham, A. L. 1991 [1954]. *The Wonder That Was India*. Delhi: Rupa.

Bose, Sugata, and Ayesha Jalal. 1998. *Modern South Asia*. New York: Routledge, 1998.

Chatterjee, Partha. 1993a. *The Nation and Its Fragments*. Princeton: Princeton University Press.

———. 1993b [1986]. *Nationalist Thought and the Colonial World: A Derivative Discourse?* Minneapolis: University of Minnesota Press.

Davies, Philip. 1989. *Monuments of India*, Vol. 2. New York: Viking.

Doniger, Wendy. 1999. "Presidential Address: 'I Have Scinde': Flogging a Dead (White Male Orientalist) Horse." *Journal of Asian Studies* 58, no. 4 (November): 940–960.

Eaton, Richard. 2000. *Essays on Islam and Indian History*. New Delhi: Oxford University Press.

Embree, Ainslee, ed. 1988. *Sources of Indian Tradition I*. 2nd ed. New York: Columbia University Press.

Flood, Gavin. 1999. *An Introduction to Hinduism*. Cambridge: Cambridge University Press.

Gopal, Sarvepalli, ed. 1991. *Anatomy of a Confrontation*. New York: Viking.

Gordon, Stewart. 1993. *The Marathas, 1600–1818*. New York: Cambridge University Press.

Grewal, J. S. 1990. *The Sikhs of the Punjab*. New York: Cambridge University Press.

Hay, Stephen, ed. 1988. *Sources of Indian Tradition II*. 2nd ed. New York: Columbia University Press.

Ikram, S. M. 1964. *Muslim Civilization in India*. New York: Columbia University Press.

Jackson, Peter. 1999. *The Delhi Sultanate*. New York: Cambridge University Press.

Kenoyer, Jonathan Mark. 1998. *Ancient Cities of the Indus Valley Civilization*. Karachi: Oxford University Press and the American Institute of Pakistan Studies.

Kulke, Hermann, and Dietmar Rothermund. 1998. *A History of India*. 3rd ed. New York: Routledge.

Metcalf, Thomas. 1994. *Ideologies of the Raj*. New York: Cambridge University Press.

Olivelle, Patrick. 1998. *Upanishads*. New York: Oxford University Press.

Ramusack, Barbara. 1999. "Women in South Asia." In *Women in Asia: Restoring Women to History*, Barbara Ramusack and Sharon Sievers, eds. Bloomington: Indiana University Press.

Richards, John. 1993. *The Mughal Empire*. New York: Cambridge University Press.

Schimmel, Annemarie. 1980. *Islam in the Indian Subcontinent*. Leiden: E. J. Brill.

Thapar, Romila. 1987. *A History of India*. Vol. 1. New York: Penguin Books.

4

The Nationalist Movement

Pratap Bhanu Mehta

On August 12, 1858, the British Parliament passed the Government of India Act. This act formally transferred to the British government all the rights that the British East India Company had acquired over Indian territories. India was now to be formally governed by the British Parliament.

Indian society went through a profound transformation between 1858 and 1947, the year of India's eventual partition and independence. During this period, the country began to experience more fully and systematically the implications of what historians refer to as colonial modernity. The colonial government brought to India, with varying degrees of success, a whole set of modern political institutions, such as the modern state, a modern army, a civil service, a judiciary, and limited experiments with representative government. New forms of property rights in agriculture, new trading practices and tariffs, and investment in railways were transforming the economy beyond recognition. Meanwhile, the introduction of western education and ideas was compelling Indians to rethink the value of their own traditions.

At the same time, Indians were becoming more and more uncomfortable with their subordinate status. They resented the ideological justification that lay behind the British Empire—that Indians were backward and inferior and needed to be dominated. And they began to argue that, although British rule (known as the Raj) may have bequeathed some benefits to India through the introduction of modern ideas and institutions, the presence of the British was ultimately detrimental to the interests of Indians. Modern India was formed in this crucible of colonial penetration and Indian resistance to it.

The exact nature and origins of both the colonial state and nationalist responses to it are an object of contention, in part because the character of colonial rule revealed itself only gradually. As discussed in the previous chapter, the British East India Company first gained a foothold in India in 1757, after defeating the forces of the nawab of Bengal; in the hundred years that followed, it extended its dominion only incrementally (see Map 3.2). Although the company introduced profound changes in the territories it governed and real power was vested in its hands, it never declared itself to be an independent source of state sovereignty. Instead, it made use of the symbolic paraphernalia and legal instruments of the Indian kingdoms it encountered, including the Mughal Empire (1526–1857) that it was eventually to replace. It continued to present itself as a trading company, albeit one that could provide a vast range of services, including military and commercial expertise for hire. It was only with the Crown's formal acquisition of sovereignty over India in 1858 that the extent of British power became clear.

Some regional kingdoms were better than others at foreseeing the threat that the British East India Company posed. In Mysore in southern India, for example, Haidar Ali and Tipu Sultan continually fought battles against the company during the last three decades of the eighteenth century. There was cultural resistance as well: for the author of a text called *The Pleasure of All Gods*, written in Sanskrit around 1787, the seizure of power by "the white faced upstarts was like a recurrence of the age of demons" (Ray 1998: 508). These acts of political and cultural resistance were retrospectively incorporated into a nationalist historiography as the forerunners of the nationalist movement. At the time that they occurred, however, they were motivated more by regional ambitions than by any pan-Indian concerns.

In Bengal, where British power was first consolidated, there were early stirrings of a cultural self-consciousness. Members of the educated classes began to reflect on the myriad ways in which British rule was different from prior forms of governance, seeking to understand why the Raj had been able to consolidate itself. Out of these debates emerged a movement known as the Bengal Renaissance, which contributed two enduring themes to subsequent Indian nationalism (see Kopf 1969). The elements of a pan-Indian nationalism can be found embodied in texts such as Mritunjaya Vidyalankara's *Rajbali* (1808), among the first modern histories of India to be written along pan-Indian lines. And Bengali writers began a critical assessment of Hindu society and a process of social reform that would also be an enduring aspiration of Indian nationalism. One of the early reformers was Rammohun Roy (1772–1833), who campaigned for the abolition of sati (the practice of widow burning). Roy founded the Brahmo Samaj, a group that aspired to reform Hinduism along rationalist lines. But these efforts were along cultural lines, and there was no explicit ideology that called for displacing British power. Roy himself, treated in retrospect as the harbinger of modern India, had in 1809 welcomed the transition from Mughal to British government as the passage from a despotic government to a "milder, more enlightened and more liberal one." It was only after the 1857 revolt (see below) that Bengali commentators began explicitly to see their acts of cultural resistance in terms of political consequences. The most famous instance of this new wave was Bankim Chandra Chatterjee's novel, *Anandamath* (1882), in which India is a mother to be worshiped and whose song "Bande Mataram" (Mother! I bow to thee) became a nationalist rallying cry (see Kaviraj 1995).

■ The Revolt of 1857

For Indian nationalism, 1857 is a significant date. In that year much of the Ganges plain and central India revolted against the British. These revolts were a product of three grievances. Indian soldiers in the British army engaged in a widespread mutiny based on rumors that the cartridges of their rifles were being smeared with pig and cow fat—anathema to Muslims and Hindus, respectively. In the province of Awadh, peasants and artisans, unhappy with new forms of taxation, joined these soldiers in large numbers. Finally, the rulers and peasants of the Maratha territories tried to seize the opportunity to get rid of the British. Out of these events emerged the icons of the 1857 revolt: the image of the rani of Jhansi, for example, who died fighting on horseback while resisting the annexation of her kingdom, became an inspiration for nationalists for generations to come.

The 1857 revolt was haphazard but widespread. In the small towns of north India, religious leaders called for a jihad (holy war) against the British. During the revolt, thousands of *ghazis* (warriors of the faith) drawn from the religious order of the Sufis fought against the British. Astrological prophecies foretelling the end of British rule abounded (for a general study, see Sen 1957; see also Bhadra 1988). All sides practiced immense brutality, but ultimately the British prevailed, helped by significant Indian collaboration. The revolt was infused by an emerging sense of patriotism, but the aspiration to end British rule was framed in the context of restoring the old monarchies and empires of India, and Bahadur Shah Zafar, the last Mughal emperor, was installed as the nominal head of the revolt. The year 1857 saw the last serious struggle for Indian independence that aimed at restoring old monarchies and aristocracies. Subsequently, the Indian nationalist movement would take a distinctly forward-looking trajectory, in which the rights of old monarchies and empires were as suspect as those of the British.

The British learned significant lessons from this revolt. The Crown decided to put an end to the mismanagement of India, abolishing the British East India Company and crowning Queen Victoria as empress of India. India was now governed directly by the British government through its representatives in India.

■ The Birth of Modern Nationalism

The nationalist movement in the modern sense began in the 1880s and is symbolically associated with the founding of the Indian National Congress party (commonly known as the Congress Party) in 1885.

Victoria Memorial in Calcutta, built 1906–1921, one of the most attractive of the buildings constructed in honor of the queen

Unlike previous forms of resistance to the British, the goal of the new nationalism was not the reestablishment of any inherited monarchy or the restoration of an earlier status quo. Instead, it was the introduction of some form of self-rule for Indians. Although the precise form of that self-rule remained debatable, there was little dissent from the idea that it would have to be in some way democratic.

The instruments of this movement were also modern. The nationalists effectively used the printing press, then new to India, as a vehicle for mobilization. They used forms of association that were relatively new in India—like political parties and voluntary organizations—and that claimed to represent the general interest and to be united by overarching principles rather than by kinship or inherited ties. This newly emerging political consciousness was the direct result of the introduction of English-language education in India. The British had hoped that English-language education would create a native elite beholden to the British; instead, the educated middle class became the vanguard of Indian nationalism.

A plethora of reform and revivalist movements sprang up in various parts of India during the 1880s and 1890s. The objectives and tone of these movements varied considerably: they did not yet, in the first instance, seek the capture of state power. They were imbued by a growing consciousness that the economic relations between India and Britain were detrimental to the former. Arguments against India's economic exploitation began to be articulated in books such as Dadabhai Naoroji's *Poverty and Un-British Rule in India* (1901). These books catalogued the mechanisms by which the British were hurting the Indian economy. For example, preferential tariffs made British imports cheaper at the expense of local industry, and the pressure on farmers to grow cash crops like indigo, rather than food crops, was making them even more vulnerable to famine. Such arguments gave impetus to the ideas of *swadeshi*, the boycott of goods manufactured in Britain and the emphasis on indigenous production. They took concrete form in Bal Gangadhar Tilak's Ganapati festivals and protests against excise duties on Indian cotton. Popularly known as *lokmanya* (beloved of the people), Tilak (1856–1920) was a Brahman scholar from Maharashtra who set up home rule leagues in his province to agitate against British rule.

Elsewhere, there were movements directed against the intrusiveness of the colonial state in the regulation of social institutions such as marriage. Many of these movements were less opposed to the substance of the British reforms than to the fact that they emanated from the British. Indeed, Indians undertook their own social reforms.

It was also Tilak, along with Aurobindo Ghosh in Bengal and Lala Lajpat Rai in the Punjab, who first contemplated mass action and effective insurrection (see Brown 1994; Sarkar 1980). Although each of the three had a primary base in his own region, they were able to join in opposing the proposed partition of Bengal in 1905, a plan seen as a conspiracy to divide Hindus and Muslims. This agitation (1905–1907) was significant in a number of ways. It had antecedents in Tilak's agitations in Maharashtra but was a new benchmark in the nationalist movement. It quickened the pace of agitations in Punjab, Madras, and Bombay. Displaying the willingness of certain segments of the movement to seriously use violence as a means, it brought street agitation and a whole repertoire of agitational techniques like strikes, boycotts, and public rallies to new heights.

Following repression of this movement, the British introduced concessions designed to increase Indians' share of power in a way that would not undermine British control. The Minto-Morley reforms of 1909 increased the number of Indians who could be elected to legislative bodies and permitted them to make resolutions and discuss the budget. These reforms also enshrined the principle of separate electorates, whereby each community (Hindus and Muslims in particular) would vote only for the representatives of their community. Many nationalists regarded this method of constituting electorates as a way of dividing Indians so that they would not be able to challenge British power.

■ Gandhi and the Trajectory of Indian Nationalism

The most decisive transformation in the nationalist movement was brought about by Mohandas Karamchand Gandhi. Born in Porbandar (in what is now the state of Gujarat) in 1869, as a young man Gandhi practiced law in South Africa (1893–1914), where his protest against the racist policies of South Africa's government brought him into political prominence. During this period, he laid out the foundations of many of the ideas in a tract titled *Hind Swaraj* (1909). He resolutely emphasized nonviolence as a method of protest, provided a searching critique of modern industrial civilization, and articulated his vision of a decentralized village democracy. On his return to India in 1915, he tried out his strategy of nonviolent noncooperation in three local actions: an agitation against the colonial state's exorbitant revenue demands in Kheda, a conflict between industrialists and workers in

Ahmadabad, and a protest in Champaran against the European planters' requirement that peasants grow indigo.

The year 1919 was significant in two respects. First, the Montagu-Chelmsford reforms of 1919 further involved Indians in governing their own affairs. As was the case with the 1909 reforms, the Montagu-Chelmsford reforms continued to uphold the principle of separate electorates while at the same time transferring financial responsibility to Indians. These reforms introduced the principle of dyarchy: areas such as education, health, and agriculture became the responsibility of provincial legislatures, in which Indians had greater participation, whereas such important issues as revenue and law enforcement were reserved for the central British authority. It is interesting to note that the division of powers between the central government and the states in independent India followed much of the pattern established by the 1919 reforms.

In 1919 there was also widespread opposition to a series of government measures known as the Rowlatt Acts. They allowed the government to perpetuate the repressive legislation enacted during World War I, under which the government could hold Indians without trial. The British response to this opposition was severe, ultimately culminating in the infamous Jallianwalla Bagh massacre at Amritsar in Punjab, in which 379 unarmed civilians were gunned to death.

After this incident, Gandhi wove together an ambitious program of noncooperation. It included mobilizing a whole range of nonviolent techniques to grind government machinery to a halt: strikes, boycotts of foreign-made clothes, peace marches, and collective protests all became the standard repertoire of the Indian nationalist movement. Gandhi mobilized around issues that could appeal across all classes and religious divisions. He joined forces with Muslim leaders like the Ali brothers (Rahamat and Shaukat). He supported poor peasants boycotting the payment of revenue demands but went along with a proposal that they continue to pay rent, thus mobilizing peasant support of the Congress Party while preventing Indian landlords from becoming alienated.

Throughout this period, Gandhi set high moral standards for the nationalist movement. For example, in 1922, when peasants killed twenty-two policeman at Chauri-Chaura in Gorakhpur, Uttar Pradesh, Gandhi called off the noncooperation movement, much to the disappointment of his followers. He argued that the violence that had resulted from the movement was, even if in an ostensibly nationalist cause, inexcusable.

During this time, Gandhi's prestige and hold on the population were undeniable. He became a figure onto which many and often contradictory hopes became projected, and the force of his personality allowed the nationalist movement, momentarily at least, to transcend the contradictions that might otherwise have beset it. The source of Gandhi's success is not easy to identify. Most of his followers, including close associates, did not share much of his ideology, yet his effect was palpable. Jawaharlal Nehru (1889–1964)—another leading Indian nationalist, one of Gandhi's principal followers, and subsequently the first prime minister of independent India—described the effect Gandhi had on Indians in general:

> The dominant impulse in India under British rule was that of fear, pervasive, oppressive, strangling fear. . . . It was against this all pervading fear that Gandhi's quiet and determined voice was raised: Be not afraid. . . . So suddenly as it were, that black pall of fear was lifted from people's shoulders, not wholly, of course, but to an amazing degree. The Indian people did not become more truthful than they were, nor did they change their essential nature overnight; nevertheless a sea change was visible as the need for falsehood and furtive behaviors lessened. It was a psychological change, almost as if some expert in psychoanalytical method had probed deep into the patient's past, found out the origins of his complexes, exposed them to his view and thus rid him of that burden. (Nehru 1946)[1]

Gandhi had transformed the Congress Party into a mass organization capable of representing a wide spectrum of groups and classes. Equally significant was his organizational imagination, which consolidated these gains. The party was now better organized at the provincial level, and the provincial committees conducted much of their recruitment and campaigns in the local languages. This strategy allowed the party to co-opt a wide variety of linguistic groups and ensured that no single Indian language dominated. (It also laid the basis for the practice of linguistic accommodation that the modern Indian state was to follow.) Further, each province was asked to send a number of delegates—proportional to its population—to the annual party sessions to guard against the packing of key positions by delegates from a particular province. The Congress Party became an established organization, with funds deriving from membership dues, a permanent staff of career political workers, organizational elections, and so on. It was now in a position to mediate between different sections of Indian society.

A new period of agitation arose in the 1930s and lasted, with interruptions, until 1935. In 1929, the Congress Party had for the first time officially declared that it would not be satisfied by incremental concessions and that its ultimate goal was *purana swaraj* (complete freedom). It was in this context, and with the increasing effects that the worldwide economic depression was having on the Indian economy, that the civil disobedience campaign was launched in 1930. Among the many demands that Gandhi chose to highlight was the abolition of a tax on salt and a reduction in rents for India's peasants. Many of Gandhi's trusted colleagues, including Nehru, had some misgivings about emphasizing so seemingly trivial an issue as salt. But characteristically, Gandhi had picked an issue close to the hearts of the Indian masses. The anti–salt tax campaign had an electrifying impact across the subcontinent, and many Indians and Britons alike were impressed by the sacrifices and discipline of thousands of ordinary people committed to nonviolent protest. Despite the noble aims and the electrifying start that widened the reach of the Congress Party, the civil disobedience campaign began to flag as 1930 went on, and its appeal, though widespread, was uneven. Indian landlords began to fear peasants who were refusing to pay rents; Muslim peasant debtors started to rise up against Hindu moneylenders; and as British repression of civil disobedience grew, significant sections of the population were increasingly attracted to revolutionary violence.

Gandhi himself, along with large sections of the Congress Party, was uncomfortable with this revolutionary fervor. Gandhi opened negotiations with Viceroy Lord Irwin in 1931, and many nationalists were disappointed that he had, for the second time in his career, called off a movement just when it was reaching a crescendo.

The Gandhi-Irwin pact offered only promises of limited Indian self-government, safeguards for minorities, and the eventual creation of a federation. This outcome disappointed those who had hoped for more concessions. Under pressure from below, the civil disobedience campaigns were renewed in 1932. During the following year, about 120,000 Indians were arrested, including significant numbers of women. Although the demand for women's suffrage had been voiced as early as 1917, the civil disobedience campaigns were the first occasion of women's significant involvement in politics. Gandhi looked upon women as embodying the very qualities that he took to be necessary for carrying out his programs. Under his influence, large numbers of middle-class women emerged from the seclusion of housework into politics. (See Chapter 8 for a discussion of the role of women in contemporary India.)

But the Congress Party continued to gain some and lose some. Although these campaigns extended its geographical reach, it began to lose support among many middle-class and wealthy farmers and especially among Muslims. The Muslims felt uneasy with the way in which such Hindu causes as cow protection often became the focus of disobedience campaigns. In the coming years, this emerging disaffection proved costly.

The upshot of all this activity was the Government of India Act of 1935, which gave some Indians a significant taste of representative government. This act extended the franchise, still based on property qualifications, to about 35 million voters. At the provincial level, for the first time it brought all government departments under the control of elected Indian ministers. The British kept sufficient powers to dismiss ministries and bring provincial governments under the direct sway of the governor and civil servants, and matters of finance and defense were still mainly controlled by the central government. The act also projected a future federation in which there would be representatives not only from the British Indian provinces but from the princely states as well.[2]

Most Congress leaders, like Nehru and Subhas Chandra Bose (1897–1945), were deeply dissatisfied with the Government of India Act. But after a combination of introspection and calculation, the Congress Party took a pragmatic line and decided to participate in the elections scheduled for 1937. The elections turned out to be a triumph for the party. The Congress Party won clear majorities in five provinces: Madras, Bihar, Orissa, the Central Provinces, and the United Provinces. It made an impressive showing in Bombay, Assam, and the North West Frontier Province. In Punjab, Bengal, and Sind, regional parties formed the majority. Indian political parties now acquired a taste of functioning within parliamentary norms, rather than engaging in extraconstitutional protest. Congress-controlled ministries began themselves to curtail some of the more radical peasant movements that were springing up. Congress now appeared to many to be not just a repository of their protests against the British but a party that would inherit the mantle of power. Congress Party membership in the United Provinces alone jumped from 65,733 in 1936 to 1,472,456 in 1938; nationally, it jumped from 635,504 to 4,511,858 during the same period.

When World War II broke out, the British were still determined to hold onto India. For many Indians, the war was a conflict between new and old imperial powers. Britain's claim to be fighting for freedom and democracy seemed less than credible to a population under colonial subjection. The economic dislocation caused by the war—especially the catastrophic famine in 1942 that is estimated to have taken close to

3.5 million lives in Bengal and Orissa, together with rising inflation, falling wages, and rural unemployment—made conditions propitious for a deepening conflict between Indian nationalism and the colonial state. The immensely popular nationalist Subhas Chandra Bose (see below) fled from house arrest in India to collaborate with the Japanese and Germans in an armed struggle against the British in India. To prevent further such collaboration, Sir Winston Churchill quickly dispatched Sir Stafford Cripps to open talks with Indian leaders. Sir Stafford proposed that India be granted "dominion status," with Indians having a substantial degree of self-government and Britain retaining formal sovereignty over the country. Gandhi described Cripps's proposals as a postdated check on a failing bank. The British were unwilling to concede to the Congress Party's demand that defense matters be immediately turned over to Indians. In April 1942, Gandhi drafted a resolution calling on the British to leave India. A version of this resolution was adopted by the Congress Party on August 9.

The August 9 resolution formally launched the "Quit India" movement, whose slogan "do or die" captured some of the intensity of the movement. It was the largest civilian uprising in India since the revolt of 1857, though it was never clear who controlled it. Much of the senior Congress Party leadership had been swiftly put into prison, leaving the movement to be orchestrated by lower-level leaders, students, and urban workers. In late September the movement took on the dimensions of a significant agrarian revolt, with peasants attacking all manner of state institutions like railway lines, revenue offices, and police stations. British administration virtually collapsed in parts of Bihar, eastern United Provinces, Bombay, and Orissa. The British ultimately

Government of India Press Information Bureau

Gandhi and Nehru at the historic meeting in Bombay, August 1942, at which the "Quit India" resolution was adopted

brought things under control by the summer of 1943 through the largest deployment yet of British military forces on Indian soil, but their vulnerability was quite apparent.

Meanwhile, Bose, a nationalist leader from Bengal whose popularity as a Congress Party leader during the 1930s had come almost to rival Gandhi's (the two later had a falling out), had managed to organize an Indian National Army (INA) of some 45,000 soldiers. Many of them were deserters from the British Indian Army; some had been taken prisoner by the Japanese during their campaign in Southeast Asia and had broken ranks; others were civilian recruits among the Indian plantation workers in Malaya. Although the INA did not come even close to its aim of removing the British, even in defeat it performed a significant function. First of all, it attacked the British Indian Army, which had been the key instrument of imperial control. Second, the trial of its officers aroused nationalist passions immensely. Even though the Congress Party had formally distanced itself from Bose's methods, it took up the defense of the INA officers with alacrity and used the trial to launch what was arguably the last mass movement on an all-India scale. Even the previously loyal armed forces were stirred into a political consciousness, which culminated in significant mutinies in the Indian Navy led by M. S. Khan. The armed forces, the last preserve of British loyalty, seemed to be crumbling. In 1946 the British sent a cabinet mission to discuss the terms of independence.

But the road to independence was beset by deep divisions that ultimately led to one of the most colossal human tragedies of modern times: the partition of India and the violence that accompanied it. To understand how the events of 1946–1948 came into being, one has to understand in some depth the one issue that the Congress Party could not successfully resolve: the relationship of minorities to Indian nationalism.

■ Muslims and Indian Nationalism

The consolidation of British rule had a significant impact on India's Muslims. For the first time since their arrival on the Indian subcontinent almost a millennium earlier, Muslims found themselves without significant political power. This situation generated new vulnerabilities and called for new adjustments, and Indian Muslims—like their Hindu neighbors—engaged in a process of self-reflection and debate about their future.

Government of India Press Information Bureau

Subhas Chandra Bose

These debates incorporated a wide variety of views about coping with the new predicament and involved a wide range of issues, including reform of Muslim theology and the creation of Muslim modernism, gender relations and the education of women, and reformulations of Muslim law. But politically, there were two issues around which much of the anxiety centered. What form of political representation would safeguard Muslim interests in India? How could Muslims retain the institutions and practices that were considered important to their identities? It would be a mistake to think of relations between Hindus and Muslims during precolonial times as characterized either by complete harmony or implacable hostility. Islam had sunk deep roots in India, and significant elements of syncretism had emerged out of that encounter. But there also had been significant moments of conflict and competition.

Muslim employment in high public offices had decreased considerably in the period from 1857 to the early twentieth century, and there was great resentment on the part of Muslims against the Hindu middle classes and the commercial groups that succeeded them. During the 1880s, Sayyid Ahmad Khan, a prominent reformist leader from Aligarh and founder of the Aligarh Muslim University, sought to ally the landed Muslim gentry of the United Provinces with the colonial state. To bring about this alliance, he argued that there were two nations in India: Hindu and Muslim. These nations were hostile to one another, and only British power could protect Muslims. Fueling Muslim anxiety during this period were the cow protection movement, aimed at outlawing cow slaughter; the *shuddhi* movement, aimed at reclaiming Hindus who had converted to Islam; and the increasing assertiveness of Hindus in public spaces, especially near Muslim shrines.

Religious conflict often derived its momentum from economic concerns. Hindu peasants and Muslim landlords in the Ganges Valley region had opposing interests, as did Muslim tenants and Hindu landlords along the Malabar coast. Muslim peasants in Bengal were suspicious of Hindu moneylenders in Bengal, and the Hindu commercial classes were pitted against older Muslim gentries in the United Provinces. Hindus and Muslims began to compete for greater British patronage. These conflicts would inextricably intertwine with overt religious issues to produce sporadic but widespread rioting in early-twentieth-century India.

Despite these conflicts, hostility between Hindus and Muslims was not a foregone conclusion. There were significant moments of political cooperation. Mohammed Ali Jinnah, who was later to become the founder of Pakistan, was for some time a member of the Congress Party and was heralded as an ambassador of Hindu-Muslim unity. And Muslim leaders like Maulana Azad remained key figures in the Congress Party even after the establishment of Pakistan.

But perhaps the single most important issue to bedevil Hindu-Muslim relations was the question of Muslim representation. As a minority in India, Muslims wanted adequate representation to safeguard their interests. Although their demands often were presented as if there were a single, monolithic Muslim community, actual Muslim politics continued to be fractured by class and regional distinctions. No pan-Indian Muslim organization had any prominence until the 1930s.

The definition of an Indian Muslim was first used as a significant political category to award the Muslims their own electorates during the 1909 Minto-Morley reforms, and the 1935 Government of India Act extended the principle of communal electorates even further. As a result of the 1935 act, Muslims in Muslim-majority provinces like Punjab and Bengal were ensured dominance in provincial assemblies, and they formed ministries in these provinces in 1937. At the same time, Muslims in Muslim-minority provinces began to feel more vulnerable because the act eliminated from local government in those provinces the British officials whom many Muslims had come to regard as a safeguard for their interests. It was Muslims in Muslim-minority provinces who turned to Jinnah and the newly revived Muslim League in 1935. Although the league did poorly in the 1937 elections, the accession of

Congress Party ministries in Muslim-minority provinces gradually began to fuel Muslim anxiety. During the 1930s, Sayyid Ahmad Khan's earlier assertion that India consisted of two nations began to gain ground, although its political consequences were still unclear. For some, like the great poet and thinker Iqbal, the idea meant that Muslims were a nation *within* India; for others, like the Cambridge student Rahamat Ali, who coined the term *Pakistan,* Muslim nationhood had an irrevocable territorial dimension.

In his famous presidential address to the Muslim League at Lahore in 1940, Jinnah envisaged a Muslim federation based on the existing boundaries of undivided Punjab and Bengal. Whether he envisaged this federation as working within an Indian union or whether it was to acquire complete sovereignty remains a matter of some dispute. Be that as it may, he was not willing to accept anything less than an equal sharing of power between Hindus and Muslims in any Indian central government. Many Hindus thought that Jinnah's demand was unfair: not only would Muslims dominate Muslim-majority provinces, but also they would have power at the center beyond what their numbers justified. Protracted negotiations yielded no result that all sides could accept. Meanwhile, the Muslim League and right-wing Hindu organizations like the Hindu Mahasabha were fomenting Hindu-Muslim tensions. Their activities lead to widespread rioting in the 1940s and had a palpable effect on the hopes of any settlement.

National Archives

Mohammed Ali Jinnah, president of the Muslim League and later the first president of Pakistan, August 1945

The upshot of the deadlocked negotiations and worsening Hindu-Muslim violence was the partition of India in 1947—the result that no one had wanted but all conspired to get. A new state of Pakistan was carved out by dividing Punjab (in the northwest of India) and Bengal (in the east) and joining them to Sind, Baluchistan, and the North West Frontier Province. Jinnah called this unhappy solution "the maimed, mutilated and moth eaten state" (see Hasan 1994). The irony was that it left Muslims in Muslim-minority provinces in India without any safeguards other than the goodwill of the majority. The partition of Bengal and Punjab unleashed an unprecedented human catastrophe, as Sikhs and Hindus were expelled from Pakistani territory into India, and Muslims from some parts of India moved into Pakistan (although a large number of Muslims chose to remain in India and now constitute about one-tenth of India's population). The violence that accompanied these migrations was of untold brutality: estimates of casualties range between 1 and 2 million. India became independent under the shadow of the violence of partition.

■ Interpreting Indian Nationalism

In the simplest terms, the Indian nationalist movement aspired to displace British power. But as it gained momentum, its tasks also became more complex. It had to fashion out of India's staggering diversity of religions, languages, and regions a workable conception of national identity. It had to provide a serious critique of all those features of Indian society that had over the years weakened it and made it debilitatingly oppressive. It needed to confront issues like caste, the treatment of untouchables, and the position of women in society. In sum, it was forced to engage in a plan of social reform, but it had to do so in a manner that did not condemn all of India's past to the dustbin of history. The nationalist movement had to allow Indians to transcend the worst excesses of their own tradition without making that tradition despicable, and it had to provide a positive agenda of economic development and social justice around which Indians could fashion a forward-looking identity for themselves.

There were various views on how each of these tasks was to be accomplished. The nationalist movement was remarkably successful in weaving a nation out of India's diverse inheritance. The organization of the Congress Party along linguistic lines allowed each region to have at least some, if not always an equal, share in power at the center. It managed to provide a forum in which varying regional interests could come together and engage in the normal rough-and-tumble of politics. If it is true that the British provided an administrative structure that to some degree gave India an unprecedented coherence, it is also true that the Congress Party facilitated the emergence of political links across different regions within the realm of civil society. This reach was uneven and often contested. Yet by the time of independence, India not only had a state but a political party that could knit state and society together.

Congress was able to act as a mediator among various classes in society: peasants and landlords and moneylenders, workers and capitalists. Although this conciliatory approach prevented the party from seriously challenging the most privileged sections in society—reform agendas seldom upset the status quo to any significant degree—it also prevented a class-based polarization of Indian society that might have led to violent, catastrophic revolutionary movements.

In retrospect, what is remarkable about the Congress Party is the degree to which political leaders of very different political styles and ideological persuasions learned to work together and compromise. Nehru and Gandhi were as different as two leaders could be, both in ideology and in personal style. Yet they managed to work together and carry along with them an assortment of key figures from both the left and the right. This process was not without its failures: the inability of Gandhi to accommodate the radical nationalism of Bose is perhaps the most important instance of such a failure. Nevertheless, if democracy requires the consistent ability to make compromises, to recognize other leaders, to inculcate a sense of self-restraint, and to tolerate difference and eschew ideological purity, then the Congress Party in large measure was responsible for producing a generation of leaders who understood this. Many of these qualities, then, albeit with certain imperfections, helped to consolidate constitutional and democratic politics after independence (see Kohli 1988).

During the nationalist movement, the idea of India became the repository of an immense range of contending hopes and corresponding fears. From its antiquity and depth, its geographic contours, and its intricate cultural and social facets, modern India has had to fashion a new identity for itself. But these elements had to jostle with many of the aspects of modernity that have shaped India in equal measure: the presence of a modern state, the rise of new forms of politics that constantly questioned inherited identities, the aspirations of democracy and egalitarianism, and the ambitions of industrialization. Different aspects of the nationalist movement recombined these elements in different forms. The interest of Indian nationalism is precisely that it was a deep, serious, and multifaceted debate on the meaning of India and what it meant to be an Indian.

■ Ideas of India

On the extreme fringes of Indian nationalism but nevertheless casting a persistent shadow on Indian politics were an assortment of what we now think of as Hindu nationalists. The most articulate version of Hindu nationalism was found in the writings of Vir Vinayak Damodar Savarkar (1883–1966), a Maharashtrian Brahman who spent many years in prison for insurgency against the British. According to Savarkar, Hindus are united not as a religious category but rather by their geographic origin, a sense of racial connection, and an allegiance to Sanskritic culture. Those who shared these traits were true "Indians." Muslims and Christians lay outside the fold of the Indian nation as defined in these terms. An associate of Savarkar, K. D. Hegdewar (1898–1940), founded the Rashtriya Swayamsevak Sangh, which to this day continues as the organizational arm of Hindu nationalism (see Jafferlot 1993 for a history).

Although this movement did not capture the center of Indian politics, it shaped the nationalist movement in significant ways. The organizations associated with it were resolutely involved in anti-Muslim campaigns and violence, and the presence of its sympathizers often tied the Congress Party's hands when it came to yielding concessions to Muslims. Its adherents considered Gandhi too sympathetic to Muslims; indeed, Gandhi was assassinated by a Hindu nationalist in 1948. Although this version of Indian nationalism still does not enjoy the support of the majority of Indians, the resurgence of contemporary Hindu nationalism owes a lot to it. It is the single most exclusivist conception of Indian nationhood, against which more pluralist conceptions of Indian nationalism have constantly had to act.

It would be fair to say that there were at least two prominent visions of a pluralist India. Unlike Hindu nationalism, these visions were founded not on resentment of others but on a concept of an India that would be an exemplar of values that all societies could emulate.

The first was Gandhi's India. It was an India that would draw on what Gandhi thought were India's deep wells of spirituality. India's diverse religious traditions would provide the foundations of its moral values. Gandhi insisted that religion would be the source of tolerance rather than conflict. India would carve out a distinct path for itself by avoiding two of the central pillars of western civilization: industrialization and a strong, centralized state. Neither of these, Gandhi argued, held much promise for improving the lot of the countless inhabitants of India's villages. India's distinctive trajectory would lie in emphasizing small-scale forms of production that made each household self-reliant, that did not depend on exploiting nature and fostering endless consumption throughout the needless proliferation of wants.[3] Even though Gandhi's hopes in this regard were idealistic and exaggerated, his vision acknowledged the centrality of rural life to any account of India. At independence, India was more than four-fifths a rural country, and any sense of nationhood that did not tap into the lifestyles and aspirations of its rural population was bound to be a failure. Whatever his failures, Gandhi rescued rural life from the condescension it was subject to by other forms of nationalism and gave it its rightful place as an essential part of modern India. Perhaps more enduringly, Gandhi is almost unique among twentieth-century leaders in eschewing all forms of political violence. Nearly all modern political ideologies have either explicitly embraced violence as a legitimate means of political action or have implicitly come to accept the inevitability of violence in politics and social life. Gandhi's radical insistence on nonviolence will remain a haunting reminder of the moral imperfections of these political ideologies.

Like Gandhi, Nehru's vision of India was deeply pluralistic, but in a different sense. Nehru, too, argued that India's identity lay in its pluralism, but for him the country was a propitious ground for cultural mixing: "an ancient palimpsest upon which layer upon layer of thought and reverie had been inscribed, and yet no succeeding layer had completely hidden or erased what has been written previously" (Nehru 1946: 49–51).[4] He was less sympathetic than Gandhi to any claims that India's religions might provide the groundwork for a shared set of values. India had to don the "garb of modernity." By that, Nehru meant that a forward-looking Indian identity could emerge only within the institutional framework of a modern state. This state would rest on resolutely secular foundations: it would derive its legitimacy from upholding a distinctly modern conception of the rule of law, the protection of broadly liberal rights, and the rights of minorities. Also, Nehru was more optimistic than Gandhi about the prospects of economic progress through the application of state power and scientific knowledge. This view was not based, at least in Nehru's mind, on a slavish imitation of the West. Instead, India would attempt to avoid both the unbridled acquisitiveness of capitalism and the abridgement of liberty that socialism entailed.

By 1947, it was Nehru's modernist imagination that triumphed, and much of independent India was to be fashioned along lines that he envisaged. Although Gandhi had done much to restore India's self-confidence, his political and economic ideas were swiftly sidelined. Much of Nehru's India remains, at least formally, intact. India is a functioning democracy, and although it has abandoned state-led growth, it is deeply committed to economic growth and a modern state. But for many confronting the uncertainties unleashed by modernization, the question of what it means to be an Indian remains a haunting one. Many are being tempted by the exclusionary simplicities of Hindu nationalism. How far Nehru's India will endure remains to be seen. But if the history of Indian nationalism has taught us one thing, it is this: the story of modern India is the story of Indians constantly struggling to discover and articulate what it means to be Indian.

■ Notes

1. For information on Gandhi more generally, see Brown 1989.

2. In 1935, there were some 600 princely states. Britain exercised sovereignty over India in two ways. It directly ruled most of India's territory. But in some areas, it entered into arrangements with existing princes, whereby they would formally retain sovereignty over their kingdoms but accept the British as the paramount power in India. The British would have rights to intervene in the affairs of these kingdoms if they were thought to be detrimental to British interest. These states were, occasionally reluctantly, absorbed into independent India. For more on this see Copland 1997.

3. Gandhi's collected works run to some ninety volumes. The best short selection, thematically organized, is Gandhi 1988. Also see Parekh 1988.

4. Jawaharlal Nehru's 1946 work, *Discovery of India,* remains in many ways the best introduction not only to Nehru's own outlook but also to complex issues in Indian history.

■ Bibliography

Bhadra, Gautam. 1988. "Four Rebels of Eighteen Fifty Seven." In *Selected Subaltern Studies,* Ranajit Guha and Gayatri Spivak, eds. New York: Oxford University Press.

Brown, Judith. 1989. *Gandhi: Prisoner of Hope.* New Haven, Conn: Yale University Press.

————. 1994. *Modern India: The Origins of an Asian Democracy.* Oxford: Oxford University Press.

Copland, Ian. 1997. *The Princes of India in the Endgame of Empire, 1917–1947.* Cambridge: Cambridge University Press.

Gandhi, M. K. 1988. *Selected Writings of Mahatma Gandhi*, edited by Raghavan Iyer. Delhi: Oxford University Press.

Hasan, Mushirul, ed. 1994. *India's Partition: Process, Strategy, and Mobilization.* Delhi: Oxford University Press.

Jafferlot, Christophe. 1993. *The Hindu Nationalist Movement in India.* New York: Columbia University Press.

Kaviraj, Sudipta. 1995. *The Unhappy Consciousness: Bankim Chandra Chatterjee and the Making of Indian Nationalism.* Delhi: Oxford University Press.

Kohli, Atul, ed. 1988. *India's Democracy.* Princeton: Princeton University Press.

Kopf, David. 1969. *British Orientalism and the Bengal Renaissance, 1773–1835.* Berkeley: University of California Press.

Nehru, Jawaharlal. 1946. *Discovery of India.* New York: John Day.

Parekh, Bhikhu. 1988. *Gandhi's Political Philosophy.* London: Macmillan.

Ray, Rajat. 1998. "Indian Society and the Establishment of British Supremacy, 1765–1818." In *The Oxford History of the British Empire: The Eighteenth Century*, P. J. Marshall, ed. Oxford: Oxford University Press.

Sarkar, Sumit. 1980. *Modern India.* Delhi: Macmillan.

Sen, S. N. 1957. *Eighteen Fifty Seven.* Delhi: Publications Division.

5

Indian Politics

Shalendra D. Sharma

The triumph of democracy in a historically improbable environment such as India is nothing short of extraordinary. For more than half a century, India has been a constitutional democracy with a parliamentary system of government. Indians are justly proud to be citizens of the world's largest democracy and see that democracy as a precious national accomplishment. Today, democracy has become such an indelible part of the nation's political consciousness that—despite the disillusionment with "politics as usual"—most Indians continue to maintain a deep philosophical commitment to democracy and embrace the fundamental idea that the state's authority must derive solely from the uncoerced consent of the majority, tested regularly through open competitive elections.

Following the 1996 general election, the *New York Times* commented on April 18:

> What seemed important was not so much which of the dozens of political parties was up or down, or which local candidate from the 15,000 running across India was likely to win. What permeated the mood was something as old as independent India itself—the sheer pleasure of taking part in a basic democratic rite, the business of appointing and dismissing governments, that has survived all the disappointments that Indians have endured in the past half-century. In a troubled land, democracy means there is hope.[1]

In September and October 1999, India held its thirteenth general election since gaining independence in 1947.[2] That election, the fifth held

63

within a decade, produced for the eighth time since 1989 a coalition government made up of some eighteen disparate parties.

Yet, even as India has secured virtually all the requirements associated with a mature and resilient democracy, the nation's ability to provide effective governance has hardly improved. Indeed, some believe that the problems of governability have actually worsened. It seems that the progressive empowerment of popular sectors and the deepening of democratic practices have created new problems. Paradoxically, even as India's peoples enjoy the right to exercise popular sovereignty and its Parliament has become ever more representative of society, this "deepening" of democracy also seems responsible for exacerbating political fragmentation and the nation's inability to produce stable and effective government. In fact, rampant corruption and violence have infected the body politic. For example, on September 29, 2000, former prime minister P. V. Narasimha Rao was found guilty of illegal financial transactions, and Laloo Prasad Yadav, a former chief minister of Bihar (India's most economically backward state), was out on bail after being charged with looting the exchequer in a state-run animal fodder scheme. Large numbers of elected legislators in Bihar and in Uttar Pradesh (India's most populous state) have criminal records or have criminal investigations pending against them. Moreover, participatory democracy has not translated into a compelling alternative to top-down development models. Indeed, persistent socioeconomic inequalities mock the formal political equality of democratic citizenship (for details, see Sharma 1999).

■ The Democratic Structure

The Constitution of India, adopted in 1950 after three years of intense debate in the Constituent Assembly (elected indirectly from the various provinces in 1946), proclaimed India as a sovereign federal democratic republic. The constitution's 395 articles and ten appendixes (known as schedules) make it one of the longest and most detailed in the world. Following the British parliamentary pattern, the constitution embodies the citizens' fundamental rights, similar to the U.S. Bill of Rights. These civil rights take precedence over any other law of the land; they include the individual rights common to most liberal democracies, such as equality before the law; freedom of speech, association, assembly, and religion; the right to constitutional remedies for the protection of civil rights; and the right to own and sell property. In addition, the constitution outlaws the traditional Indian system of social stratification based on caste and prohibits discrimination on the grounds of religion, language, race, ethnic background, sex, or place of birth. It also gives "minorities" the right to establish and administer their own educational institutions and to preserve a distinct language, script, and culture.

An interesting feature of the constitution is the directive principles of state policy, which describe the obligations of the state toward its citizens. The dictates of the directive principles are not enforceable by a court, in contrast to the fundamental rights. Rather, they are intended to guide the government in framing new legislation. They include such orders as "the state shall direct its policy towards securing . . . that the ownership and control of the material resources of the community are so distributed to subserve the common good" and "the state shall promote the interests of the weaker sections of society."

The key institutions of national governance are the executive (composed of the president and the Council of Ministers), the Parliament, and the highest judicial system in the land, the Supreme Court. It is important to note that, although executive power is formally vested in the president (who is the head of state), the president exercises these powers on the advice of the Council of Ministers, which is headed by the prime minister.[3] Hence, both in theory and practice, power is concentrated in the hands of the prime minister, the de facto head of the Indian executive. It is the prime minister who determines the composition of the Council of Ministers and assigns departmental portfolios to the cabinet, which is made up of fifteen to twenty individuals. In India, the nature and composition of the Council of Ministers and cabinet

Government of India Press Information Bureau

Prime Minister Nehru congratulates Dr. Rajendra Prasad, president of the Constituent Assembly, on the occasion of the signing of the new Constitution of India, January 14, 1950

have varied, depending on the prime minister in power. The prime minister's office is also supported by a secretariat (currently over 300 strong) and senior bureaucrats, technocrats, economists, politicians, and their assistants.[4]

India's Parliament consists of a bicameral legislature made up of the Lok Sabha (House of the People—the lower house) and the Rajya Sabha (Council of States—the upper house). In 2000 the Lok Sabha had 546 seats. Except for two members who are nominated by the president as representatives for the Anglo-Indian community, all others are popularly elected.[5] Seats in the Lok Sabha are allocated among the states on the basis of population: each state is roughly divided into electoral districts made up of about 1.5 million people. The usual term is five years, and under the rules of the constitution, the Lok Sabha must meet at least twice a year, with no more than six months between sessions. However, the president may dissolve the house and call new elections if the sitting government loses its majority in Parliament.

The Rajya Sabha is a permanent body that meets in continuous session. It has a maximum of 250 members, all but twelve of whom are elected by the state legislative assemblies (the Vidhan Sabhas) for six-year terms.[6] The Rajya Sabha permits more extended debates. Home to

The circular Parliament building, in which the Lok Sabha
and the Rajya Sabha have their chambers

a large number of elder statespersons, it is designed to provide stability and continuity to the legislative process (thus, it is not subject to dissolution as is the Lok Sabha). Nevertheless, the authority of the Rajya Sabha in the legislative process is subordinate to that of the Lok Sabha.

The power to make policy decisions in India is concentrated at the highest levels of authority, with the prime minister, his or her cabinet, and high-level officials and bureaucrats (through their control of the various government ministries) taking the initiative. The government has primary responsibility to draft legislation and introduce bills into either house of Parliament, although financial bills for taxing and spending (known as money bills) can only be introduced in the Lok Sabha. The central government (or the center) is aided in its activities by some 17 million government employees (known collectively as "public services"), about 5,000 of whom are officers of the elite Indian Administrative Service (IAS).[7]

Finally, an independent judiciary is an important component of the Indian system. The Supreme Court is the ultimate interpreter and guardian of the constitution and the laws of the land.[8] Headed by a chief justice and twenty-five associate justices, the Supreme Court sees that all legislation passed by the central and state governments is in conformity with the constitution. It also has the power of judicial review, original as well as appellate, regarding the constitutionality of any other enactment.[9] Although in practice the executive branch of government has often managed to limit the Supreme Court's powers of judicial review—and although the court has not always handled cases effectively, including those dealing with religious minorities and the rights of women—it is an institution of some significance and in recent years has begun to reassert its authority.

India's federal system has vested significant legislative powers with the central government, but the constitution also specifies powers that are divided between the central government and the states. Below the central government, there are twenty-eight state governments and six union territories, with populations ranging from 400,000 for the union territory of Sikkim to 140 million for the largest and most populous state, Uttar Pradesh. The states do not have individual constitutions; they are governed by the provisions of the federal constitution. The constitution specifies that all the states must have similar governmental structures, with a popularly elected bicameral or unicameral legislature in each, headed by a chief minister who is responsible to the assemblies.[10] A governor, appointed by the central government, has the power to disagree with a bill and refer it to the president of India; the governor also has the power to appoint, with the approval of the legislature, the state's chief minister.

The strength of the central government relative to that of the states is further apparent in the constitutional provisions (laid down in the Seventh Schedule of the constitution) for central intervention in state jurisdictions. The central government has exclusive authority over ninety-seven matters of national importance, including defense, foreign affairs, transportation, communications, interstate trade and commerce, and finances. Moreover, Article 3 of the constitution authorizes Parliament, by a simple majority vote, to establish or eliminate states and union territories and to change their boundaries or names. The central government can also dismiss any state government by means of president's rule. The center also exerts control over state governments through the financial resources at its command. In a real sense, it "acts as a banker and collecting agent for the state governments" (Hardgrave and Kochanek 1993: 130). Under the rules of the constitution, financial resources flow from the central government to the states through a system of discretionary divisible taxes and grants-in-aid, making the states dependent on the center for their regular budgetary needs, as well as for their capital expenditures. The central government also allocates and distributes substantial development funds and grants through its five-year plans. The resources available under the plans are substantial, given the center's exclusive control over taxation and foreign financial flows.

Although India's federal government exhibits all the features of a highly institutionalized modern unitary state, appearances can be deceiving. Despite the constitutional powers of the central government, the provincial governments are not without significant constitutional powers of their own.[11] In the words of B. R. Ambedkar, chairman of the constitution-drafting committee, "the states of the union of India are as sovereign in their field which is left to them by the Constitution as the Center in the field which is assigned to it" (Palmer 1961: 97). Under the constitution, states have exclusive authority over sixty-six items, including public order, welfare, health, education, local government, industry, agriculture, and land revenue. With regard to the agricultural sector and land revenue, the constitution assigns primary responsibility to the state governments; the center is reduced to providing guidelines, leaving the actual task of legislating and implementing rural development policies to the states. In fact, Paul Appleby, who at the request of the Indian government conducted a comprehensive review of the country's administrative system in the early 1950s, was astounded to discover how much the center was dependent on the states for the actual implementation of major national programs and how little real authority the center seemed to have in the vital areas of policy and administration. Appleby has lucidly captured this paradox: "No other large and important government . . . is so dependent as India on theoretically subordinate but actually rather distinct units responsible to a different political control, for so much of the administration of what are recognized as national programs of great importance to the nation" (Appleby 1953: 21).

Below the state governments is an array of formal and informal governance structures, known simply as local self-government and understood as the administration of a locality (a village, town, city, or any other area smaller than a state) by a body representing the local inhabitants. Those who supported the idea behind local self-government, articulated most forcefully by the 1957 *Mehta Study Team Report,* argued that local self-government, or "democratic decentralization," could play a vital role in the process of political legitimation and offer a means for developing a sense of participation in the citizenry.[12]

The district is the principal formal subdivision within the state governments.[13] In 2001 there were 537 districts in India, averaging 4,000 square kilometers in size and approximately 1.8 million people. The district collector, a member of the Indian Administrative Service, and the district judge (who is appointed by the state government and is in no way subordinate to the collector) are the most important officials in district administration. Districts are further subdivided into *taluqs* or *tehsils,* comprising anywhere from 200 to 600 villages. The *taluqdar* or *tehsildar* and the occasional village *patwari* (accountant)—the most important state government representatives at this level—are responsible for overseeing government programs, maintaining land records, and collecting revenue.

Finally, Article 40 of the constitution directs all levels of government to engage in the "democratic decentralization of Indian administration" by reviving or creating *panchayati raj,* "traditional village councils for self-government," and to "endow them with such powers and authority as may be necessary to enable them to function as units of self-government" (Government of India 1952: 6–7). Most states have since introduced a fairly institutionalized system of *panchayati raj,* and the seventy-third constitutional amendment, passed in 1992, stipulates that all *panchayat* members be elected for five-year terms in elections supervised by the Election Commission.[14]

Village *panchayat* in Uttar Pradesh

■ General Elections in the 1990s

Overall, India's quasi-federal political system and its ability to hold regular, free, and fair elections has long provided a peaceful outlet for its citizens' diverse aspirations and competing demands. For example, the twelfth general election (held in February–March 1998) was aptly described by the media as a "grand civic festival." However, it was also a daunting logistical undertaking. Roughly 63 percent of the 600 million eligible voters elected 790 representatives to the two legislative bodies of Parliament and 4,100 members to the state legislatures. According to the former chief election commissioner, M. S. Gill, approximately 4.5 million staff members supervising "no fewer than 900,000 polling stations from the high Himalayas to the desert of Rajasthan, including areas that can be reached only on the back of an elephant," were deployed to ensure that the election was carried out in an orderly and fair manner (Gill 1998: 164–168). This remarkable exercise in democracy cost approximately Rs 6.7 billion (6.7 billion rupees), or about U.S.$165 million.

However, hopes that the twelfth general election would end the political uncertainty and fragmentation that had plagued India during the 1990s were dashed because the results produced yet another fractured verdict. Although some forty-one parties won at least one seat, the Hindu nationalist right-of-center Bharatiya Janata Party (BJP) emerged as the largest single party in the Lok Sabha with 179 seats (still far short of a majority). Sticking to formal propriety, President K. R. Narayanan (a veteran Congress politician) invited Atal Bihari Vajpayee, the BJP parliamentary leader, to form the government and gave him ten days to prove his majority. It was a sharp role reversal for the BJP, which in its earlier incarnation, as the Jan Sangh, was considered a political outcast with which no mainstream party would actively cooperate. Vajpayee, who represented the eloquent and moderate voice of the BJP, was able to distance himself from the hard-line image projected by his predecessor as party leader and from the often violent bigotry associated with the party's organizational base, a grassroots cultural organization known as the Rashtriya Swayamsevak Sangh (RSS), or National Volunteer Association. After conducting intense negotiations with and making major concessions to an unruly collection of disparate parties, the BJP-led thirteen-party coalition narrowly passed the test of a parliamentary vote and took over the reins of office. However, the precarious coalition, which commanded a parliamentary plurality but not a majority, remained hostage to unpredictable political calculations, extortive demands, and threats to withdraw support. Potentially, it could be pulled down at any time.

It seems that even before the new BJP-led government took office, plots were being hatched to bring about its downfall. Masterminding this move was the Congress (I) Party, the party of the Nehru-Gandhi dynasty and the main opposition party in Parliament before the twelfth general election.[15] Congress (I), under the leadership of Sonia Gandhi (the widow of slain former prime minister Rajiv Gandhi), set out to persuade some of Vajpayee's more mercurial partners to desert the coalition. Evidently, this task hardly proved difficult: some of the coalition partners began to air their dissatisfaction even before the new government took office. Most notably, the imperious and insulting behavior of Jayaram Jayalalitha toward the prime minister could hardly be missed. Jayalalitha, whose All-India Anna Dravida Munnetra Kazhagam (AIADMK) held eighteen critical seats, was an indispensable component of Vajpayee's ruling coalition.[16] However, she had joined the coalition on the condition that her two nonnegotiable demands be met and met quickly. The first (and implicit) demand was that Vajpayee intervene to prevent government lawyers from pressing corruption charges against Jayalalitha in the courts; the second, often voiced openly, was that Vajpayee use his power as prime minister to dismiss the ruling party in the state of Tamil Nadu, the Dravida Munnetra Kazhagam (Jayalalitha's arch-nemesis) for alleged misconduct. After months of constant tantrums and threats to pull down the government, Jayalalitha and her party finally exited from the coalition in a dramatic fashion. In mid-April 1999, the coalition government led by Vajpayee lost a vote of confidence in the Lok Sabha by just one vote. The Vajpayee government was history just thirteen months after it took office. Although Jayalalitha provided few reasons for her withdrawal, it was widely believed that her motive was to avoid standing trial for corruption—something that her alliance with the BJP had not prevented. Sonia Gandhi's overtures may have persuaded the beleaguered Jayalalitha that a Congress-led government would be more supportive.

Despite frantic efforts to put together a majority coalition, Sonia Gandhi finally had to admit failure. The bid by Congress (I) to reclaim power unraveled after the leader of the Samajwadi Party, Mulayam Singh Yadav, refused to back a government headed by a "foreigner" like Sonia Gandhi.[17] At the direction of the president of India, the cabinet requested the dissolution of the Lok Sabha and called for a fresh election. Because of the vagaries of the upcoming monsoons, the election was postponed until September 1999. In the interim, the BJP-led coalition was invited back as a "caretaker" government. Eventually, the election was held over five separate polling days, beginning on September 5, 1999. Some 60 percent of the more than 600 million eligible voters cast their ballots. The counting of ballots began on October 6, and the (almost complete) results were known within forty-eight hours.

The election returned the BJP-led National Democratic Alliance (NDA) to power with thirty-four additional seats (from 265 to 299), giving it a more stable majority. However, the electoral outcome hardly represented a mandate for Hindu nationalism: the NDA's expansion was the result of the BJP gaining new coalition allies rather than broadening its mass support. Indeed, the BJP itself did not increase its tally of votes or seats. Nevertheless, the election signified that the BJP had come of age.

Unlike the Congress Party, which clings to the hope of returning to the good old days of one-party dominance with a member of the Nehru-Gandhi family at the helm, the BJP has embraced the basic reality of modern Indian politics: that alliances with a host of political parties are the key to electoral success. The BJP has emerged as a genuinely national political party with a base in virtually all parts of the country; it is no longer strong only in the Hindi-speaking belt. Like the Congress

Party of the past, the BJP has become the nucleus of party politics—the central mass toward which other parties gravitate or from which they are repelled. To occupy this centrist position, the BJP has avoided confrontation and worked shrewdly to shed much of its narrow doctrinal and jingoistic ideological baggage. It has increasingly focused on concrete programmatic issues rather than on overarching visions of *ramrajya* (an idealized polity associated with the Hindu god Lord Rama). Indeed, the BJP's decision to seek popular support on the basis of the NDA manifesto (which deliberately excluded controversial elements of its past platforms) illustrates the extent to which it has become pragmatic and instrumental in order to move into the mainstream.

Yet there are no guarantees of stability, given the inherent volatility of Indian politics. The thirteenth general election also underscored the fact that India faces an indefinite period of unstable coalition governments. How and why, amid a "deepening" of democracy, India has experienced political fragmentation and instability and the implications of all this for governance are issues discussed in the following sections.

■ State-Society Relations and the Crisis of Governability

Changes in postindependence India's state-society relations are at the root of its governability problems. To better understand these complex processes—in particular, why it is more of a challenge to govern India today than during the Nehru years (1947–1964)—a brief historical overview is necessary.

Considering the high mortality rate of democracies in postcolonial settings, democracy in India long appeared something of an anomaly. At the time of independence, it was widely believed that India was the least likely of the newly emergent nations to sustain democracy.[18] To the skeptics, liberal democracy and the practice of representative government was too alien a system to survive in a country nostalgic for "traditions" and compromised by irreconcilable divisions. Indian democracy, they believed, superficially imposed from the top and lacking enduring roots in society, would eventually succumb to the crushing inertia of traditionalism and destructive parochialism. Indeed, the bloody riots that followed partition and the subcontinent's ancient enmities and entrenched inequities lent credence to the view that India lacked the conditions in which the values, norms, and institutions of liberal democracy could survive and flourish. Yet this rigidly hierarchical social order, whose population crossed the billion mark at the beginning of the new millennium, has so far defied the odds. Not only has India maintained its national and territorial integrity, but for much of the five decades since independence, the country has shown remarkable political stability. India stands virtually alone among the newer nations in preserving a relatively open system of parliamentary government and holding free, fair, and competitive elections. It embraces the idea that all the diverse groups and communities in the country can aspire to dignity and ultimately share in economic prosperity and political power. What explains this Indian "exceptionalism"?

Perhaps the most compelling answer has been provided by Sunil Khilnani. In his eloquent book *The Idea of India* (1997), Khilnani argues that democracy in India is the result of neither deep-rooted Indian traditions nor the legacy of British colonial rule. Rather, democracy in India arose from choices made by a progressive segment of the Indian nationalist elite, who nurtured democratic norms and practices and instilled a strong participatory democratic ethos in the Congress Party. There is little doubt that India's success with democratic institution building owes much to the collective wisdom of the nationalist leadership—individuals like Mohandas Gandhi, Jawaharlal Nehru, Rajendra Prasad, Babasaheb Ambedkar, Vallabhai Patel, C. Rajagopalachari, and others—who gave life to the Indian Constitution, a document that not only enshrined the principles of parliamentary democracy but did much to add to and transform the rudimentary political and institutional scaffolding of late colonialism into tools for democratic reconstruction. In practice, these founding fathers remained committed to the principles of parliamentary democracy and to the rules of civility, political accountability, and respect for constitutional and judicial procedures. They were able to arouse popular passion and allegiance and to assert a solidarity with the masses that allowed them to reconcile differences without precipitating political-institutional decline. In addition, they helped to forge an awareness about India that did not exist earlier: that the Indian union is greater than the sum of its parts, its pluralism is the source of its strength, and its multitudinous problems are best resolved through representative institutions and mediated politics. Even during the dark days following partition, leaders like Nehru were unequivocal in their rejection of the ideology of religious exclusivity and the demands of Hindu fundamentalists for a nonsecular, theocratic Hindu state. With consummate skill and resolve, Nehru assuaged the anxieties of the religious minorities and the so-called weaker sections of society and constructed a tolerant secular order that gave India a distinctive place in the international community.

However, since the early 1970s the sense of optimism that accompanied independence has dissipated. The previous commitments to the ethics and customs of parliamentary democracy—respect for the rule of law, the accountability of leaders, the norms of political civility and tolerance—have given way to an ugly arbitrariness, arrogance, corruption, and violence at all levels. The causes of this decline are complex and interrelated, often occurring in tandem with each other.

Whereas the Nehru-era nationalist leadership planted and nurtured the seeds of democracy, the post-Nehru leadership did just the opposite. A large volume of literature documents how and why the actions of power-hungry political elites, in particular former prime minister Indira Gandhi (1966–1977, 1980–1984), and their loyalist apparatchiks squandered the political-institutional capital so carefully built by an earlier generation of Congress Party leaders. The basic argument is that a centralized, autocratic, and confrontational style of personal rule became the norm during Indira Gandhi's sixteen-year tenure, consistently bypassing the decisionmaking institutions of government (the cabinet, Parliament, and civil service) and greatly weakening their capacity to amplify their authority and legitimacy. Even the judiciary was subordinated to the executive branch, as increased administrative discretion removed administrative actions from judicial review, and new laws provided for preventive detention and arbitrary arrests without any recourse to the courts. As the bulk of the strategic positions in these institutions became rewards for palace courtiers, the consequence was predictable: the institutions and their managers lost not only their legitimacy but also their professionalism and spirit (see Baxi 1982). Lloyd and Susanne Rudolph (1987: 84) bluntly sum up the two contrasting political eras since independence, one associated with Nehru and the other with Indira Gandhi:

> Unlike her father, Mrs. Gandhi depleted India's political capital by eroding the autonomy, professional standards, and procedural norms of political institutions and state agencies. She tried to make those responsible for Parliament, the courts, the civil services, and the federal system answerable to her. The effort succeeded, to varying degrees, in orienting their conduct to her personal will. A paradoxical consequence was to diminish the legitimacy and effectiveness of the state. Centralization based on personal loyalty and obedience to a monocratic executive lessened the state's capacity to amplify itself through multiple agencies extending beyond the limited control and attention of one person. Jawaharlal Nehru was the schoolmaster of parliamentary government, Indira Gandhi its truant.

Indira Gandhi

Government of India Press Information Bureau

Perhaps the most egregious legacy of Mrs. Gandhi's long reign was the progressive weakening of the Congress Party. Since the 1920s, when Mohandas Gandhi transformed the party into a mass organization, the "Congress system" had dominated Indian public and political life, providing the link between the political center and the sprawling periphery and bringing a measure of coherence and stability to an otherwise fragmented system. Although the Congress Party never won an absolute majority of the popular vote, India's system of plurality elections (that is, whichever candidate gets the most votes wins) in single-member districts enabled the party to win consistently large parliamentary majorities, especially during the twenty-five years following independence. (Those majorities have allowed the party to rule continuously at the national level and in most states for all but twelve years between August 1947 and March 2002.[19]) The Congress Party's unquestioned dominance in the first decades of independence rested in part on its prestige as India's premier anticolonial and nationalist organization and in part on the formidable administrative-organizational capacity of its committees at the local, state, and national levels. In addition, there were intricate networks of political favors and factional alliances (both within the party and between party factions and non-party interest groups) stretching from New Delhi to the tens of thousands of rural villages.

The destruction of the pillars of the venerable Congress system began imperceptibly in the mid-1960s, as a result of forces coming from both the state and society. As the head of the Indian state, Indira Gandhi was Machiavellian, obstructionist, and uncompromising, and the criminalization of politics under her son and apparent heir, Sanjay (who died in a 1980 plane crash), contributed greatly to the party's organizational decline. Gandhi repeatedly demonstrated disregard for both constitutional and legal constraints, winking at the violations and transgressions of her coterie and using her position to centralize power to perpetuate her cult of personality and further her dynastic ambitions. As the Rudolphs (1987: 134) have aptly noted, her "imperious, self-righteous," and harsh governing style (in particular her reliance on "populist waves" to secure electoral majorities and her habit of arbitrarily reconstituting party committees) resulted in the erosion of intra-party democracy and accelerated political and institutional decline.

Under this arbitrary system, members of the Congress Party no longer entered state or national politics by getting elected to local party committees and then moving up through the party ranks by distinguishing themselves in community work. Nor did they have to gain the confidence and support of their colleagues and their constituencies. Instead, they had to demonstrate their allegiance and deference to the prime minister. Similarly, the process of selecting party candidates for election to the district and state legislative assemblies and to the Lok Sabha became centralized in New Delhi and managed by the prime minister and her close circle. In many cases, individuals chosen to run on the Congress Party tickets had no grassroots base and only a loose affiliation with the party; they were selected because they could collect large sums of money for the party coffers and because they were loyal to Indira Gandhi. In fact, nepotism and corruption became such a pervasive part of the political culture that the new breed of Congress Party politicians engaged in an orgy of self-aggrandizement and manipulation of the political process. They used their power to enrich family members, participate in elaborate kickback schemes with businesses, or thwart the democratic process by enrolling bogus party members in order to fix elections—to name only a few examples. Indeed, the thoroughness of the Congress Party's degeneration was made vividly obvious in June 1975, with the imposition of a twenty-month-long authoritarian "emergency regime," and again in 1978, when it changed its name to Congress (I) for Indira Gandhi, which sadly epitomized the transformation of one of the twentieth century's great political organizations into a family dynasty.[20]

By the 1980s, India's political structures were deeply fractured and polarized. The personalization and centralization of power had not only eroded the government's professional and institutional autonomy but also reduced the Congress system and its intricate networks to a shell of its former self. In effect, the Congress Party came to resemble a lame Leviathan; it was a party omnipresent but hardly omnipotent, one that reacted but could not effectively govern or promote economic development. Under these conditions, Gandhi had to rely even more on populist appeals and demagogic manipulation to consolidate her political base and to keep the opposition at bay. But in the absence of structured and dependable institutions operating within accepted rules of political conduct and established legal-judicial procedures, populist waves were too ephemeral and superficial to respond to the needs of a complex and variegated society. Under such conditions, politics became even more personalized and erratic. Populist slogans and hard-to-fulfill promises became a substitute for performance.

Unwilling (and now lacking the political tools) to engage in meaningful conciliatory dialogue with a growing array of disaffected and restive groups, Gandhi in characteristic fashion met challenges (real and perceived) with disregard for democratic rules and procedures, substituting harsh decrees for a government of laws. She made strident appeals to pro-Hindu religious themes, which reentered the political scene with a vengeance after an absence of some three decades. She recklessly misused governmental and constitutional powers, exercising discretionary control over financial grants to the states, arbitrarily dissolving state governments and assemblies, and toppling popularly elected opposition ministers and replacing them with handpicked loyalists. These actions had the effect of aggravating factionalism within the Congress Party, widening the gulf between the party and society, and exacerbating communal and secessionist demands.

Nowhere was this more visible than in the tragedies of Punjab and Kashmir. To the short-sighted political elites, the growing social unrest and violence in Assam was more evidence of antinational forces trying to destroy national unity. Quick to equate any form of popular opposition (especially by ethnoreligious and regional groups) with disloyalty and treason, they sought harsh authoritarian measures to protect the country. The deadly, self-perpetuating cycle of violence in Punjab, Kashmir, Assam, and elsewhere in India became the sad harvest of this modus vivendi. Indira Gandhi's high-handedness, her need to shore up her political base among the Hindu majority, and her tendency to view even reasonable and legitimate minority and regional demands and aspirations with suspicion prevented her government from coming up with prudent and constructive solutions to these complex problems.

The sequence of events that led to the Punjab tragedy is instructive. Starting in the late 1970s, Mrs. Gandhi and her son Sanjay began to meddle in the internal affairs of Punjabi politics in an effort to impose their will over the ruling moderate Akali Dal Party. They harnessed the support of the arch "Indira loyalist" Giani Zail Singh, who used the militant Sikh fundamentalist preacher Bhindranwale to weaken the Akali Dal's leadership by dividing Punjabi politics along religious lines. However, this strategy set off the tragic events that ended in the assault on the Golden Temple in June 1984, increased support for the Sikh separatist movement, the assassination of Indira Gandhi on October 31, 1984, and the intensification of violence against the Sikhs, which quickly spread throughout the country. Similarly, it was Gandhi's tactics that paved the way for the rise of murderous agitations in Assam and Mizoram. Paul Brass, a leading scholar of Indian politics, states: "The relentless centralization and ruthless, unprincipled intervention by the center in state politics have been the primary causes of the troubles in the Punjab and elsewhere in India since Mrs. Gandhi's rise to power" (Brass 1988: 212). In a sense, then, the Indian state, once seen by society as the mediator of conflict, had become the source of conflict.

When Rajiv Gandhi assumed the office of prime minister in 1984, the political legacy he inherited was greatly compromised. The entire process of intraparty democracy at the local, district, and state levels, including the All-India Congress Committee and the Congress Working Committee (two of the party's highest organs), had ceased to function effectively or have any voice independent from that of the prime minister. Because he was the heir of the Nehru family, and also because there was sympathy for his tragic loss, Rajiv Gandhi received 48 percent of the popular vote and 77 percent (or 415 seats) of the 545 seats in the Lok Sabha. However, his five-year term (1984–1989) was characterized by numerous political blunders (largely the result of his overdependence on a small group of bungling "back-room boys"). His problems were aggravated by the Bofors scandal, by his widely perceived pro-rich and pro-urban economic liberalization policies (his preference for Gucci loafers and Porsche sunglasses did not help), and by his failure to redeem his election pledge to clean up the Congress Party and "return it to the people."[21] He squandered the initial advantages he enjoyed as the legitimate inheritor and rejuvenator of the Congress Party.

India's ninth general election (held in 1989) saw the Congress (I) Party spin into a precipitous political freefall, dropping from 415 to 197 seats. However, the new minority Janata Dal (National Front) govern-

A campaign poster for Rajiv Gandhi, Delhi, 1984. The slogan (in Hindi) on the poster reads: "A new challenge, a new message: [when] the hand is strong, the country is unified."

ment, a coalition of several disparate parties led by V. P. Singh, was overwhelmed by factionalism and by irreconcilable policy differences with its coalition partner (the BJP), and it collapsed after a little more than two years. Rajiv Gandhi's assassination by Tamil separatists during the 1991 election campaign (the tenth general election) decidedly helped to tilt the electoral balance in favor of the Congress Party, now under the leadership of the veteran P. V. Narasimha Rao. The minority Rao government (1991–1996) was sustained by its alliances with an array of regional parties and introduced a long-overdue economic liberalization program. But hopes that the seventy-year-old Rao might try to revive the rules of the Nehru era and reverse the party's organizational decline were soon dispelled. Beset by scandal after scandal, the Rao administration soon fell into disrepute. It also became apparent that competing factions within the Congress Party continued to have both a vested interest in and great devotion to the continuation of dynastic rule. The "courting" of Rajiv Gandhi's Italian-born widow, Sonia, by various factions showed how paralyzed the Congress Party had become. Indeed, the simultaneous devotion of the Congress factions to democratic principles and dynastic monarchy is one of the great puzzles of contemporary Indian politics.

■ India's Democratic Paradox

The eleventh general election, held in 1996, marked an important moment in Indian politics. H. D. Deve Gowda, a self-proclaimed "peasant's son" from the southern state of Karnataka, became the first Indian prime minister who could speak neither Hindi nor English. Although Deve Gowda's United Front government (a loose agglomeration of leftist, regional, and caste-based political parties) governed India for only eighteen months, the poignancy of the moment was hard to miss.[22] It seemed that at last power had slipped from the hands of the upper-caste westernized elites into those of India's popular majorities. However, the complex processes that brought Deve Gowda and others like him to the pinnacle of power were not new.

The universal right to vote instituted in 1951 had one very powerful effect: it empowered the masses, making their numbers count. And in the course of the half-century that followed, Indians from all walks of life came to understand the power and utility of democracy. The "deepening of democracy," reflected in the spread of democratic ideas, competitive politics, and universal suffrage, has helped spur unprecedented political activism among formerly passive groups and has served as an effective vehicle for the political empowerment of the country's previously excluded and subordinate groups. A broad alliance of the lower castes and classes collectively referred to as the "Other Backward Castes" (estimated to be about 40–45 percent of the population),[23] the "Scheduled Castes" or Dalits (20–25 percent of the population),[24] Muslims (12–15 percent), and other groups and communities that had endured generations of neglect and oppression has entered the political arena, translating their numbers into political power. Today their representatives occupy influential positions, including some of the highest offices in the land. Their political organizations and parties are formidable political machines, forming governments or determining the nature and fate of governments. As the old certitudes of the Hindu order—in which the lower-caste "inferiors" were expected to show ritualized deference to their propertied upper-caste "superiors"—have crumbled, so have the days of de facto control of passive lower-caste voters by the upper castes and classes. This sharp erosion of upper-caste/upper-class political dominance is nothing short of a quiet revolution.[25]

But why has this transformation of the political system into a truly representative form of majority rule not resulted in stable and effective governance? Moreover, why has the extension of popular sovereignty not translated into an effective challenge to the structural foundations of socioeconomic and political domination in India? Part of the problem, according to some theorists, stems from the fact that Indian society—what Mohandas Gandhi once called that layer upon layer of inbuilt resentment, inequality, and oppression—is sorely lacking in "social capital."[26] In other words, although India is blessed with a robust civil society and a rich and vigorous associational life, the associations usually reflect the narrow caste, ethnic, regional, and religious-communal loyalties (including patriarchy, class domination, and other tyrannies) that are deeply embedded in civil society. As a result, these potentially divisive tendencies often define India's associational life. And not surprisingly, despite India's resilient democratic institutions and relatively long experience with constitutionalism, political participation (especially voting) still continues to be a largely collective behavior rather than the exercise of individual choice envisioned by liberal theory. Thus, the shallowness of social capital has prevented the representatives of the state and civil society from creating forums through which they can identify and agree on common goals.

However, the social capital approach provides only part of the answer. In India, the high levels of political mobilization in the absence of a strong and responsive state and political parties have served to fragment rather than unite society. Instead of responding to the demands of an increasingly mobilized population, the country's weak and overburdened political institutions have reinforced, if not exacerbated, socioeconomic and political cleavages. The efforts of a great number of voluntary associations and nongovernmental organizations (NGOs) to build durable and inclusive representative institutions have had little success, failing to enable those sharing common interests to unite politically.

Thus, India's democratic renaissance has a dark side. It is true that the new political awakening has provided unprecedented opportunities to a diverse society—once tightly regulated by westernized political elites and by the strict rules and taboos of Brahmanic Hinduism—to explore its multifaceted and checkered histories. But that society seems at the same time to have become a prisoner of its own discursive frameworks and narrative accounts. Political parties compete increasingly along caste, religious-communal, and ethnoregional lines, with such loyalties the most significant determinant of electoral outcomes.[27] In this atmosphere, it is not surprising that parties of all stripes place partisan interests above the public good, often pathetically outbidding each other (through promises of costly state entitlements and other guarantees) to consolidate their bases and garner new support.

The trend is unambiguous. Members of the upper castes (20–25 percent of the population) have been gravitating toward the once-obscure Hindu-nationalist Bharatiya Janata Party, whose commitment to good governance, "traditional values," and the transformation of India into a disciplined Hindu nation-state has struck a particular chord, especially among the propertied classes in the Hindi-speaking heartland.[28] The Samajwadi Party, confined mainly to Uttar Pradesh, claims to be the party of the state's backward castes, and the Bahujan Samaj Party represents the interests of the Dalits. Meanwhile, the secular, or "modernist," Indians, who fear the BJP's militant Hindu nationalism, continue to cling to the incorrigibly "top-down" Congress Party.

The heterogeneous lower castes and classes, unified largely in their desire to settle scores with their former upper-caste "masters," suffer from many internal contradictions that have made common action extraordinarily difficult. In their strident campaigns against upper-caste exploitation, the lower-caste political leaders rarely invoke universal principles of rights and justice. Instead of demanding that the state accord universal rights, protections, and provisions to all its citizens, especially the "weaker sections," they often insist that their particular communities and groups are most deserving of state entitlements. Not surprisingly, such an environment has produced a motley array of self-serving regional chieftains, political fixers (including criminal gangs, the so-called *goondas* and *dacoits*), local power brokers, and political freelancers. These typically pose as the saviors of their communities, promising to sweep away the debris of the past and usher in a new order. They are often all too ready to circumvent institutional and legal procedures and, if need be, maliciously engage in political demagoguery to inflame their communities. Although it is important to repeat that social pluralism is not necessarily antithetical to the formation of an inclusive political community, weak political institutions and chauvinistic politics in contemporary India have engendered societal fragmentation and alienation rather than integration.

Ironically, from the start, the Indian state became an unwitting accomplice in creating and reinforcing caste-based identities at the expense of common, or national, citizenship. In its effort to correct the systematic injustices and deprivations suffered by the lower castes and other underprivileged communities, the constitution abolished "untouchability" and outlawed discrimination on the basis of caste and religion. (See Chapter 11 for a further discussion of caste.) The first amendment to the constitution (which became law in 1951) also introduced a wide array of "compensatory discrimination" programs (India's version of affirmative action) by reserving 22.5 percent of all central government jobs for individuals belonging to Scheduled Castes and Tribes.[29] Similar reservations were made for admission to educational institutions. Over time, these reservations have been extended to the Other Backward Castes (OBCs). In 1980, the report of the Backward Classes Commission (also know as the Mandal Commission), chaired by B. P. Mandal—a former chief minister of Bihar and himself a member of a backward caste—proposed an even wider-ranging "compensatory discrimination" program for the 52 percent of the population, including Muslims, classified as "backward." The report recommended that 27 percent of all central and state government jobs and 27 percent of all spaces in government universities and affiliated colleges should be reserved for members of the 3,743 castes and subcastes identified as "backward." For more than a decade, this report was shelved. Then, in 1990, the new OBC-dominated Janata Dal coalition government under then prime minister V. P. Singh announced its intention to implement the commission's recommendations.[30] This decision aroused strong passions, convulsed Indian society (some higher-caste students even set themselves on fire in protest), fueled caste wars, and was instrumental in causing the government's downfall. Although implementation was stayed by the Supreme Court pending a ruling on the constitutionality of the measure, no political party has publicly opposed "reservations," since none wants to alienate itself from the large backward-caste electorate.

In 1991, the newly elected Congress Party government under Prime Minister P. V. Narasimha Rao sought to mollify opposition to the reservations issue by adding a 10 percent reservation for the poor of the higher castes. In November 1992, the Supreme Court upheld the reservation for OBCs, with the vague provision that it be "need-based," but struck down the additional 10 percent as constitutionally impermissible. Such public policies and decisions have only served to sharpen caste enmities in a classic case of how noble intentions can turn sour. Since the late 1980s, India has experienced renewed religious and communal discord, as the forward, or elite, classes and castes, the Scheduled Castes, the various backward castes and classes, and competing religious and regionally focused groups have fiercely contested and some-times violently fought over every scrap of the state's largesse. Indian society, it seemed, had been irreversibly realigned in ways so as to strengthen caste, communal, and ethnoregional identities.

In summary, as India's national Parliament and some two dozen state assemblies have become more pluralistic and representative of the country's diversity and numerous social cleavages, one outcome has been the emergence of enormous challenges for India's political and economic development. More than ever before, crucial decisions regarding the allocation of resources are heavily influenced by political considerations, rather than by sound technical and developmental cri-teria. With considerable fanfare, politicians make regular visits to their constituencies to inaugurate projects and to receive petitions for new ones. Ruling parties routinely distribute government resources and perks to reward supporters and to create new bases of support while withholding resources from opposition supporters and perceived and real "hostile" communities. Such a system has accentuated deep-seated communal and caste allegiances and antagonisms and has produced widespread graft and corruption, leaving few resources for meaningful human development.

Given the prevailing patterns of state-society relations, how can India resolve its pervasive developmental dilemma? I suggest that the resuscitation of public institutions and the renegotiation of state-society relations are imperative for India.

■ The Resilience of Indian Democracy

For all its limitations, India remains the world's largest constitu-tional democracy, with a functioning Parliament, a political regime of laws and institutions, civilian control of the military, a free press, numerous political parties, and free elections for which millions of vot-ers turn out. Moreover, democracy has provided the glue that holds together this nation of some 1 billion people and twenty major lan-guages. No doubt, although a palpable sense of concern exists regard-ing the future of good governance in India, there is nevertheless some hope. Some developments bode well for India's democracy.

First, despite the fact that caste and communal loyalties are still the most significant determinant of electoral outcomes, the proliferation of political parties has also given the Indian voter a wide menu of choices. That has enabled the largely illiterate Indian electorate, on critical occasions, to demonstrate an uncanny wisdom and sophistication. Since 1947, only a quarter of incumbents have been returned to power. In elections since 1987 for state-level governments, less than 15 percent of incumbent administrations have been returned to power. Moreover, the Indian electorate is increasingly splitting its vote among different parties—in both state and national elections—as if to show their preference for deadlocked parliaments. If the emerging trends hold, the message is clear: the volatile voter with a strong bias against incumbents has a low threshold for ineffective or bad governments; no party can take its rule for granted; and ideologically polarized parties must shed their extremism if they are to be successful. Electoral success now depends on a party's ability to reach out to individuals in diverse social settings while conveying a political agenda with generalized rather than sectoral appeal. This underscores the fact that fears about the Hindu nationalist BJP may be exaggerated. As noted earlier, the BJP has softened its Hindu chauvinism and moved increasingly to occupy the political center, the traditional mainstream of Indian politics.

Second, although Indians often bemoan the recurring instability associated with coalition governments, it is important to recognize that India's mind-boggling diversity can be effectively reflected in a broad-based coalition government. Indeed, it is the very deepening of democracy that has made the national Parliament and state assemblies more representative of civil society. Contrary to the conventional view, the various coalition governments have not necessarily worsened governability. Rather, by facilitating a measure of the much-needed decentralization of power from New Delhi to the states, the various coalitional configurations have restored some vitality to regional grassroots democratic institutions. Moreover, under today's coalition governments, politics remains highly pluralistic. Since the prime minister and cabinet are chosen by multiple political actors, their power is also constrained by multiple constituencies.

Third, in recent years India's judiciary, including the Supreme Court and the high courts in a number of states, has reasserted its authority. The courts have sought to weed out corruption at all levels, pursuing civil and criminal cases involving several former ministers in the central government and in the states (including former prime minister P. V. Narasimha Rao and the former chief minister of Bihar, Laloo Prasad Yadav). Most startling, India's once compliant Election Commission has undertaken an energetic and unprecedented campaign to make political parties and their leaders accountable. Besides demanding that political parties must file returns of their expenditures both for parties and for individual candidates, the commission has also begun to clamp down on the flagrant use of money to influence voters. In the process, many of the country's seemingly invincible rulers have been humbled. The fact that the Election Commission has used its power to deploy large numbers of security forces to polling stations has helped to prevent violence and vote fraud.

Finally, although this point belies conventional logic, it seems that India's political instability has had little effect on the country's overall macroeconomic performance. Indeed, India's economic performance in recent years has been remarkable. After slowing down in 1997–1998 (in response to a weak harvest and the effects of the Asian financial crisis), the gross domestic product increased an average of 6.25 percent in the subsequent two years—among the highest rates of growth in the world. Moreover, the balance of payments has remained comfortable despite the regional slowdown, turmoil in international capital markets, international sanctions, and the sharp increase in oil prices.

In India, the dominant issue on the political agenda is no longer whether democracy can survive, but whether it can become a meaningful way for diverse sectors of the populace to exercise collective control over the public decisions that affect their lives. Indeed, there is growing recognition that although democracy cannot guarantee the complete fulfillment of a country's socioeconomic and political objectives, it is nevertheless a precondition for their pursuit and thus an intrinsic value in its own right.

■ **Notes**

1. For the mood of the populace during the 1996 general election, in which a record 530 million voters participated, see "Joy and Order as India's Voting Starts," *New York Times*, April 18, 1996.

2. In February and March 1998, India held its twelfth general election. Given the daunting logistics, the election was held over thirteen days in four stages.

3. The president of India occupies the same position the Crown does in Britain. India's presidents, with few exceptions, have been distinguished elder statesmen (no women so far), who have generally performed their rather perfunctory duties with dignity. The president is elected by the members of the Lok Sabha, the Rajya Sabha, and the Vidhan Sabhas for a five-year term and can stand for reelection. Presidents are subject to impeachment by Parliament for violation of the constitution.

4. Malik (1993: 86) notes that "in some ways the prime minister's secretariat resembles the U.S. president's executive office. It is entrusted not only with preparation of the agenda for cabinet meetings and maintenance of the records of cabinet proceedings but also with coordination of the administration of different departments of the government headed by the members of the council of ministers."

5. Under this system, political parties can gain commanding positions in the Parliament without gaining the support of a majority of the electorate. For example, the Congress Party, which has dominated Indian politics until recently, never won a majority of votes in parliamentary elections. The best-ever Congress Party performance in parliamentary elections was in 1984, when it won 48 percent of the vote but garnered 76 percent of the parliamentary seats. In the 1991 general elections, the Congress Party won 37.6 percent of the vote and 42 percent of the seats.

6. The members of the Rajya Sabha are elected indirectly, rather than by the citizens at large. The terms in the upper house are staggered so that one-third of the members stand for election every two years.

7. Officers of the IAS are an elite corps drawn primarily from the affluent and educated upper castes. In 1990, only about 150 out of a candidate pool of approximately 85,000 recruits received appointments in the IAS.

8. India has a single judicial system, with the Supreme Court at the head of the judicial hierarchy, high courts in each of the states, and district courts. According to the constitution, the Supreme Court should consist of a chief justice and not more than seven other judges (although Parliament is authorized to change the number of judges and has done so).

9. It is important to note that India has a unified judicial system (see note 8). That is, there are no separate state courts, but instead each state has a high court that is subordinate to the Supreme Court. The Supreme Court also covers the disputes arising between the central and the state governments, as well as cases involving two or more states. Robert Hardgrave and Stanley Kochanek (1993: 101) aptly note that although "the scope of judicial review in India is not as wide as in the United States . . . the Court held more than 100 Center and state acts invalid, either in whole or in part, and most of its decisions have been unanimous."

10. Most states have unicameral legislatures. However, Andhra Pradesh, Maharashtra, Tamil Nadu, Uttar Pradesh, Bihar, Pondicherry, and Jammu and Kashmir have bicameral legislatures, with the lower house or legislative assembly (the Vidhan Sabha) being the real seat of power. The upper house or legislative council (the Vidhan Parishad) serves as an advisory body. The largest Vidhan Sabha is in Uttar Pradesh, with 425 members, and the smallest, with thirty members, is in Pondicherry.

11. Norman Palmer has argued that the "Indian union is not strictly a federal polity but a quasi-federal polity with some vital and important elements of unitariness" (1961: 94).

12. The team's report is named after its chairman, Balwantray Mehta, a former chief minister of Gujarat state. For the report's detail, see Government of India (1957).

13. Local self-government is divided into urban and rural categories. The Census Report of 1961 has laid down definite criteria for determining urban localities: a population of over 5,000 or more, a density of not less than 1,000 persons per square mile, and at least 75 percent of the working population being engaged in nonagricultural occupations.

14. An independent Election Commission established in accordance with the constitution is responsible for the conduct of parliamentary, state legislature, and presidential elections. The commission prepares, maintains, and periodically updates the electoral roll, which indicates who is entitled to vote, supervises the nomination of candidates, registers political parties, monitors the election campaign (including the candidates' funding), organizes the polling booths, and supervises the counting of votes.

15. The Congress Party changed its name in 1978 to Congress (I), recognizing Indira Gandhi.

16. Despite its name, the AIADMK is confined almost entirely to one state, Tamil Nadu.

17. Of course, political considerations were also at work. Yadav feared an erosion of support from one of his core constituencies, the Muslims, who seemed poised to return to the Congress Party.

18. The classic works on this topic include Eugene Staley's *The Future of the Underdeveloped Countries* (1954) and Selig Harrison's *India: The Most Dangerous Decades* (1960), in which the authors argue that "centrifugal pressures" could ultimately overwhelm the new state, resulting in chaos and Balkanization.

19. The Congress Party was in power at the national level from independence in August 1947 to March 1977, from May 1980 to November 1989, and from June 1991 to May 1996. Its share of the vote declined steadily from around 47.8 percent at its peak in 1957 to 37.6 percent in 1991, barring the unusual "sympathy vote" of 48.1 percent in 1984 after Indira Gandhi's assassination. As noted earlier, under India's electoral system a candidate needs to obtain only the greatest plurality of votes, not necessarily a majority, to win. Hence, 40 to 50 percent of the popular vote can produce legislative majorities of 60 to 75 percent in Parliament. For example, in the years of Congress Party dominance, from 1947 to 1967, when the party held more than 70 percent of the seats in Parliament, it never received more than 50 percent of the vote in parliamentary elections.

20. Not surprisingly, from 1969 to 1977 the Congress Party had five presidents, a turnover no doubt aimed at preventing the consolidation of power by any potential challenger.

21. In 1987, Rajiv Gandhi's government was rocked by charges that the Swedish arms manufacturer AB Bofors had paid an illegal commission to win an artillery contract. The government's stonewalling on a full-scale inquiry and press exposés of illegal transactions involving the prime minister's closest friends—including evidence that came perilously close to directly implicating the prime minister himself—contributed to the government's defeat in 1989.

22. The United Front produced two prime ministers in its less than two years of power. Both were from the Janata Dal, a party that has since dissolved and regrouped as part of the Janata Dal (United).

23. The term *backward castes* (also referred to in the 1950 constitution as "Other Backward Classes") is used to refer to a broad range of subcastes of intermediate ritual status in the Hindu caste hierarchy. These castes fall between the elite upper castes (the forward castes) and the lower, Scheduled Castes (previously known as "untouchables," now often referred to as Dalits, or "oppressed ones") and Scheduled Tribes. The Indian Constitution recognizes the backward castes and the Scheduled Castes and Scheduled Tribes as "disadvantaged lower castes" or "weaker sections" and has allowed them remedial solutions, such as reserving legislative seats, government posts, and places in educational institutions for these groups. Yet it is important to note that the low castes are not a monolithic group. Divided into literally thousands of subcastes, they, like the upper castes, are governed by strict rules and ritual taboos.

24. The Dalits, or the former "untouchables" in the Hindu caste order, are referred to as Scheduled Castes. They represent the most exploited and the poorest sectors in society.

25. For a detailed analysis across regions of the emergence of the Other Backward Castes as a political coalition, see Frankel and Rao 1989–1990.

26. "Social capital" refers to the institutions, relationships, and standards that shape and determine a society's social interactions.

27. The Hindi satirist Harishankar Parsai captured this reality in a telling literary piece. He claimed that he had convinced Lord Krishna to contest a seat in the state assembly. He wrote, "We talked to some people active in politics. They said, 'Of course. Why shouldn't you? If you won't run in the election, who will? After all, you are a Yadav [a dominant Other Backward Caste], aren't you?' Krishna said, 'I am God, I don't have a caste.' They said, 'Look, Sir, being God won't do you any good around these parts. No one will vote for you. How do you expect to win if you don't maintain your caste?'"

28. Although the upper-caste Hindus were gradually eased out of political power in the major southern states in the 1960s and 1970s, this process did not take place in the Hindi-speaking heartland until the 1980s. Squeezed by the assertiveness of the lower castes, the upper castes, traditionally supporters of the Congress Party, have flocked to the BJP because it is widely perceived to be the true protector of their interests. It is important to note that the BJP is part of a larger "Hindu family." The parent organization, the Rashtriya Swayamsevak Sangh, founded in 1925, stands for the consolidation of all Hindus into a united community. The BJP's main goal is to unite Hindus politically to achieve national power and to transform India into a Hindu nation-state. The Vishwa Hindu Parishad (VHP) is involved in mass-mobilization activities, while the Bajrang Dal serves as the armed wing, often using violence and intimidation against opponents.

29. Comparable reservations for the Scheduled Castes and Scheduled Tribes were also made by state governments.

30. Although Singh declared that the reservations were being implemented to correct social injustices, his political opponents saw it as a cynical move to shore up his support among the backward castes.

■ Bibliography

Appleby, Paul. 1953. *Public Administration in India: Report of a Survey.* New Delhi: Government of India, Cabinet Secretariat.

Baxi, Upendra. 1982. *The Crisis of the Indian Legal System.* New Delhi: Vikas.

Brass, Paul, 1988. "The Punjab Crisis and the Unity of India." In *India's Democracy: An Analysis of Changing State-Society Relations,* Atul Kohli, ed. Princeton: Princeton University Press, pp. 169–213.

Dasgupta, Joytindra. 1988. "Ethnicity, Democracy and Development in India." In *India's Democracy: An Analysis of Changing State-Society Relations,* Atul Kohli, ed. Princeton: Princeton University Press, pp. 144–168.

Frankel, Francine. 1988. "Middle Classes and Castes in India's Politics: Prospects for Accommodation." In *India's Democracy: An Analysis of Changing State-Society Relations,* Atul Kohli, ed. Princeton: Princeton University Press, pp. 225–261.

Frankel, Francine, and M. S. A. Rao, eds. 1989–1990. *Dominance and State Power in Modern India.* 2 vols. Delhi: Oxford University Press.

Freire, Paulo. 1970. *Pedagogy of the Oppressed.* New York: Herder and Herder.

Gill, M.S. 1998. "India: Running the World's Biggest Elections." *Journal of Democracy* 9, no. 1: 164–168.

Government of India, Planning Commission. 1952. *First Five-Year Plan.* New Delhi: Government of India.

————. 1957. *Report of the Team for the Study of Community Projects and National Extension Services.* 3 vols. New Delhi: Government of India.

Hardgrave, Robert, and Stanley Kochanek. 1993. *India: Government and Politics in a Developing Nation.* 5th ed. New York: Harcourt Brace Jovanovich.

Harrison, Selig. 1960. *India: The Most Dangerous Decades.* Princeton: Princeton University Press.

Hirschman, Albert. 1970. *Exit, Voice, and Loyalty: Responses to Decline in Firms, Organizations, and States.* Cambridge: Harvard University Press.

Khilnani, Sunil. 1997. *The Idea of India.* New York: Farrar, Straus and Giroux.

Kohli, Atul. 1988. *India's Democracy: An Analysis of Changing State-Society Relations.* Princeton: Princeton University Press.

————. 1990. *Democracy and Discontent: India's Growing Crisis of Governability.* New York: Cambridge University Press.

Kothari, Rajni. 1970. *Politics in India.* Boston: Little, Brown.

Malik, Yogendra. 1993. "India." In *Government and Politics in South Asia,* Craig Baxter, Yogendra Malik, Charles Kennedy, and Robert Oberst, eds. Boulder, Colo.: Westview Press.

Palmer, Norman. 1961. *The Indian Political System.* Boston: Houghton Mifflin.

Putnam, Robert. 1993. *Making Democracies Work: Civic Traditions in Modern Italy.* Princeton: Princeton University Press.

Rudolph, Lloyd, and Susanne Rudolph. 1987. *In Pursuit of Lakshmi: The Political Economy of the Indian State.* Chicago: Chicago University Press.

Sharma, Shalendra D. 1999. *Development and Democracy in India.* Boulder, Colo.: Lynne Rienner Publishers.

Staley, Eugene. 1954. *The Future of the Underdeveloped Countries.* New York: Harper and Row.

Weiner, Myron. 1967. *Party Building in a New Nation: The Indian National Congress.* Chicago: University of Chicago Press.

6

International Relations

Sumit Ganguly

As India enters the new millennium, its foreign policy is undergoing a profound transformation. The original pillars that supported it have either collapsed or rest on shaky foundations. These architectural features were composed of a commitment to nonalignment, a global redistributive economic order, and a belief—at least in the abstract—in universal nuclear disarmament. Each of these principles has eroded over time.

As early as the late 1960s, for example, India's commitment to the global elimination of nuclear weapons was mostly rhetorical (Ganguly 1983). Though some of the antinuclear rhetoric persists, the country is well on its way to being a full-fledged nuclear weapons state (Ganguly 1999a). The end of the Cold War and the simultaneous Soviet collapse led to the rapid disintegration of a second component of India's foreign policy structure, nonalignment.[1] The commitment to global redistributive economic justice also lost ground in the 1980s because of the ebbing of superpower competition and the intellectual shift to the principles of neoclassical economics as the primary mechanism for promoting economic growth (Thakur 1994).

India's national leaders continue to invoke the language associated with these three original goals. Nevertheless, for all practical purposes, they have been abandoned. Today India's foreign policy goals and strategies reflect those of any large, ethnically diverse, and economically weak state. They include the protection of national sovereignty, the preservation of territorial integrity, and the pursuit of national economic development.[2] A larger moral or ethical vision no longer informs India's rhetoric about transformation (or preservation) of the global order in such areas as climate change, human rights, and nonproliferation. Though couched in terms of idealistic principles, India's goals reflect its own national needs and imperatives.

■ The Past as Prologue

What factors, both material and conceptual, led India initially to pursue a transformational foreign policy agenda? The answer can be traced to the early days of the Indian nationalist movement. One of the principal leaders of this movement, Jawaharlal Nehru, had a specific vision of world order based on distinctive and deeply held values. He was able to define India's key national interests without much hindrance because few others in the nationalist leadership had his international exposure and knowledge (Gopal 1984). V. K. Krishna Menon, another British-trained lawyer with socialist credentials, shared Nehru's intellectual leanings. Among other matters, they had an innate distrust of the United States and some, albeit grudging, admiration for the Soviet Union's industrial achievements.

Despite their seemingly lofty visions of world order, however, a good deal of pragmatism also informed Nehru's and Menon's thinking. The two were acutely aware that India's material weaknesses, most notably its acute poverty, precluded it from playing a significant role in global affairs and from protecting its vital interests. They pursued the strategy of nonalignment to keep India away from the titanic superpower struggle in the post–World War II era. Specifically, they feared that India's involvement in the Cold War would have profoundly adverse consequences for its political and economic development. Any close association with either superpower, they suspected, would draw India into military pacts and lead to the militarization of Indian society. They also were determined to avoid excessive defense spending for fear of strengthening the military at the cost of economic development.

Nehru directed India's foreign policy in pursuit of these ends during his entire career in public office (1947–1964). The Indian Foreign Service, the diplomatic arm of the state, simply translated and implemented directives from the highest quarters. Policy initiation was not its role. One important consequence of Nehru's dominance of foreign policy issues was the inhibition of the growth of the country's foreign policy making institutions (Tharoor 1982). The failure to develop institutional mechanisms for the formulation and conduct of foreign policy proved costly for India after his death.

Nehru actively campaigned for decolonization in Asia and Africa and became a prominent advocate for pan-Asian solidarity (Gupta 1964). Along with other postcolonial nationalists, such as President Achmad Sukarno of Indonesia, President Gamal Abdul Nasser of Egypt, and Marshall Josef Broz Tito of Yugoslavia, he boosted the nonaligned movement, which sought to promote the peaceful settlement of international disputes, economic development, and decolonization. At the global level, he campaigned for universal nuclear disarmament. In 1954, for example, in conjunction with the Republic of Ireland, India introduced a resolution in the United Nations General Assembly calling for a complete cessation of nuclear weapons testing. Some forty years later, this resolution would become the basis of the Comprehensive Test Ban Treaty.

Under Nehru's tutelage, India's adherence to these goals was complex and, as some have argued, uneven (see Perkovich 1999). The tensions in India's foreign policy were most evident in the realm of nonalignment. For example, India failed to unequivocally condemn the Soviet invasion of Hungary but expressed early reservations about the U.S. role in Vietnam. Later, Prime Minister Indira Gandhi hedged on the question of the Soviet invasion of Czechoslovakia (Mansingh 1984: 138).

This lack of evenhandedness had important adverse consequences for India. In 1960, when Indian forces marched into the Portuguese colonial enclave of Goa (on the west coast of India) after protracted negotiations for Portugal's withdrawal failed, the United States and the majority of the western powers sharply condemned the Indian action (Rubinoff 1971). Two years later, when India had to defend its borders against Chinese aggression, the United States only grudgingly came to its assistance (Subrahmanyam 1976).

The disastrous Sino-Indian border war of 1962 laid bare the inherent weaknesses of India's military and diplomatic strategies (see Hoffman 1990). The inadequacy of India's military capabilities proved costly, as the People's Republic of China (PRC) came to occupy some 14,000 square miles of disputed territory. In the aftermath of this war, although India still refused to abandon nonalignment, it fundamentally altered its defense policies. It embarked on a significant program of military modernization, which would entail a dramatic reappraisal of its security policies (Thomas 1978).

Eventually, after the 1971 Indo-Pakistani war (which was preceded by the 1965 Indo-Pakistani war), India for all practical purposes dispensed with the practice of nonalignment (Horn 1982). To counter the emergent U.S.-China link, India forged diplomatic and security relationships with the Soviet Union, which served India well in terms of its national security for the next two decades. The Soviets, desirous of good relations with India to counter U.S. and Chinese influence in South Asia, gave India unstinted diplomatic support regarding its dispute with Pakistan over Kashmir; they also provided substantial amounts of sophisticated weaponry at highly advantageous prices (Racioppi 1994).

Nehru's immediate successor, Lal Bahadur Shastri (1964–1966), although he had no experience at all in foreign affairs, deftly coped with the consequences of the September 1965 Pakistani attack on India (Brines 1968). Shastri successfully negotiated a peace accord with his Pakistani counterpart, Mohammed Ayub Khan. His imprint on the policymaking process was minimal, however, since he died shortly thereafter, in January 1966.

■ The Limits of Nonalignment

Shastri's successor in office was Nehru's daughter, Indira Gandhi. Ironically, the jettisoning of Nehru's vision of foreign policy started under her leadership (1966–1977; 1980–1984). Unlike her erudite and brilliant father, she had few intellectual proclivities and little formal education (Malhotra 1991). Although initially unsure of herself in office, she quickly became a ruthless practitioner of hardball politics at both domestic and international levels. Publicly, she and her circle of advisers continued to reiterate the lofty Nehruvian principles that supposedly were the basis of India's foreign policy. Thus, India opposed the Nuclear Nonproliferation Treaty (NPT) of 1968 on the grounds that it was discriminatory. (It prohibited the nonnuclear states from acquiring nuclear weapons while placing no equivalent restrictions on the actions of the nuclear weapons states.) Gandhi also used the nonaligned movement to press for a global redistribution of the world's resources. In practice, however, after weathering her first foreign policy crisis in 1966–1967, she started to dismantle the structure that her father had so carefully constructed.

The crisis of 1966–1967 had domestic roots but profound foreign policy consequences. The near-collapse of agricultural production in India's key regions—as a result of two consecutive poor monsoons—

caused India to turn to the United States for food assistance. The United States was willing to provide such assistance, but it wanted India to curb its strident criticisms of the U.S. conduct of the Vietnam War. Simultaneously, the United States wanted India to reform its agricultural procurement practices, to adopt more market-friendly economic policies, and to dismantle significant barriers to foreign investment (Ganguly 1988–1989). U.S. president Lyndon Johnson adopted a "short-tether" policy, which made continued food aid dependent on a change in India's public diplomacy on the Vietnam question. In the end, however, despite some cost, the Indian foreign policy establishment made few concessions except in the realm of economic policymaking.

This experience made Indira Gandhi acutely aware of India's vulnerability to external pressures. Consequently, when the United States began an attempt at rapprochement with the PRC in 1970, she made overtures toward the Soviet Union. These overtures culminated in the twenty-year Indo-Soviet Treaty of Peace, Friendship, and Cooperation. A key clause in the treaty amounted to a virtual security guarantee for India (Donaldson 1974), but it came in for some domestic criticism on the grounds that it compromised nonalignment.

The treaty paid off handsomely for India during the 1971 Indo-Pakistani war, when the Soviets twice blocked United Nations Security Council resolutions condemning India for its military intervention on behalf of the beleaguered Bengali population of East Pakistan (Sisson and Rose 1990). After the 1971 war, India moved even closer to the Soviet Union and distanced itself further from the United States. Again, Indira Gandhi's pragmatic and nonideological approach to foreign and defense policy goals carried the day.

This bilateral relationship with the Soviet Union, though highly beneficial to India, did entail certain diplomatic costs. India's closeness to the Soviet Union kept its relations with the United States both frosty and distant. Its relations with the PRC also remained in limbo, apart from a fitful attempt to improve relations in 1978. This attempt, made during the coalition government led by the Janata Dal (People's Party), floundered when China attacked Vietnam during Indian foreign minister Atal Bihari Vajpayee's visit to China—and when the Chinese told Vajpayee that they were teaching Vietnam a "lesson," just as they had taught India one in 1962. Finally, India's ties with the Soviet Union also inhibited the development of better relations with the states of Southeast Asia.

The robust Indo-Soviet relationship was disturbed in the wake of the latter's invasion of Afghanistan in December 1979. At the time of the invasion, India had an interim government under Prime Minister Chaudhuri Charan Singh. It is a little-known fact that the Charan Singh government, despite its shaky status, sharply upbraided the Soviets for their invasion of a sovereign state.[3] When Indira Gandhi resumed office in January 1980, she publicly reversed course. Under her instructions, India's permanent representative to the United Nations simply echoed the Soviet position that the regime in Afghanistan had invited the Soviets in (Horn 1982). This switch proved costly for India in both symbolic and material terms. At the level of political symbolism, India's international image was tarnished because it was the only democratic state that appeared to uncritically accept the Soviet explanation for its actions in Afghanistan. It also proved costly in material terms, as the Association of Southeast Asian Nations (ASEAN) became wary of India's overtures in its direction.

Despite the bonds that India had forged with the Soviet Union, Indira Gandhi and her advisers realized that they could not indefinitely afford to alienate the United States. Accordingly, in 1981 she met with President Ronald Reagan in Jamaica at a North-South summit. She also visited the United States at President Reagan's invitation in 1982. The changes that took place in Indo-U.S relations as a consequence were largely cosmetic. Nevertheless, the visit provided a basis for an improvement in relations under Gandhi's son and political successor, Rajiv.

Indian dependence on the Soviet Union continued during Rajiv Gandhi's government (1984–1989). However, his fitful attempts to reform the hidebound and near-stagnant Indian economy contributed to further improvements in Indo-U.S. relations. As India moved to slowly dismantle the complicated regulatory apparatus that had governed investment and trade regimes, U.S. firms took a new interest in the Indian economy. With the growth of commercial ties, some government-to-government contacts also widened. When Rajiv Gandhi visited the United States, a major memorandum of understanding was signed, which enabled India to purchase various high-technology items that previously had been unavailable because of U.S. export restrictions.

Closer to home, India's relations with most of its neighbors suffered. India had become drawn into the civil war that wracked Sri Lanka, helping to negotiate a peace accord between the Sri Lankan government of Junius Jayawardene and the principal Tamil insurgent group, the Liberation Tigers of Tamil Eelam (LTTE). India sent a mission, the Indian Peace Keeping Force (IPKF), to help monitor the peace. The LTTE, however, failed to adhere to the terms of the accord, and very quickly the IPKF's role changed into one of military enforcement. The IPKF was ill suited for the mission at hand, and after a bloody experience of nearly two years, it withdrew at the request of the next president, Ranasinghe Premadasa.[4]

Relations with India's long-standing adversary, Pakistan, also deteriorated during Rajiv Gandhi's tenure in office. Undeniable evidence emerged about Pakistan's support for the Sikh insurgents in the Punjab, and despite repeated warnings to Pakistan, that support continued unabated.[5] Although many Indians were in favor of some kind of retaliation, India did not offer similar aid to insurgents in Pakistan's Sind province. But the Brasstacks military exercises of 1986–1987 may have in part been a response to the Pakistani actions.

■ The Brasstacks Crisis and Beyond

In late 1986 and early 1987, India carried out its largest peacetime military exercise, Brasstacks. It involved tests of some newly developed battlefield tactics and the coordination of some rapid-movement armored formations. Though firm evidence is still unavailable, it is reasonable to conclude that one of the goals of Brasstacks was to send a message to Pakistan. To the dismay of General Krishnaswami Sundarji, the chief of staff of the Indian Army and the architect of the exercise, the Pakistani response proved to be unexpectedly vigorous. Fearful of being caught in an escalatory spiral, Prime Minister Rajiv Gandhi and Minister of State for Defence Arun Singh sought U.S. and Soviet intercession. Primarily as a consequence of U.S. help, the crisis was brought to a close (Bajpai et al. 1995).

The end of the Cold War and the collapse of the Soviet Union led to a fundamental reappraisal of India's foreign policy goals and choices. Indian decisionmakers realized that Russia, the principal successor state to the Soviet Union, had neither the inclination nor the resources to provide India with the same guarantees that the former Soviet Union had offered, particularly against a belligerent China. Consequently, Indian leaders, most notably Rajiv Gandhi, tried to improve relations with the United States and China. Under his successor, P. V. Narasimha Rao, India embarked on a "look east" policy designed to cultivate better relations with the states of Southeast Asia. Rao's efforts to improve ties with the Southeast Asian nations neatly dovetailed with the economic reform process that he and his finance minister, Manmohan Singh, undertook in 1991 to rescue India from the depths of an acute financial crisis. These efforts resulted in India obtaining observer status in ASEAN and full membership in the ASEAN Regional Forum (ARF).

Although India met with some success in its attempt to court the ASEAN states, its relations with the United States and China were more problematic. Fundamental differences of interest continued to plague both relationships. With the United States, the disputes largely focused on India's pursuit of a nuclear weapons program. Sino-Indian relations were affected by the limited progress in settling the border dispute and the low priority that China accorded to India in its foreign policy calculations.

■ The End of the Cold War

In the 1990s, India faced several critical foreign policy choices. One involved a response to Saddam Hussein's invasion of Kuwait. India, which had long had good relations with Iraq, found itself in a quandary. It could hardly endorse the invasion. At the same time, it did not wish to alienate a major supporter in the Arab world and a critical supplier of oil. More to the point, it had several thousand expatriate workers in Iraq. In the end, Indian leaders decided to adopt a cautiously supportive policy toward the U.S-led coalition forces in the Gulf. In a departure from past practices, it even allowed U.S. aircraft to refuel in Bombay (Ganguly 1991b). This decision, however, was overturned once the matter was made public, and several political leaders, most prominently Rajiv Gandhi, sought to embarrass the ruling regime.

Relations with the United States, which had shown some signs of improvement in recent years, again became contentious as the decade of the 1990s drew to a close. In large part because of the lack of a more solid relationship with the United States in such areas as trade, investment, and security, the ties fell victim to a single and deeply nettlesome issue, nonproliferation. In the mid-1990s, India and the United States found themselves at loggerheads over the U.S. decision to pursue an unconditional and indefinite extension of the NPT. From the inception of the treaty in 1968, India had been staunchly opposed to it.

When the NPT Review Conference started in New York, India did not attend the formal proceedings but nevertheless sought informally to forge a Third World coalition against the unconditional extension of the treaty. The Indian efforts proved futile, and the U.S. initiative prevailed. Subsequently, India took a far more active stance at the Geneva Conference on Disarmament, which was attempting to draft a Comprehensive Test Ban Treaty.[6] India, which had proposed the treaty as early as 1954, now emerged as one of its most vocal critics on the basis of a number of technical reservations. In particular, India objected to the unwillingness of the nuclear weapons states to make some firm commitment toward the elimination of nuclear weapons; it also questioned the loopholes that allowed the nuclear states to test the reliability of their stockpiles through laboratory experiments. In the end, India's objections were overruled, and the treaty was sent to the United Nations General Assembly for a vote.

It has been argued in some quarters that India's decision to test a set of five nuclear devices in May 1998 stemmed in considerable part from the seemingly relentless pressure that was being applied to make it renounce its nuclear weapons program (Ganguly 1999a). The tests were carried out under the auspices of the coalition dominated by the Bharatiya Janata Party (BJP), without significant consultation or prior public debate. Nevertheless, apart from some self-aggrandizing opposition from the Congress Party, the tests were mostly popular among the Indian electorate.

Closer to home, the Indian nuclear tests spurred the Pakistani political leadership to test their own nuclear weapons. In the aftermath of these tests, following several months of acrimony, India and Pakistan appeared to embark on a path toward rapprochement. The high point of this process involved Prime Minister Vajpayee's visit to Lahore, Pakistan, in February 1999 to inaugurate a bus service between Lahore and New Delhi. But the good feelings that the Lahore visit occasioned proved to be short-lived. In early May 1999, Indian army patrols discovered that several Pakistani army units of the Northern Light Infantry had made significant incursions across the Line of Control in Kashmir near Kargil (Kargil Review Committee Report 2000). Faced with this colossal intelligence failure, the Indian politico-military leadership acted quickly, and within two months the intruders had been dislodged. In the aftermath of this conflict, Indo-Pakistani relations remained deeply strained.

In a renewed effort to impove relations with Pakistan, Prime Minister Vajpayee invited General Pervez Musharraf to the historic Indian city of Agra for a summit in July 2001. Despite a promising start, the summit failed to accomplish much. Many mutual recriminations followed in the aftermath of the summit and India-Pakistan relations continued down a desultory course.

In the aftermath of the terrorist attacks in the United States on September 11, 2001, relations between the two countries worsened. India sought to link its own troubles with Pakistan over the disputed area of Kashmir to the U.S.-let effort against global terror. Pakistan, quite understandably, sought to distinguish its support for the Kashmiri insurgents from support for terror, insisting that it was aiding a freedom struggle in Kashmir. Pakistan's insistence on maintaining this distinction suffered an important blow in the wake of a terrorist attack on India's parliament on December 13, 2001. Two Pakistan-supported terrorists organizations, the Jaish-e-Mohammed and the Lashkar-e-Taiba, claimed responsibility for the attack.

Under substantial pressure from India and the United States, General Musharraf made various pledges to cut off ties to these radical groups. Despite his public commitment to end support to theses organizations, terrorist attacks aimed at India continued, leading to a steady worsening of India-Pakistan relations. Another terror attack on an Indian military base at Kaluchak in the state of Jammu on May 30, 2002, deepened the ongoing crisis. As India moved substantial numbers of troops to the Pakistani border, Pakistan retaliated in kind. Many western commentators raised the prospect of a nuclear war between the two countries. In an effort to defuse tensions, the United States, along with a number of other western powers, undertook a series of diplomatic initiatives. Toward mid-July 2002, tensions subsided as General Musharraf reiterated his pledges to end support for the insurgency in Kashmir. Indian officials, willling to reduce some force deployments, nevertheless expressed skepticism about Musharraf's willingness to abide by his commitments.

■ Institutional and Societal Factors in the Policymaking Process

The making of India's foreign policy (except for dealings with its immediate neighbors, especially Pakistan) has been and remains the concern of only an elite group. During the Nehru years, the prime minister held the foreign policy portfolio himself. Subsequent prime ministers usually have had a minister for external affairs. Key foreign policy decisions reflect the ruling party's political and ideological orientation and are the result of cabinet-level discussions. Immediately below the level of the ministers is the highest-ranking bureaucrat, the foreign secretary, drawn from the ranks of the elite Indian Foreign Service (IFS). Entry into the IFS, in turn, is through a highly competitive national examination. Currently, the IFS has approximately 700 serving officers.

Government of India Press Information Bureau

Prime Minister Vajpayee (right) and Pakistan prime minister Nawaz Sharif (center) wave to the crowds after crossing the border into Pakistan by bus, February 20, 1999

It also has a second tier of officers who are drawn from other national services; these officers mostly perform administrative and security functions.

■ The Role of Parliament and the Cabinet

In parliamentary systems, legislators, whether they belong to the ruling party or the opposition, are expected to oversee foreign policy formulation and implementation. India's parliamentarians, with marked exceptions, have not performed this task with any degree of skill.

During the Nehru era, some members of Parliament did demonstrate an interest in and an understanding of India's foreign policy. Minoo Masani, for example, an ardent critic of Congress Party governments and a member of the pro-U.S. (and long defunct) Swatantra Party, was known for his parliamentary eloquence on matters pertaining to foreign policy. Frank Anthony, a member of Parliament from the Anglo-Indian community, showed considerable interest in foreign affairs. George Fernandes, a trade union leader and defense minister, also took an interest in foreign affairs. More recent entrants to Parliament, however, have shown considerably less interest in the conduct of India's external relations.

This relative lack of interest and expertise should not obscure the fact that Parliament can wield significant power in certain areas pertaining to foreign policy. For example, it has the power to ratify both bilateral and multilateral treaties. But in practice, various administrations have deemed it unnecessary to present minor treaties for ratification (Bandopadhyaya 1991).

The record of the cabinet's role in foreign policymaking has also been quite uneven. Under Nehru, it hardly played any significant role. The prime minister simply made his decisions and then informed the cabinet. In effect, the cabinet became little more than a rubber-stamp organization.

A similar trend continued under Nehru's daughter, Indira Gandhi. (Unlike Nehru, however, she did not have a larger vision that animated her foreign policy goals.) Under her leadership, the various cabinet committees, including that of external affairs, were folded into the unified Political Affairs Committee (PAC). Since then, the prime minister has chaired this committee, which includes the ministers for external affairs, defense, finance, and home affairs. The PAC, then, is the primary body for the formulation and conduct of foreign affairs.[7] Except in its earliest years, the PAC routinely deferred to Indira Gandhi. In subsequent years, serving under less dominant personalities, it has shown greater independence.

■ The Mass Media and Other Institutions

Apart from the individuals who have institutional responsibilities for the formulation and conduct of the country's foreign relations, a small handful of influential journalists in the English-language press and research analysts based primarily in official, quasi-official, and independent think tanks attempt to influence foreign policymaking.

The think tanks include the Ministry of Defence's Institute for Defence Studies and Analysis, the independent Centre for Policy Research, the dovish Institute for Peace and Conflict Studies, and the Congress Party–affiliated Rajiv Gandhi Centre for Contemporary Studies. It is difficult to ascertain the extent to which these organizations directly or indirectly affect the formulation of Indian foreign policy. Nevertheless, it appears reasonable to conclude that they do play some role in influencing key debates and decisions.

Within the elite English-language press, three news magazines stand out for their coverage of foreign affairs: *India Today*, *Outlook*, and *Frontline*. All three magazines generally have an independent political stance, though *Frontline* has a pronounced left-wing bias on most economic issues, whether at domestic or international levels. In recent years, some of the major English-language dailies, such as the *Hindu* and the *Times of India*, have employed full-time foreign and strategic affairs correspondents. Some of these individuals probably wield influence in the corridors of South Block, the home of the Ministry of External Affairs. Determining their ability to influence specific issues and decisions, however, is impossible. Suffice it to say that they play a consultative role and, on occasion, serve as channels for the ruling regime to use in building support for existing policies.

Since the 1990s, with the onset of various forms of economic deregulation, television has become an important means for the dissemination of news about foreign affairs, and access to television has become emblematic of membership in India's growing middle class. The state-run television network, Doordarshan, now competes with the Cable News Network (CNN) and the British Broadcasting Corporation (BBC) to provide Indians with news from abroad. It seems reasonable to assume that the dramatic growth in the number of television viewers has contributed to a more informed populace, and in the future, this knowledge may well have important consequences for India's foreign and defense policies.

Some signs of such consequences of television may already be visible. For example, when Indian forces repulsed the Pakistani intruders along the Line of Control in Kashmir, many enterprising television reporters provided on-the-spot coverage, making the Kargil war India's first televised conflict. If the conflict had not ended within two months and if larger numbers of Indian soldiers had been killed, the television coverage could have affected foreign and defense policy choices.

Despite the growth of television and print coverage, the mass electorate in India, though increasingly politically sophisticated, demonstrates little sustained interest in the nation's foreign policy. There are, of course, exceptions. In northern India, the physical proximity of Pakistan and the presence of large numbers of postpartition immigrants from Pakistan help to sustain an interest in Indo-Pakistani relations. In the state of Tamil Nadu, there is interest in the plight of fellow Tamils in Sri Lanka. Similarly, illegal immigration from Bangladesh has become an electoral issue in such northeastern Indian states as West Bengal and Assam. Nevertheless, the vast majority of India's electorate is more interested in immediate issues of domestic politics than in the remote complexities of world affairs (Ganguly 1991a).

■ The Future of India's Foreign Policy

The tasks that face India's current foreign policy decisionmakers are challenging. At a procedural level, India must strengthen its institutional capacity for the formulation and conduct of its foreign relations. Doing so will require improving the recruitment processes and training of its diplomatic service personnel; a reliance on talented generalists will no longer suffice. In at least two issue areas, those of international economics and arms control, India will have to develop a group of career bureaucrats who have sufficient professional training to tackle increasingly complex subjects. It will also need to provide a group of trained individuals to improve the workings of the National Security Council (NSC). The normal bureaucratic corps cannot generate the specialized expertise that the NSC staff calls for. Finally, to ensure that the Parliament plays a viable role in foreign policymaking, the parliamentary committee on foreign affairs will need to be adequately and appropriately staffed.

At a more substantive level, the preeminent tasks faced by future administrations will involve the management of India's newly acquired and much-contested nuclear weapons status. To this end, it will have to place its future relations with the United States on a more secure footing. It will also need to stabilize its relations with Pakistan and the People's Republic of China. Positive advances in Indo-Pakistani relations will largely depend on Pakistani initiatives and policies. As long as Pakistan remains unreconciled to Indian control over the disputed state of Jammu and Kashmir, there will be few tangible and durable improvements in Indo-Pakistani relations.

The Sino-Indian relationship is also likely to remain competitive.[8] India and China, except on rare occasions, have divergent goals and support different causes. More to the point, Indian strategists legitimately fear China's growing military prowess and its willingness to disburse nuclear weapons and ballistic missile technology to India's principal adversary, Pakistan (see Tellis 2001).

For good or ill, Indian decisionmakers have come to see the South Asian region as their political and strategic preserve, and India will continue to play the role of a regional security manager. Any developments in Bangladesh, Nepal, and Sri Lanka that could have materially adverse consequences for India will draw its attention and even intercession. The key questions that will confront India's decisionmakers are the means and approaches that they will adopt to deal with regional contingencies. For example, during the brief existence of the Janata Dal administration under Prime Minister Inder Kumar Gujral in the mid-1990s (which followed another Janata Dal administration under V. P. Singh), India displayed remarkable generosity in dealing with Bangladesh on the contentious and politically charged issue of water sharing. It remains to be seen if future governments can also craft such

Government of India Press Information Bureau

Prime Minister Vajpayee (right) greets visiting Chinese premier Zhu Rongji in New Delhi, January 14, 2002

imaginative policies, designed to allay the fears and suspicions of India that many of its smaller neighbors harbor (Ganguly 1999b).

In another sphere, that of India's foreign trade and economic policies, much will depend on the country's ability to press forward with the domestic economic reforms that it began in 1991. If the reforms proceed apace, India can attract significant amounts of foreign investment and newer forms of technology. If these investments prove to be substantial, they will in turn influence India's foreign relations with key investor nations such as the United States. In such a situation, even if there were differences in particular issue areas, the overall relationship would still remain viable. The central question that looms before India's leaders is whether they can adapt to a changed structure of world politics, set new priorities, and develop the necessary institutional mechanisms for pursuing those priorities.

■ Notes

1. As Inder Kumar Gujral, a former Indian foreign and prime minister, told the author, "Who are you going to be nonaligned against?" Personal communication, New York City, September 1991.

2. For a particularly good discussion of the concept of Westphalian sovereignty, see Krasner 1999.

3. Personal communication with a senior Indian diplomat, New York City, October 1992.

4. For an analysis of the IPKF's role in Sri Lanka, see Muni 1993. For reasons that led to this involvement, see DeVotta 1998: 457–473.

5. Personal communication with a senior retired Indian Foreign Service Office, New Delhi, July 1988.

6. For a discussion of Indian diplomacy at these two meetings, see Perkovich 1999.

7. In 1998, when a Bharatiya Janata Party–led coalition came to power, it created a National Security Council (NSC). The NSC is largely a consultative and deliberative body and is composed of the secretaries of home affairs, external affairs, and defense. A senior bureaucrat serves as the national security adviser. The first person to hold this position was Brajesh Mishra, a retired senior foreign service officer.

8. For the extraordinary difficulties that are likely to be encountered in attempts to improve Sino-Indian relations, see Garver 2001.

■ Bibliography

Bajpai, Kanti, P. R. Chari, Pervaiz Iqbal Cheema, Stephen P. Cohen, and Sumit Ganguly, eds. 1995. *Brasstacks and Beyond: Perception and the Management of Crisis in South Asia*. New Delhi: Manohar.

Bandopadhyaya, Jayantanuja. 1991. *The Making of India's Foreign Policy: Determinants, Institutions, Processes and Personalities*. New Delhi: Allied.

Brines, Russell. 1968. *The Indo-Pakistani Conflict*. New York: Pall Mall.

DeVotta, Neil. 1998. "Sri Lanka's Structural Adjustment Program and Its Impact on Indo-Lanka Relations." *Asian Survey* 38, no. 5 (May): 457–473.

Donaldson, Robert. 1974. *Soviet Policy Toward India: Ideology and Strategy*. Cambridge, Mass.: Harvard University Press.

Ganguly, Sumit. 1983. "Why India Joined the Nuclear Club." *Bulletin of the Atomic Scientists* 39, no. 4 (April): 30–33.

———. 1988–1989. "Of Great Expectations and Bitter Disappointments: Indo-U.S. Relations During the Johnson Administration." *Asian Affairs* 15 (winter): 212–219.

———. 1991a. "Foreign Policy Issues in the Ninth General Election." In *Alliance Politics and Minority Governments in the Ninth and Tenth General Elections in India*, Harold Gould and Sumit Ganguly, eds. Boulder, Colo.: Westview Press.

———. 1991b. "India Walks a Middle Path in the Gulf Conflict." *Asian Wall Street Journal Weekly*, March 4.

———. 1999a. "India's Pathway to Pokhran II: The Sources and Prospects of India's Nuclear Weapons Program." *International Security* 23, no. 4 (spring): 148–177.

———. 1999b. "India: Policies, Past and Future." In *India and Pakistan: The First Fifty Years*, Selig S. Harrison, Paul H. Kreisberg, and Dennis Kux, eds. Cambridge: Cambridge University Press.

Garver, John W. 2001. *Protracted Contest: Sino-Indian Rivalry in the Twentieth Century*. Seattle: University of Washington Press.

Gopal, S. 1984. *Jawaharlal Nehru*. London: Jonathan Cape.

Gupta, Sisir. 1964. *India and Regional Integration in Asia*. New York: Asia Publishing House.

Hoffman, Steven. 1990. *India and the China Crisis*. Berkeley: University of California Press.

Horn, Robert. 1982. *Soviet-Indian Relations: Issues and Influence*. New York: Praeger.

Kargil Review Committee Report. 2000. *From Surprise to Reckoning*. New Delhi: Sage.

Krasner, Stephen. 1999. *Sovereignty: Organized Hypocrisy*. Princeton: Princeton University Press.

Malhotra, Inder. 1991. *Indira Gandhi: A Personal and Political Biography*. Boston: Northeastern University Press.

Mansingh, Surjit. 1984. *India's Search for Power: Indira Gandhi's Foreign Policy, 1966–1982*. New Delhi: Sage.

Muni, S. D. 1993. *The Pangs of Proximity*. New Delhi: Sage.

Perkovich, George. 1999. *India's Nuclear Bomb*. Berkeley: University of California Press.

Racioppi, Linda. 1994. *Soviet Policy Toward South Asia Since 1970*. Cambridge: Cambridge University Press.

Rubinoff, Arthur. 1971. *India's Use of Force in Goa*. Bombay: Popular Prakashan.

Sisson, Richard, and Lee E. Rose. 1990. *War and Secession*. Berkeley: University of California Press.

Subrahmanyam, K. 1976. "Nehru and the China-India Conflict of 1962." In *Indian Foreign Policy: The Nehru Years*, B. R. Nanda, ed. Delhi: Vikas Publishing House.

Tellis, Ashley J. 2001. *India's Emerging Nuclear Posture: Between Recessed Deterrence and Deployed Arsenal*. Washington, D.C.: Rand Corporation.

Thakur, Ramesh. 1994. *The Politics and Economics of India's Foreign Policy*. New York: St. Martin's Press.

Tharoor, Shashi. 1982. *Reasons of State: Political Development and India's Foreign Policy Under Indira Gandhi, 1966–1977*. New Delhi: Vikas.

Thomas, Raju G. C. 1978. *The Defense of India: A Budgetary Perspective of Strategy and Politics*. New Delhi: Macmillan.

7

India's Economy

John Adams

Every morning more than 1 billion Indians start the ordinary routines of daily life: bathing, praying, eating, going to work, shopping for the family's needs, and walking to school. By the time night falls, some 175 million families are fed, provisioned, tired, and mostly in good humor. The mission of this chapter is to explain how India's economy looks to the people who energize it by their diverse tasks in the processes of making a living, trading their products and services with each other, and sharing and enjoying the fruits of their labor.

This bottom-up view of India's economic activities shows how Indians perceive their roles and duties in the tasks of production, exchange, and consumption. The intent is twofold: to try to convey people's aims and actions in the material or economic realm of their lives and to apply and make real concepts that are vital to understanding the operations of one of the world's most complex and dynamic economies. Like most of the world's peoples, Indians not only strive to meet their daily needs but also are engaged in the quest for an expanding standard of living for themselves and their children. In some ways, this is the same view that workers and families in the United States have of their economy: not something remote or "out there" but part of the habits and practices of working, providing, and "getting by."

In other ways, the average Indian family and the average U.S. family differ sharply. For one thing, by the simplest yardstick, an American is about seventy-four times richer than his or her Indian counterpart. The total income of an economy in one year is known as its gross national income (GNI). When GNI is divided by total population (POP) the result is average income per person, or per capita income (GNI/POP). In 2000, per capita income in the United States was $34,260, but in India it was $460.[1] Explaining how such large differences can exist and persist in the world's comity of nations is the task of growth economics. One reason is inadequate education: 33 percent of Indian men and 61 percent of Indian women are illiterate. Educated populations are much more productive and wealthy than those that do not make effective use of their potential human capacities. Another explanation is health: 53 percent of Indian children under the age of five are malnourished, so that their growth, strength, energy levels, and learning abilities are reduced. A measure of widespread technological sophistication and the use of machines is the per capita consumption of electricity: an Indian uses 347 kilowatt hours per year, compared to an American's 11,796. Ease of transportation and communication facilitates economic activities. Indians have nineteen telephones for each 1,000 people, whereas Americans have 644 per 1,000 (World Bank 2000: 232, 264–267). For Indians to move toward U.S. standards of living, these crucial gaps will have to be closed.

The ready availability of jobs sharply differentiates the horizons of U.S. workers from those of Indian workers. Most Americans who want to find steady jobs can obtain them. Most Indians worry, more than anything, that if they lose their jobs, they cannot find others. Managing poverty and the fear of falling off the economic and social ladder are at the heart of most Indian families' concerns. Coping with affluence and competing in the rush to ride the U.S. escalator of success equally dominate Americans' lives. International opinion polls suggest that most Indians give their degree of "happiness" roughly the same crude score that Americans do. Understanding Indians' acceptance of their poverty equates to understanding how they can apprehend abundance in the midst of want. For the typical Indian family, even one living at the edge of the margin of poverty, the perception is of "enough," and the wish is for "a little more." Although there are millions of families in desperate deprivation, most couples and their children have adequate food, clothing, and shelter and have accommodated to their conditions, although their piles of possessions would be dwarfed by Americans' piles, as modern worldwide television makes only too evident.

To capture this seeming paradox—that most Indian families "get by" even when they are measurably poor—the theme of this chapter is "abundance in poverty." It suggests the enormous potential Indians have to extend the economic gains of the past fifty years and make themselves a much more prosperous nation. Hope for a more bountiful future is not a delusion.

■ The Rural Economy and Agriculture

As in most poor countries, the heartbeat and soul of the Indian economy rests in village-based agriculture. Many Indians, even sophisticated businesspeople or educated professionals who live in giant metropolises like Mumbai (Bombay) or Delhi, retain deep and affectionate ties to their ancestral villages. They visit their remaining kinfolk, make pilgrimages to family shrines, and dream of retiring in imagined idyllic rural bliss. More than a century has passed since most Americans adjusted their lives to the cycle of the seasons and the needs of their crops and livestock, rather than to the mandates of the factory whistle or the office time clock. In India's 550,000 villages, people are never far from the odors, sounds, and textures of plowed soil, crop production, livestock rearing, or harvested grains. Half of India's families still rely on farming for their immediate livelihoods, and many others make their living by selling or processing vegetables, fruits, raw milk, fibers, or grains. Industries depend on the farmers' foodstuffs, cotton, oilseeds, and silk as inputs into hundreds of factories. India's agriculture is the basis for many of India's exports: cotton textiles, jute carpet backing, fruits, vegetables, and leather goods. Contrary to the conventional international perception, India exports more food and farm products than it imports and is not a food-deficit country.[2]

Life in an Indian village is rich and complex, even if the typical community has no more than 500 to 2,000 inhabitants.[3] By taking a close look at a single village, it is possible to learn much about the organization of India's rural economy and to see how economic relationships are linked with landownership, the caste hierarchy, and social attitudes. Of course, no village is perfectly typical, but at the same time, Indian village life has common components everywhere. Wangala is a village in Karnataka state in south-central India.[4] In this part of India, villages are nucleated; that is, they feature tight clusters of houses in the midst of the village fields. Wangala is served by canal irrigation, which permits the growing of sugarcane as a cash crop, along with paddy (rice) and other produce. Most farmers possess bullocks (castrated male cattle), which are used for tilling the fields and pulling wooden carts. Many own one or more milch cows, some goats and sheep, or a pair of blue-gray water buffalo, which are used for plowing and are a source of rich milk. Today, peasant families own tractors, power tillers, and other farm equipment.

Wangala lies mostly northwest of a small country crossroads. To the west, which is to the left on Figure 7.1, a rutted dirt road connects Wangala to Mandya, a commercial town, with sugar milling, farm supplies, and a lively shopping area or bazaar. Bangalore, one of India's largest cities and an emerging global software production nexus, is only a couple of hours distant. Buses stop at Mandya several times a day. The figure's codes for the buildings identify shops and a café, which in this part of India is called, grandiosely, a "hotel-u." Some people travel to Mandya each day to work. Selling sugarcane, buying fertilizer, shopping for household goods, and earning money in Mandya are activities that link the villagers to the larger Indian economy. Still, to a high degree, the families in Wangala are most closely tied to each other within the web of relationships that characterize the community's economy.

There is a strong correspondence between caste and house quality and location. The leading Peasant families have large homes lining both sides of Headman Street, and they truly form the spatial and social core of Wangala's society. (It is customary to capitalize caste names like Peasant or Potter. I use *caste* to mean *subcaste* or *jati*. India's *jati* groups are endogamous, meaning that people almost always marry someone from their *jati,* usually in an arranged marriage.) The Peasants

Bullocks pull a roller to separate grain from chaff

Figure 7.1 Diagrammatic Sketch Map of Wangala Village

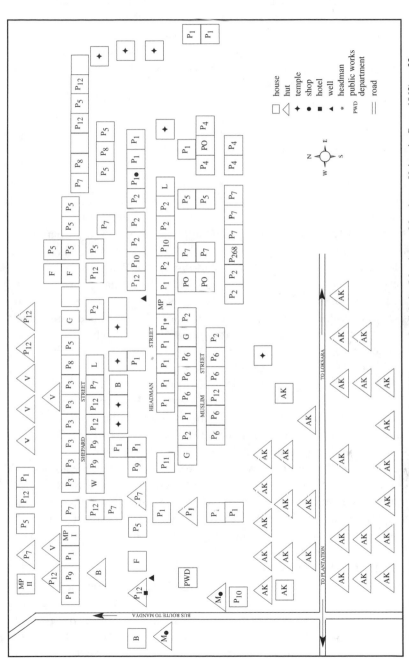

Source: Scarlet T. Epstein, *Economic Development and Social Change in South India* (Manchester: Manchester University Press, 1962), p. 22.

Notes: Castes: Lingayat Priest (L), Peasant (P), Potter (PO), Goldsmith (G), Blacksmith (B), Fisherman (F), Madras Peasant I (MPI), Madras Peasant II (MPII), Washerman (W), Muslim (M), Untouchable AK (AK), Untouchable Vodda (V). Peasant lineages: Headman (1), Mallegowda (2), Kadegowda (3), Tuparegowda (4), Kadeholade (5), Kalasegowda (6), Chaudegowda (7), Bevaregowda (8), Chamegowda (9), Hallegowda (10), Nanjegowda (11), no lineage (12).

are landowners and are divided into eleven kinship groups, or lineages, which themselves cluster together. Altogether there are 128 Peasant households, and they hold 89 percent of the village lands.[5] The average family has only about 4 acres, some of which may be wet, or irrigated, and the remainder dry, where only rain-fed crops can be grown. The second-largest group in the village comprises the low-status Harijans, who constitute nearly 20 percent of all families, thirty-five in all, but have less than 7 percent of the land. (I use *Harijan,* Mohandas Gandhi's term for the former Untouchables, to refer to the agricultural worker *jatis.* It means "Children of God." Harijans and service-caste people perform what are regarded as ritually polluting tasks in the course of their daily work: cleaning latrines, handling leather products, washing dirty clothes, or cutting hair and shaving beards. In earlier times, particularly, priests and landlords, who were at the top end of the caste hierarchy, disdained work and looked down on the farming and commercial castes. Ideas asserting the "dignity of work" or that "hard work is a good thing" do not fit well into this set of attitudes and customs.) Most Harijans are farm laborers working for the Peasants, and they are very poor. They live in thatched huts rather than mud or brick houses, and their isolation from village society is reflected in their peripheral locations on the margins of Wangala. Harijans cannot use the village's two wells or take water from the canal and pond where upper-caste women wash their laundry and cooking pots and so must rely upon a small pond some 200 yards away.[6]

A third large grouping of families and castes lives in Wangala. There are Potters, Goldsmiths, Blacksmiths, Fishermen, Priests, and Washermen, as well as the two Muslim shopkeepers. Most of these families have abandoned the occupations suggested by their caste titles, if indeed they ever practiced them at all, and now own land, work for Peasants, or have found new jobs in the growing regional economy.[7] A century ago, the array of services and products offered by these specialist castes made the village economy more or less self-contained and self-reliant, although there were always significant connections to the outside world, such as crop and crafts sales, tax payments, and outside work and shopping. The acceptance of the family's inherited caste position, the availability of adequate food and services, the sheer fullness of everyday village life, the security of family and kin, and the pageantry of festivals and weddings have combined for 2,000 years or so, and still combine today, to create a pattern of living that is humanly rich and materially sufficient for most. This sense of abundance, albeit in the midst of poverty, should not be romanticized because the verity of social division and economic hierarchy reinforced by sharp disparities in power is equally pervasive.

An overview of the economy of an Indian village must recognize that stability and perceived abundance constitute only one aspect of rural life. Another aspect of village life is inequality sustained by inherited prerogative. The first and foremost principle is the importance of landownership in determining a family and caste's status, power, and wealth, all of which are passed from generation to generation.[8] This principle extends beyond the village to dominance of the landed castes in regional, state, and national politics. It explains why the Indian government caters to farmers with free or subsidized irrigation water, electricity, and fertilizer, at massive cost to the national and state treasuries. It explains why agricultural incomes in India are not taxed, no matter how large they are. It explains why farmer castes have immense weight in most state and national parties and preeminent standing in most incumbent governments.

A second, contrasting principle hinges on the other reality of the hierarchy of village life. The marginalized Harijan, or Dalit, castes are poor and numerous, characteristics that make them potentially important in democratic elections when they are angry, organized, and active. As time has passed, this fundamental cleavage between the landed castes and the agricultural workers has deepened, especially in north India, has become a strong factor in elections, and sometimes has been the basis for armed and murderous clashes in the most riven villages. Dalit parties seek power as a way of obtaining better schooling, more seats in universities, greater job opportunities, and the respect and equality their members are guaranteed by the Indian Constitution.

At the national level, India's agricultural sector is the sum of all the farming activities that take place in the villages. As in Wangala, two leading Indian farm products are rice and sugarcane. The second major foodgrain is wheat. Barley, maize, sorghum, other millets, peas, and beans fall in the foodgrain category.[9] In addition to sugarcane, other crucial cash and plantation crops are oilseeds, cotton, jute, tea, coffee, rubber, spices, cashews, coconuts, vegetables, and fruits. Probably the most important single indicator of economic success in India since 1950 has been the output of foodgrains because the nation has given the highest priority to feeding itself without reliance on unpredictable foreign sources.

Many families watch the prices of key foods like rice, wheat, and cooking oils. When there are shortages and prices rise, all families, and most critically poor families, suffer because food expenditures absorb anywhere from a large slice to virtually all of their budgets. The poorest will not be able to find enough work at wages high enough to cover their food bills.[10] Shortfalls in food production and the accompanying high prices are blamed on the incumbent state and national governments, even though failures of the monsoon rains in large measure may be responsible. At such times, there will be discontent and unrest, and if elections are being held, there is a good chance the government in office will be voted out or at least find its majority reduced. Table 7.1 provides a synopsis of the growth of major components of India's agricultural sector since 1950/51. (India's accounting year runs from April to March and falls across two calendar years.) For comparison, the rising size of the population is shown. Since 1950/51, the output of rice has more than quadrupled. The story of wheat is more impressive, with an elevenfold increase through 2000/01.[11]

Rice and wheat outputs have both benefited from the application of Green Revolution technologies. In the late 1960s, India's farmers began planting new high-yielding varieties of wheat seeds that were the product of international and Indian research. These seeds were highly responsive to the application of fertilizers but required controlled doses of irrigation water to flourish. Conditions in northwest India, centering on the state of Punjab, known for its web of canals and its entrepreneurial farmers, were most favorable, and yields per acre soared. Gradually, the methods of the Green Revolution have spread widely in India, and now new varieties of rice are enabling farmers in India's eastern region, its poorest, to raise their outputs and incomes. The minor grains, peas, and beans are often planted in dry areas and have not been much affected by the Green Revolution, so their growth in output has lagged far behind that of the two major foodgrains.

Table 7.1   Foodgrains, Sugarcane, and Population, 1950/51–2000/01
               (millions of tons; millions of persons)

Year	Rice	Wheat	Foodgrains	Sugarcane	Population
1950/51	20.58	6.46	50.82	57.10	361.09
1960/61	34.58	11.00	82.02	110.00	439.23
1970/71	42.22	23.83	108.42	126.40	548.16
1980/81	53.63	36.31	129.59	154.30	683.33
1990/91	74.29	55.14	176.39	241.10	846.30
2000/01	91.04	72.35	211.60	293.50	1,024.02

Source: Government of India, *Economic Survey 1997/98,* tables 8.3 and 8.6, for crops; Jagran, *India at a Glance 1998,* edited by R. K. Thukral for the *Dainik Jagran* (Hindi daily newspaper), Kanpur, India, 1998, 21–23.

Winnowing grain

Overall, foodgrain output has risen by 4.2 times in the fifty years since independence, but during the same span of time, the population has almost tripled. An implication is that Indians on average have somewhat more food per family than earlier, but a lack of work, income, and purchasing power means that many of the worst-off adults and children do not have enough to eat. As in Wangala, the marginalized Harijans or Dalits are most affected.

Commercial crop production has climbed, but less dramatically than the output of foodgrains. Sugarcane harvests have increased five-fold, but overall the commercial crops, including cotton, jute, and tea, have not done particularly well. India's agriculture will require heavy investment and continued research on better farming methods and seeds, if yields per hectare are going to rise to higher levels. The increased use of chemicals and pesticides carries with it threats to wildlife and biodiversity and, in addition, is yet another source of drinking-water pollution in India's already contaminated waterways. On the whole, though, the achievements of growing enough food and meeting industry's needs for raw materials are strong components of India's economic success after 1950. The success in agriculture not only provides foodstuffs for the towns and cities and inputs for industry but raises incomes so that rural families become a larger market for the products of industry: clothing, motor scooters, fertilizers, bicycles, and television sets. Agriculture and industry's linked growth has been a key feature of India's expanding economy.

■ Commerce and Industry

Most modern, rich economies have vigorous commercial and industrial sectors. India has a long history of commercial and industrial enterprise, but only recently has agriculture diminished in proportionate size, allowing urban business activities to move to the forefront.[12] In 1980, agriculture was responsible for generating 38 percent of India's gross national product (GNP), but this proportion fell to 27 percent in 2000, not because agriculture shrank but because other activities grew more speedily. The share of industry in GNI rose from 24 to 27 percent over the same time span. Banking, transportation, communications, and government services captured a 46 percent share of output in 2000, up from 34 percent in 1980 (World Bank 2002: 236). This shift in economic structure is a predictable companion of economic growth and rising per capita income. It is indicative of India's progress along the road to economic maturity. Some vignettes depicting representative workers will help in understanding the range of jobs and

John Adams

Boiling sugarcane juice to make *gur*, an Indian brown sugar kinds of enterprises that make up India's expanding commercial and industrial sectors.[13]

Ritu's husband pushes mail carts in the main post office in Madurai, a temple city in south India. She and her family live in a one-room shack in a colony of squatters on unused public land. Rent is paid to a local mafia don, who bribes the police so that they will not evict the settlers. Her widowed mother helps care for her two young children. Ritu makes sweets every day and takes them to a spot on the sidewalk outside an office building where she and other women sit and gossip. She sells enough, usually to regular customers, to add Rs 20 per day (20 rupees per day, or about U.S.$0.42) to the family's income. It is not hard work, she enjoys talking to her friends, and she feels more independent than she would if she stayed at home all day. Still, when evening comes, Ritu is responsible for cooking meals, cleaning her home, caring for the children, and meeting the commands of her husband and mother.

Swamy works in a cotton spinning mill in Ahmadabad in Gujarat state in northwest India. He belongs to a union and has worked in the factory for fifteen years. He lives in the village where he was born and rides a company bus to work every morning. He has acquired some land, which his father and brother proudly farm. Swamy's position is a comparatively high-paying and secure one, but he and other workers read newspapers and attend union discussions. They fear that they may lose their jobs as competition grows in the world economy. They know that their equipment is old and must be replaced, but they are suspicious that management is skimming profits and not investing enough in the business. Swamy and his friends support politicians who espouse job protection, high-tariff "India-first" trade policies, and government assistance to failing private businesses.

Near the center of Ahmadabad, Akbar runs a small metalworking shop, which makes steel cabinets, by hand and to order. His brother works with him. Their business is on a street with many similar shops. It is typical in Indian cities for tailors, metalworkers, door makers, and auto-parts stores to cluster in the same areas. Instead of fostering cutthroat competition, such congregating helps customers find and choose dealers, makes it easier to get supplies in and products out via shared transportation, and permits potential rivals to keep an eye on each other. Akbar and his brother live in four rooms behind their shop with their wives and six children. They are hardworking and thrifty. The growth in Ahmadabad's population and economy enables them to make a good living, and they are thinking about moving to a new industrial

park set up by the state government and hiring some nonfamily workers. If they did that, though, they would have to pay taxes, which they
now avoid, and could no longer tap illegally into power lines to obtain
free electricity.

Lakshman is an attorney (called an "advocate" in India) in New
Delhi. He and his firm consult with multinational companies, seeking
to expand their presence in India's emerging telecommunications sector. India's laws and regulatory practices have been slow to change,
making bidding for cellular telephone contracts or seeking to enter
long-distance service subject to uncertainties. Much time is taken up in
dealing with government officials, none of whom seems to have a sense
of urgency or to be possessed of ultimate decisionmaking authority.
Lakshman was trained in India but has spent considerable time visiting
law schools in England and the United States. Sometimes he feels very
Indian, having tea with bureaucrats, and sometimes he feels very western over whisky at the Sheraton. His wife, Renu, is a partner in a firm
of chartered accountants. Lakshman and Renu's family is representative of India's professional middle class. They have a four-bedroom
house in a new suburb, drive a car, and travel abroad once a year at
least. Their two children are preparing for college majors in medicine
and business and hope to pursue advanced study in the United States.

Rekha has a bachelor of commerce degree from a rural college and
has worked as a clerk in a bank in Mumbai for about a year. She lives
in a small fourth-floor walk-up apartment with her father and mother
and five younger brothers and sisters. Rekha must ride overcrowded
buses to and from work. With transfers, she spends almost three hours
a day getting to the bank and back home again. She discharges her eight
hours of work time matching up and filing export-import documents.
Rekha does not enjoy her position very much, and her boss makes
coarse jokes and often touches her in ways she does not like. When she
brings her pay home, her mother puts it all into the family money
pouch. Rekha thinks that her parents should begin the search for a
groom for her. She knows that her college degree and steady salary will
make her attractive to a husband, but her father gambles and is in debt,
so there is no money for a dowry. She is neither a girl nor a wife and
sometimes wonders why her fate and security must always be dependent on the men who rule, or will rule, her existence.

These sketches describe the work and lifestyles of five workers and
their families. As of 1999, there were about 431 million full-time workers in the Indian economy. Across all India, 52 percent of males participated in the labor force, and this average did not vary much from region

to region. Children and the elderly were usually not full-time workers. For women, the picture was much different. Only 22 percent of Indian women were full-time workers, largely because they were active in their households as mothers, cooks, cleaners, and farm workers. These contributions are not measured in active labor force or GNP statistics.[14] There are great variations across India's states in women's labor force participation rates, reflecting regional attitudes toward women.

In Tamil Nadu, where Ritu's family lives, 30 percent of all women have primary jobs outside the household. High participation rates are typical of parts of India with above-average female literacy and educational levels. Fertility rates and population growth rates are lower in such states, which are found mostly in the south and west-central parts of the country. In Gujarat (Swamy, Akbar) and Maharashtra (Rekha), the respective participation rates for women are 26 and 33 percent. Conversely, across the north of India, almost all women remain in the family home or compound, and there are wide gaps between male and female literacy and educational levels. In the rich Green Revolution state of Punjab, only 4 out of every 100 women hold primary employment, and in poor Uttar Pradesh, India's most populous state, the proportion is 12 out of 100.[15] Underutilization of women's effort and talent is one reason why India's economy lags and is ill-prepared for global competition, which depends on productivity, innovation, and overall high levels of education for women and men.

Table 7.2 provides the distribution of occupations in the workforce for India and six selected states. India's census uses ten principal categories of jobs. The first four constitute the primary sector: cultivators; agricultural laborers; livestock, fisheries, and forestry; and mining and quarrying. The secondary, or industrial, sector includes household industries, small and large industries, and construction. The tertiary sector covers all forms of services: trade and commerce, transportation and communications, and other services, which include banking and government. Thinking back to Wangala, ones sees that the persistent rural character of the economy remains salient. Over India as a whole, 65 percent of all workers are either cultivators (39 percent) or agricultural laborers (26 percent). In Bihar, a large, very impoverished northern state, 81 percent of the workforce is involved in agriculture. The almost equal division of cultivators (44 percent) and laborers (37 percent) foretells what is in fact the case: intense rivalries in the villages among the landed and landless caste groupings, which spill over into contentious state politics. Bihar's acute underdevelopment is highlighted by the small shares of workers in industry, commerce, communications, and banking.

Table 7.2   Distribution of the Labor Force for India and Six States (in percent)

	Bihar	Delhi	Gujarat	Maharashtra	Tamil Nadu	Uttar Pradesh	India
Cultivators	44	1	33	32	25	53	39
Agricultural laborers	37	1	23	27	35	19	26
Livestock, fisheries, and forestry	0	1	3	2	2	1	2
Mining and quarrying	1	0	0	0	0	0	1
Household industry	2	1	1	2	4	2	2
Industry	2	23	14	12	11	5	8
Construction	1	8	2	3	2	1	2
Trade and commerce	4	24	9	9	9	6	7
Transportation and communications	1	8	4	4	3	2	3
Other services	8	33	10	10	10	10	10

Source: Government of India, "Census of India 1991," as reported in Jagran, *India at a Glance 1998,* edited by R. K. Thukral for the *Dainik Jagran* (Hindi daily newspaper), Kanpur, India, 1998, 95–98.

Because Delhi is a federal district that is almost wholly occupied by the city of New Delhi, there is little primary-sector activity. Modern industry (23 percent), trade and commerce (24 percent), and general and governmental services (33 percent) occupy most employees. Gujarat, Maharashtra, and Tamil Nadu have strong industrial sectors, and 11–14 percent of their workers are in workshops or factories. These states have above-average levels of trade and commerce and of transportation and communications services. With Delhi, they stand out for stronger construction enterprise than is found in other states. Bihar and Uttar Pradesh have some distance to advance before they replicate the income levels and transforming economic structures of India's leader states. On average, people in the more industrial states are almost twice as rich as those in the backward states.

India's industrial firms manufacture a full spectrum of chemical, electrical, engineering, pharmaceutical, and consumer goods. An idea of the range of products Indian workers turn out is provided in Table 7.3. In addition, the table shows the rapid expansion in outputs from 1987/88 to 2000/01.[16] Because the products are familiar to people living in any large country, there are parallels to the United States, subject to the realization that volumes of output are smaller in India. Indians like carbonated beverages and currently produce about 2.4 billion bottled drinks a year, up by 206 percent since 1987/88. This number may seem large, until one calculates that it constitutes about two bottles sold per year for each Indian. It is no wonder that Pepsi and Coca-Cola see

The circular arcades of Connaught Place,
New Delhi's prime shopping area

India as a huge future market, but Indian flavors have competitive appeal, and the Indian government has not made it easy for global soft drink and fast food firms to enter India.

Production of cotton yarn, as seen in the next row of Table 7.3, has been sluggish in India, for reasons Swamy and his fellow spinners understand. Yet both the growing domestic market and overseas sales present enormous growth and profit opportunities in the decades ahead. In contrast, shoe output and exports have surged. Sulfuric acid is a vital industrial chemical, and nitrogen fertilizers are a crucial farm input. Both have experienced growth of more than 70 percent. Toothpaste is a standard consumer product. An expansion of 26 percent shows the rising purchasing power of India's middle-income households. Steel rods provide the framework for concrete construction, pipes are necessary for water supplies, and sheeting is used for automobiles, buses, and metal cabinets and furniture. The rise in steel output of 209 percent is a clear indication of India's rapid industrial growth in the 1980s and 1990s. India's burgeoning middle class, exemplified by Lakshman and Renu, has translated rising incomes into durable goods purchases, as illustrated by the 138 percent rise in motorcycle and scooter sales, the 195 percent gain in the sales of refrigerators, and the 267 percent boom in car sales.[17]

Table 7.3   Commerce and Industry: Production and Growth, 1987/88–2000/01

Product	Units	1987/88	2000/01	Percentage Increase
Soft drinks	bottles, millions	778	2,381	206
Cotton yarn	tons, thousands	1,350	2,267	68
Shoes	pairs, thousands	6,749	14,153	110
Sulfuric acid	tons, thousands	3,203	5,540	73
Nitrogen fertilizer	tons, thousands	5,763	11,025	91
Toothpaste	tons	20,000	25,142	26
Steel	tons, thousands	8,807	27,200[a]	209
Motorcycles and scooters	units, thousands	1,575	3,755	138
Refrigerators	units, thousands	680	2,007	195
Motor cars	units, thousands	138	506	267
Petroleum, crude	tons, thousands	32,000	33,000[b]	3
Limestone	tons, thousands	56,328	127,891	127
Electricity	KWH, billions	202	448[b]	122
Bank offices	number	35,707	65,624	84
Manufacturing	index	100	227	127
Services	index	100	253	153
GDP	index	100	214	114
Population	people, millions	784	997	27

Sources: The two best sources of data on the Indian economy are Government of India, Ministry of Finance, *Economic Survey 2001/02* (and preceding years), which appears each spring along with the minister's annual budget speech; and Reserve Bank of India, *Annual Report of the RBI for the Year Ended June 2001* (and preceding years). The Ministry of Finance's *Economic Survey* may be found at www.indiabudget.nic.in/es2001-02/welcome. html. The RBI website address is www.rbi.org.in/.

Notes: a. 1999/2000.
   b. 1998/99.

India produces about one-half of the crude petroleum it needs. To make up the other half, oil products constitute the largest item in the nation's import bill. A fresh round of exploration may yield more strikes, but the prospects for the discovery of major oilfields are slim. Production has been flat. The next item in the table, limestone, is an input into chemicals, cement, and construction, and its output has paced overall growth. For the Indian economy to expand, electricity production has to rise more rapidly than total output because new gains require multiples of power use. The rise of 122 percent in generation is insufficient for continued expansion, and India's state governments have engaged in numerous discussions with international investors, with the result that foreign and joint ventures are becoming more common. No longer are the central and state governments the only entities trying to raise the capital for power stations and to manage distribution systems plagued by inefficiencies, nonpayment of bills, and illegal tie-ins to power lines. Expansion of the financial sector supports rapid growth, as the 84 percent expansion in the number of banks exhibits.

The final four rows of Table 7.3 furnish information on the performance of some aggregate statistics. By comparing them to the rows above, it is possible to discern with some precision which industries are leading India's development (grow faster than average) and which lag (grow slower). Total manufacturing output climbed 127 percent in the period 1987/88–2000/01. Services, including banking and transportation, expanded at a fast clip. Total gross domestic product, which combines agriculture, industry, and services, rose 114 percent. Population growth of 27 percent added 213 million citizens, but because of sustained economic growth, Indians on average were much better off than they were in the late 1980s and twice as well off as they were in 1980. This dual growth of human numbers and the economy creates problems of urban sprawl, congestion, and pollution that India's people and government have not so far seriously addressed. Current trends are not ecologically sustainable.

■ Government and the Private Sector

Almost every nation in the world wants to experience the benefits that arise from economic growth. In the latter part of the twentieth century, economists and policymakers accepted the notion that growth depends on balancing and coordinating the roles of government and market forces. Further, it is understood that as time passes and income rises, the functions and scope of the governmental and market sectors will change. The collapse of the autarkic Soviet Union and the actions of China and India to expand their connections to the world market economy have shifted their attention from communist or socialist policy frameworks toward governmental stances that are supportive of increased scope for the private sector in agriculture, industry, and commerce. In particular, the electricity, transportation, and telecommunications sectors are being moved into private hands.

India has experienced over a half-century of economic policy formulation since independence from Britain was secured. This span may be divided into three policy epochs, each of which exhibits different approaches and has yielded varied economic growth rates and development achievements.[18] The first epoch (1950–1964) was characterized by the strong hand of the central government, which sought to push forward components of the economy across a broad front. The second (1965–1979) witnessed a slowdown of growth, but the third (1980 to the present) finds India taking its place among the world's most rapidly expanding economies.

India's first prime minister, Jawaharlal Nehru, led the nation to independence. Nehru and the Congress Party, which he headed, were strongly committed to what became known as the "socialist pattern of society." Nehru did not believe that the private sector was capable of quickly initiating and upgrading a number of large-scale industries, such as chemicals, fertilizers, electrical equipment, machine tools, military equipment, railways, airlines, and insurance. In all likelihood, Nehru was correct, but his conviction has been debated ever since. India did not have the abundance of entrepreneurs, capitalists, investors, managers, and skilled technical workers required for the many tasks of early development: whole new industries, giant power stations, and massive irrigation works. Only government could undertake the combined "big push" on all these fronts and manage the "commanding heights" of the economy in a socially responsible fashion.

As a result of the Nehruvian "big push," government ownership and management spread throughout most of large-scale industry, power, irrigation, and transportation. The private sector comprised mostly farms, agricultural marketing, and small businesses. Among the big firms, most existing large enterprises, such as those in cotton and jute textiles, continued in private hands. Nehru died in 1964, but by the early 1960s, he had seen considerable movement in the direction of the realization of his vision.

From the mid-1960s until 1980, the economy did not perform well and moved unevenly through the period called "conflicting currents." The Green Revolution brought success in wheat production, exports showed spurts of growth, and the nation's saving rate went up, laying a basis for more investment. Droughts and wars with China and Pakistan played an unsettling role, though, and the economy was becoming more complex and harder to manage. Many government enterprises were not efficient performers and had to be subsidized. High tariffs to protect Indian firms from foreign imports rendered them unable to compete in the world marketplace, and exports could not provide an economic boost. Indian consumers were offered inferior radios, cars, and home appliances at higher prices than elsewhere in the world. Overstaffing became rife as politicians encouraged the public corporations to provide supporters with jobs, no matter how redundant and unnecessary. Government ownership and management of industries were accompanied by a maze of bureaucratic controls and regulations that handicapped private initiative and encouraged corruption. As a result, overall economic performance deteriorated, India's party politics became more complex and unstable, and calls for new policies became louder.

From 1980 on, many people criticized the government for being too big and taking on too many tasks. Surprisingly, the size of government has changed little since then, even though the boundaries between the public and private sectors have shifted in favor of the latter. The relative size of the public and private sectors can be measured by several yardsticks: employment shares, investment shares, or GDP shares. Continuing the motif of looking at the Indian economy from the bottom up—from the point of view of the villages, families, and workers—Table 7.4 compares the sizes of the public- and private-sector labor forces in some benchmark years, 1981, 1991, and 2001. The public sector includes central, state, and local government employment, plus workers in central and state public firms. The private sector counts include only workers in large and small enterprises and exclude farmers, shopkeepers, and rural and urban laborers. Together, these public and private employees are said to be in the "formal," or "organized," sector. The dominance of the public sector's administrative departments (e.g., the Ministries of Commerce, Education, and Finance) and enterprises (e.g., steel, power, gasoline, and soap) is plain. About two-thirds of all formal-sector workers are situated in offices or factories managed at central, state, or local government levels. Interestingly, there are more employees in the state governments than in the central government in Delhi.

Despite strong growth in output in the private sector in the 1980s and 1990s, employment did not rise significantly. India's complex and

Table 7.4 Shares of Public- and Private-Sector Employment in the Organized Sector (in percent)

	1981	1991	2001 (est.)
Public sector	68	72	68
Central government	26	26	24
State governments	33	37	35
Local governments	9	9	9
Private sector	32	28	32
Large firms	29	25	28
Small firms	3	3	4

Source: Reserve Bank of India, *Report on Currency and Finance 1997/98,* p. 20; see www.rbi.org.in/.

protective labor laws and the strength of industrial unions make it hard for private businesses to discharge workers as market conditions change. As a result, formal-sector firms keep their permanent hiring to a minimum and instead rely on short-term contractual workers or substitute machines for labor (a perverse choice in labor-rich India). Between 1981 and 1991, the proportion of formal-sector employment in large-scale private units dropped from 29 to 25 percent as the total number of workers in this sector grew by only about 10 percent. The largest expansion of employment took place in the state governments and state-owned enterprises, noted for their inefficiency and overstaffing. The estimated figures for 2001 are predicated on changes in India's labor practices in the private sector and restraints on more public-sector hiring. The private-sector components of the labor force are expanding proportionately, whereas those in the public sector are contracting.

■ Accomplishments and Prospects

By the 1970s, government ownership and management of two-thirds of the industrial sector and its attempts to regulate the expansion and operations of the private sector had become a drag on growth rather than an accelerator. Since 1950, the government's strategies at the national and state levels have been spelled out in a series of five-year plans, which are detailed in Table 7.5.[19] The last column of Table 7.5 gives the total expansion of gross domestic product achieved during each five-year period. The Nehruvian period comprised the first three plans (1951/52–1965/66), and then the next three five-year plans reflected the mixed performance of the conflicting currents period. In fact, as shown, four years in the span 1966/67–1979/80 witnessed annual plans, when the five-year planning mechanism proved too inflexible to respond to the shocks of droughts, wars, political changes, or difficulties in meeting the country's foreign payments obligations.

The slowdown of the 1970s was followed by a period of rapid expansion in the 1980s, during Plans VI and VII, which can be described as the "golden growth path" period. There are several reasons for this dramatic improvement in Indians' standard of living. Government spending was high after 1980. Middle-class consumers were acquiring motor scooters, cars, refrigerators, and air-conditioning units. There was some improvement in the government's handling of public-sector enterprises and a rise in coal production, rail shipments, and

Table 7.5   India's Five-Year Plans, 1950/51–2001/02

Plan	Years	Total Change in GDP (%)
I	1951/52–1955/56	+19.4
II	1956/57–1960/61	+22.9
III	1961/62–1965/66	+14.7
Annual plans	1966/67–1968/69	+1.1, +8.0, +2.7, by year
IV	1969/70–1973/74	+17.8
V	1974/75–1978/79	+26.6
Annual plan	1979–80	–4.9
VI	1980/81–1984/85	+31.8
VII	1985/86–1989/90	+33.9
Annual plans	1990/91–1992/93	+5.2, +0.5, by year
VIII	1992/93–1996/97	+29.2
IX	1997/98–2001/02	+30.5 (est.)

Sources: H. L. Chandhok and the Policy Group, *India Database: The Economy,* Annual Time Series Data, Volume 1, pp. 28–29; Economic and Political Weekly Research Foundation, *National Accounts Statistics of India, 1950/51–1995/96;* http://www.economictimes.com/budget.

power generation, all state-directed activities. Importantly, monsoon rainfalls were favorable, and agriculture provided a solid, if not outstanding, contribution. Export growth was better than in the 1960s and 1970s. During the 1980s, Indians seemed to acquire a taste for growth, which took precedence over conformity to ideological guideposts of the Nehruvian variety. Public opinion and the platforms of India's political parties, from left to right, shifted in favor of pragmatic policy adjustments.

By 1990/91, rapid growth and lax management of the money supply, too much borrowing, and the inability of foreign currency reserves to pay for imports and debt repayments pushed India to the brink of financial crisis. A new government, working with the World Bank and International Monetary Fund, pledged significant economic reforms. It is noteworthy that India's move to economic reforms, such as cutting tariffs, reducing restrictions on private enterprise, and relying more on private business, followed a decade of strong growth. Indians had tasted the fruits of ten years of increasing income. There was pressure on the government to maintain the pace, which benefited not only the rich and middle classes but also the poor.[20] In fact, after 1980 the number of Indian families living below the poverty line dropped steeply, to the surprise of many who thought that rapid growth would not benefit the weaker sectors of the population, but the 1990s did not see much further improvement.

Table 7.5 shows that growth in each five-year interval from 1980/81 through 2001/02 falls in the 30 percent range. Since 1991, India's national budget, five-year plans, and all dimensions of economic policy have been devoted to pro-growth policies. Most remarkable has been the shift of the locus for new investment from the public to the private sector in such areas as heavy manufacturing, banking, civil aviation, telecommunications, power generation and distribution, ports, and roads (World Bank 1997: xiii). A number of policy changes significantly enhanced India's openness to foreign investors.[21] Direct foreign investment rose to $3.2 billion in 1997/98, and portfolio investment in India's stock markets was in the $2–3 billion range.

Increases in foreign investment and mounting foreign participation in India's power, telecommunications, and other industries are only one aspect of India's rising involvement in the international economy. The expansion of the domestic economy since 1980 has been accompanied by an impressive expansion of foreign trade, but India's exports still constitute less than 1 percent of the world's total, so there is much ground to make up. Tariff simplifications and reductions have been important components of India's policy reforms. Between 1986/87 and 1995/96, India's exports more than tripled, with major gains coming in chemicals (544 percent), textiles (285 percent), polished gems (225 percent), and engineering goods (308 percent). The United States and the European Union are the chief markets for Indian goods and leading suppliers of India's imports. The growth in India's foreign sector has been based on a widening of the range of competitive exports and on diversification of India's trading partners to Southeast Asia, the Middle East, and Africa.

Globalization, policy reform, and a strong popular and governmental commitment to growth have significantly raised living standards in India since 1980. This improvement in people's well-being has been built on the foundation of Nehruvian planning. On the whole, it is fair to judge that India's economic record is one of success, although much remains to be done. Offsetting the economic gains of the past fifty years is a poor record of advancement in social fields such as literacy, education, health, clean water, and sanitation. It is a paradox that India's socialist pattern of society failed, not as a means of instigating economic development but in its educational and social programs. Pushing down population growth toward zero from its current annual rate of 1.8 percent is imperative. Changes in women's status and health will be required. About 35 percent of Indian families are still living below the official poverty line. Life expectancy is now about sixty-three years for men and women, but as India's population ages, there will be need for stronger pension and social security systems. Deforestation, erosion, and environmental deterioration will have to be reversed, and the caliber of air and water quality raised if India's economic gains are not to be offset, at least partially, by negative effects on health and the quality of life.

Abundance in poverty remains a dominant theme in the lives of Wangala's villagers and their rural compatriots, as it does in the day-to-day activities of India's working families, who are symbolized by Ritu, Swamy, Akbar, Lakshman and Renu, and Rekha. India's record of economic accomplishment since 1950 has been solid, but the future will demand better economic policies, a more educated workforce, and greater confidence in working with foreign investors and multinational companies. Ensuring that growth spreads into laggard states such as Bihar and Uttar Pradesh and reaches down to incorporate the agricultural workers and other low-caste groups will not be easy. If all goes well—and it is certainly within the capacity of India's people and leadership to ensure that it does—then the process of transforming poverty into abundance will continue its successful advance.

■ Notes

1. Dividing $34,260 by $460 produces a result of 74, indicating that Americans consume seventy-four times more than Indians on average. Incomes are taken from *World Development Report 2002,* World Bank 2002: 232–233. It is the best single source for numbers on the world's nations. Each annual volume discusses an issue of thematic importance in the global economy. GNI/POP is the most direct measure of income differences, but since many nontraded goods do not cost as much in India as in the United States, many economists prefer to use a price-adjusted comparison that includes the full spectrum of goods and services. This technique puts India's per capita income at $2,390 per year. That of the United States remains $34,260, since it is the base against which other nations are compared. By this calibration, Americans' incomes are fifteen times higher than Indians'.

2. According to a Reuters article from March 25, 1999: "India, bulging with foodgrain stocks and amid hopes of a record harvest, is suddenly faced with the problems of plenty. . . . [It is estimated that] by the end of June India will hold foodstocks of 36 million tons, 10 million tons more than required . . . [and] analysts said India could export wheat." See www.cnn.com.

3. There are many readable studies of India's village life. Among the best are: Bailey 1957; Epstein 1962; and Srinivas 1976.

4. Wangala is described in Epstein 1962. She compared Wangala with a nearby village, Dalena, to extract powerful insights about the effects of irriga-

tion, commercialization, and links to the wider regional economy on the economies and work patterns of these two small communities. Wangala and Dalena are fictitious names.

5. These numbers were true as of the mid-1950s, when Epstein did her initial fieldwork. I have visited Wangala and Dalena several times myself, and although the villages have changed, Epstein's original descriptions remain clear and valid.

6. I do not know if these rules about water use still prevail in Wangala in 2003, but such conventions remain all too common in most of India.

7. Traditionally, the Peasant households and the service-caste households were involved in a village exchange pattern known as the "jajmani system." A Washerman family might, for example, wash the clothes of several Peasant families and would, in return, receive an allotment of grain at harvest. Priests, Barbers, and Potters likewise provided services in return for stable shares of the village crops. Over time, the jajmani system has broken down, more payments are made in money for services rendered, and competitive prices have replaced customary shares. As a result, relative incomes and statuses have changed; for instance, a Blacksmith might benefit from greater need for metalworking and equipment repair, whereas a Potter would lose out to modern aluminum vessels. One street in the village is named Muslim Street, but its former residents have long since departed Wangala for external opportunities.

8. A family can lose land through mismanagement, perhaps because of illness, gambling, or alcoholism; or the absence of male heirs may leave women (a widow or unmarried sister) vulnerable. Having a member of the family make money in a factory job or by migrating to the Middle East for a time may enable a family to purchase land.

9. Millets are not eaten much in the United States but are instantly recognizable as the round black, orange, and yellow grains found in chicken and bird feed. They and the pulses (peas and beans) are very nutritious and form an important part of the diet by offering proteins and vitamins not found in rice or wheat.

10. The connection here is that when the rains fail or floods come, then crops do not need to be harvested or may never get planted. That in turn means that landowners do not hire agricultural laborers, who then do not have sufficient income to buy food that is now going up in price. Hunger and near-starvation are more often due to the absence of work than to pure food shortages. Today, for political reasons, the national and state governments are quick to provide food-for-work and other programs to prevent the famines that used to wrack India in the latter days of British rule. At present, though, some farm worker families still prefer long-term, even lifetime, contracts with landowners as a way of insuring against the risk of hunger, even though they bind themselves to a life of poverty and dependence. Farmers like such contracts, too, because they are guaranteed that the man, wife, and older children will provide labor even when wages are high and better opportunities are available.

11. All figures for 2000/01 are estimated by the author, based on 1997/98 and 1998/99 preliminary figures.

12. There was lively trade between India and the Roman Empire. For 2,000 years, India has had trading relations with the Middle East and Southeast

Asia. A century ago, Indian and British investors had created world-class cotton and jute spinning and weaving industries. Measured by size of labor force, India has been one of the world's largest industrial powers since the late 1800s.

13. These stories are, of course, apocryphal. At the same time, they are realistic enough that in each case, one could find a family that conforms to each tale.

14. The omission of women's household or secondary farm work from labor force and GNP statistics is not peculiar to India but is standard practice.

15. The rate in Delhi (Lakshman and Renu) is only 7 for every 100 people. It is traditional for many Muslim women to live in purdah, which means household sequestration. Husbands do not want their wives or daughters exposed to male contact or ogling in public view. What is interesting is that Hindu and Sikh households likewise shut women away from the outside world of jobs, education, and socializing. A further, and sad, element of the picture is that the regions that exhibit these strong inhibitions on women's lives also have low demographic sex ratios. Normally, there should be about 102 women for every 100 men in any population, but in Punjab, for example, this ratio is 88 women for every 100 men. The case of the "missing women" is easily solved: families practice selective abortion and infanticide or simply do not value girls as highly as boys and so do not provide equal measures of food, medicine, and care to girls in the first five years of life. The outcome is a loss of approximately one out of every ten potential female adults.

16. It takes over a year to gather and compile reports on the details of an economy, and India is no different in this respect. So, in early 2003, most of the recent data available are reported for 2000/01 and are almost three years old, although quick or provisional estimates exist for some key items.

17. The streets in India's cities and the country's network of highways are severely congested by automobile, bus, and truck traffic. Air pollution in the cities exceeds health standards by a large margin, causing massive health problems such as respiratory diseases and premature death. The death rate from roadway accidents is among the highest in the world. Only gradually is lead-based gasoline being phased out. Continued expansion of the automobile industry and the total consumer goods sector must be predicated on cleaner technologies and on regulations and incentives to adopt them.

18. For details on these periods, see Adams 1999: 65–88; Adams 1997: 3–19. The other chapters in this collection provide a full overview of India's economic development aims and achievements since 1950.

19. Only a few university libraries in the United States have sets of India's plans. A useful site on India is the Planning Commission. See http://planningcommission.nic.in.

20. India's annual budget and much supporting information can be located on the Internet at http://indiabudget.nic.in/. The annual Economic Survey, which can be found at the same site, is a comprehensive review of current economic trends and discusses all aspects of India's ongoing policy adjustments.

21. One of the most comprehensive sources of current information on India's reforms is the annual publication from the Reserve Bank of India, *Report on Currency and Finance 2000/01* (and other years), Bombay, 2001. The Reserve Bank's home page can be found at www.rbi.org.in/.

■ Bibliography

Adams, John. 1997. "History and Context: 1947–1975." In *Regional Handbooks of Economic Development*, C. S. LaRue, ed. Vol. 2. Chicago: Fitzroy Dearborn.

———. 1999. "India: Much Achieved, Much to Achieve." In *India and Pakistan: The First Fifty Years,* Selig S. Harrison, Paul H. Kreisberg, and Dennis Kux, eds. New York: Cambridge University Press.

Bailey, F. G. 1957. *Caste and the Economic Frontier.* Manchester: Manchester University Press.

H. L. Chandhok and the Policy Group. 1990. *India Database: The Economy.* Annual Time Series Data, Vol. 1. New Delhi: Living Media.

Economic and Political Weekly Research Foundation. *National Accounts Statistics of India, 1950/51–1995/96,* www.economictimes.com/budget.

Epstein, T. Scarlet. 1962. *Economic Development and Social Change in South India.* Manchester: Manchester University Press.

Government of India. 1998. *Economic Survey 1997/98.* New Delhi: Government of India.

———. Ministry of Finance. *Economic Survey 2001/02* (and preceding years), www.indiabudget.nic.in/es2001-02/welcome/html.

Jagran. 1998. *India at a Glance 1998,* edited by R. K. Thukral for the *Dainik Jagran,* India's largest Hindi daily newspaper, Kanpur, India.

Reserve Bank of India. *Annual Report of the RBI for the Year Ended June 2001* (and preceding years), www.rbi.org.in/.

Srinivas, M. N. 1976. *The Remembered Village.* Berkeley: University of California Press.

World Bank. 1997. *India: Sustaining Rapid Economic Growth.* Washington, D.C.: World Bank.

———. 2000. *World Development Report 1999/00.* New York: Oxford University Press.

———. 2002. *World Development Report 2001/02.* New York: Oxford University Press.

8

The Role of Women

Barbara Crossette

Not long ago, the newsmagazine *India Today* snooped around some of the more fashionable bars in Bombay and found what it identified as the modern Indian woman—dressed for success, a tequila in her hand, pointing the way to a liberated new century (Baria 1998: 32–33). "What ever happened to the Shrinking Indian Violet?" the magazine asked, recalling the stereotype of the well brought up, frequently chaperoned, slightly Victorian, easily shocked young lady of middle-class India. "She's vanished," a leading pollster from an Indian market research organization called Pathfinders told the magazine, laying out the results of a 1998 opinion survey of 5,100 teenage girls, who by a persuasive margin approved of smoking and drinking and thought that having a boyfriend was essential. The teens polled, moreover, included some "from places like Bhubaneswar in Orissa and Tonk in Rajasthan," the pollster noted. The middle of nowhere, in other words. The phenomenon was thus universal, he concluded. Those wildly liberated women form one of the images of a new India that excites advertisers and marketers, repels many advocates of women's rights, and has absolutely no relevance to most of the women in a country where a much publicized new middle class rests atop an often unrecognized mass of hundreds of millions of other Indians living in extreme deprivation, most of them women and children. India has the world's highest number of people living on $1 a day or less, a measure of absolute poverty used by international aid organizations.

Like so much else about India, more than most nations, the world of its women is a kaleidoscopic universe. Strong women populate its modern history, including the movement that led to the country's 1947 independence from Britain. In his classic work, *The Oxford History of Modern India, 1740–1975,* Sir Percival Spear saw this pre-independence period as an important time of reemergence for women in public life, aided by Christian schools for girls established during the British colonial period but drawing on ancient Indian history and mythology. "India had her own tradition of feminine culture and participation in public affairs. From Sita and Draupadi of the epics [the *Ramayana* and *Mahabharata,*] the tale ran through Rajput heroines to princesses like Rupmati of Malwa and Ahalya Bai of Indore," he wrote (Spear 1978: 281). By 1800, however, this age of princesses and heroic mythological characters had largely ended, the historian said. But nineteenth-century Indian reformers, most of them Hindus, as well as the schools run by foreign and Indian Christians, soon took up the cause of women. Famous Indians like Rammohun Roy and Swami Vivekananda in Bengal and K. Natarajan in Bombay fought for the end of practices like sati, the burning of widows on the funeral pyres of their dead husbands, and for more education for girls. Women became scholars, doctors, and social activists. By the 1920s, a group of influential women had founded the All-India Women's Conference, which soon allied itself with the Congress Party, leader of the independence movement. In the 1930s, women joined public demonstrations for independence from the British, and several thousand were arrested. Sarojini Naidu, a poet and political philosopher, was one of the most famous intellectuals of the movement. Vijayalakshmi Pandit, a sister of Jawaharlal Nehru, also became active in politics and later was a leading diplomat for the newly independent India, representing her country in Washington and at the United Nations, where she was the first woman to become president of the General Assembly.

Today, visionary women, rich and poor, lead campaigns to save the beleaguered natural environment or to promote civic responsibility. Bold women push out the social frontiers. The Indian foreign service is appointing increasing numbers of women to important diplomatic posts abroad, including as ambassadors and political or economic counselors. Kiran Bedi, the first woman to rise to the top of New Delhi's police force and prison system, served as director of India's most important high-security prison and later was put in charge of training the police in New Delhi, a city of 12.5 million people. All these influential women may be the kaleidoscope's brighter, more noticeable lights, but in a country of more than a billion people, they also are also a very small minority.

■ Poverty with a Female Face

Statistically speaking, the women of India live most of their lives at the world's lowest levels of development, on a par with their counterparts in sub-Saharan Africa. Nearly two-thirds of India's women cannot read or write. More than 60 percent of their children under five are malnourished. The majority of their homes have no flush toilets or even latrines, a situation that contributes significantly to the spread of disease. The maternal mortality rate for Indian women is one of the world's highest, at 420 for every 100,000 live births—in some areas as high as 800 per 100,000—according to the World Bank (1999). Where family planning is available, nearly three-quarters of it takes the form of sterilization, which women turn to reluctantly after they have already had at least several—often at least half a dozen—children. A European diplomat recently based in New Delhi, who was interested in seeing how aid to family planning programs was contributing to helping women, was told by neighborhood health workers that many family planning statistics are suspect because they are manipulated to show results not reflected in reality. In one area, this diplomat said, contraceptive pills were divided to be distributed among numerous women, none of whom got more than a month or two of protection, so that statistics would show that the program was reaching a large number of families. Nearly a quarter of a century ago, Sir Percival Spear looked at India's substantial strides and hopes of rapid economic development and cautioned: "Population growth was the shadow which still hung over all these efforts, the cloud which persistently obscured the sun of prosperity" (Spear 1978: 433). At the end of the twentieth century, the warning still rang true, as India's population crossed the billion mark, growing every year by a number roughly equal to the total population of Australia or Iraq. Some time in the first half of the twenty-first century, India will have outstripped China to become the most populous nation on earth—and a poorer, less healthy one.

Unlike in most industrialized and rapidly developing countries, and certainly in other democracies, the Indian population is "missing" millions of girls. For every 1,000 men reported in the 1991 Indian census, there were only 927 women—one of the world's lowest gender ratios. By the end of the decade, ratios had dropped into the 700s for women

Village woman, Uttar Pradesh

in some northern states, according to Indian women's organizations. These ratios are substantially lower not only than world averages but also than the female-to-male ratio under British colonialism. Since the life span of an Indian woman is about sixty-one years, the same as an Indian man, experts have concluded that the gender ratio must be related at least in part to the abortion of female fetuses before birth, the killing of baby girls, and the practice of depriving female children of adequate nourishment and health care, effectively shortening their lives. Social pressures—the desire for sons—have combined with illiteracy and poverty in many homes to create an unhealthy, if not dangerous, atmosphere for girls.

From puberty into young adulthood, the majority of Indian women—often Muslim and Christian as well as Hindu—are forced into arranged marriages or choose to let parents decide on a mate rather than rebel against a long-established custom important in many families. "The Indian marriage today can be understood only in the light of a past that it seeks to perpetuate; a past that was codified entirely by male lawgivers like Manu," wrote Mrinal Pande, a leading advocate of women's rights, referring to the major ancient source of Hinduism's behavioral codes.

Manu notes in his *Manu-Smriti* that a woman, being fickle and licentious by nature, must live first under the protection of her father, then her husband, and lastly her sons. No matter how westernized the families, the *Artha Veda mantra* that the priest still asks the bride's father to chant at the time of the Kanyadaan (the ritual giving away of the Hindu bride by the father to the husband) reconfirms the essentially passive status of the girl. "Here I give unto you my young virgin daughter, having adorned her with ornaments to the best of my capacity; please accept her." (Pande 1991: 59–60).

Some might argue that this ritual is not so different from a western father "giving away" his daughter in marriage. But Pande insists that an Indian wedding is rarely a joyful affair. She recommends listening to the often-doleful words of marriage songs sung by women as they gather to honor a bride.

It is a testimony to the resilience and adaptability of the majority of Indian girls and young women that they adjust well to married life in a family not of their choice, often out of deference to their parents, whom they do not want to disgrace or embarrass. Although, tragically, there are occasionally sad stories in newspapers about girls who kill themselves rather than subject their fathers and mothers to the chagrin of being too poor to afford decent dowries for their daughters and therefore being unable to find good husbands for them, younger generations of more cosmopolitan Indians put less stock in the dowry system—though weddings may be crushingly expensive. Indeed, many Indian women say that when a new husband—and his mother—are sympathetic and understanding of her background, whatever it may be, life in a new extended family can be liberating for a young woman with her own ambitions, especially if the family is educated and middle class. If family members pool their incomes, a family need not be wealthy for an Indian home to be large and comfortable, with servants to do most daily chores, not only in sprawling cities but also in rural areas where farmers have prospered because of India's Green Revolution. In a rambling Indian house open to the outdoors almost all year, there may be so many other women around for support and help with child care that a young wife may actually be freer to pursue her own goals, including a career, than she would be under her own very watchful parents or in a struggling nuclear family.

Most Indian women do not have enough economic independence to live alone, and Indian communities outside the largest cities do not have the kind of accommodations single people need. The U.S. college

A Bengali bride
arriving for her
wedding ceremony,
Tamil Nadu

© India Unveiled by Robert Arnett

graduate's dream of moving to New York or another city to establish an independent life is out of reach for young women in India. For many, marriage becomes inevitable. And when considering whether to defy an entrenched marriage system, young Indian women have to weigh many factors and take into account the real perils of rebellion, before or after marriage. They know that choosing to marry outside caste divisions—especially in conservative rural areas, where the majority of Indians still live—can bring ostracism or even death to a young couple. Among newlyweds who have been forced to accept their parents' choices, thousands of women also die each year at the hands of their in-laws because new husbands may not like their contract brides or may believe that the women they married have not come with enough dowry, often measured by newly affluent families in ostentatious household appliances, motorbikes or cars, and large amounts of cash. By 2000, the Indian Home Ministry reported more than 6,000 "dowry deaths" a year, even though the practice of demanding dowry of a bride's family is in itself now illegal (Government of India 1995). Activists say that these reported deaths probably represent fewer than half or even a quarter of the actual cases, since many suspect deaths are still registered as suicides or household accidents. A kitchen fire is the most common explanation, giving the phrase "bride burning" a literal meaning, as a young woman is doused in kerosene or other flammable liquid and set on fire near the family stove. Moreover, within extended families and in public life, Indian women face daily sexual harassment. The poorest women are vulnerable to rape by the police or public officials with power over them and the villages they live in, as Indian human rights groups have documented amply. Domestic violence is still widespread across social classes, aided by social stigmas and the economic inability of women to move out of bad relationships and live on their own.

■ Village Women on the March

But, once again, grim statistics (like upbeat magazine opinion polls) tell only part of the story. Almost everywhere in India, women themselves have begun to tackle their problems through grassroots activism against discrimination or intimidation, through small-scale credit organizations that bring them some measure of economic independence, and through new openings in politics from the local to the national level. Many newly emboldened women, still a minority but an increasingly influential one, are finding causes as diverse as consumer protection or antidrinking crusades, recognizing that alcohol is often a contributing factor to the violent behavior of spouses or other family members. No tequilas or other fashionable cocktails for these village activists, who are in many ways more revolutionary in their assertion of power than their glamorous city counterparts.

In New Delhi, the Women's Feature Service (WFS), a news agency that tracks women's movements and issues of importance to women worldwide, has been following the growth of small organizations in urban neighborhoods and rural villages across India. In early 1998, a reporter for WFS went to a conference in Ranchi, a city in Bihar, one of India's poorest states (Women's Feature Service, January 5, 1998). There she found a diverse group of 4,000 women representing local organizations of many kinds, who quickly agreed on three priority areas of concern: violence against women in domestic and public life, the failure of governments at all levels to protect them, and the dislocations women suffer when ambitious development projects are imposed on their communities without their advice or consent. A dam, for example, may swallow up land on which families depend for daily food, and there may be no certainty of compensation for the loss if local politicians ignore the plight of the dislocated. In Punjab, a reasonably prosperous state, Vineeta Gupta has been campaigning against the privatization of medical care because poor women are the first to be shut out of essential services. There are few official welfare nets in India to catch and aid the hungry or homeless. At the Ranchi conference, women watched films about campaigns against rape and about the lives of sex workers, many of them young girls sold into prostitution by desperate families. So enthusiastic were the participants that the conference broke up in near-chaos with no time to pass resolutions, the reporter noted. The women, certainly fired, were eager to begin their long journeys home to tell their neighbors that they were not alone; all over India their situation had resonance.

Women in grassroots movements, however relatively small their number in the world's second-most-populous nation, have powerful allies outside India. At the turn of the twenty-first century, the world's leading development organizations, including a range of United Nations agencies and the World Bank, which was created at the same time as the UN to finance development, have concluded that poor countries will never live up to their often-substantial potentials unless women are brought into economic and political life in far greater numbers. Development experts recognize what Indian women have long known: that stronger households with healthier children build more effective communities where the rights and needs of all are better recognized and more effectively met.

"*Literate mothers matter,*" wrote David S. Landes (his emphasis) in *The Wealth and Poverty of Nations,* his thought-provoking 1998 book about why some countries prosper and others do not (Landes 1998: 178). (In a work of more than 500 pages, Landes italicized only three sentences to underline their central importance to his analysis.) He is not alone in drawing this conclusion. When the Indian-born economist Amartya Sen won the 1998 Nobel Prize for his long work in studying the economics of poverty and development, he told an interviewer that he had trouble understanding why Indian governments continued to neglect "education, health care, social opportunity and nutrition" (Dutt 1998). Sen added that India had twice the malnutrition rate (40–60 percent of children) as sub-Saharan Africa, where 20 percent of children were then undernourished. The prevalence of illiterate mothers and what that situation says about government priorities in certain parts of India play a part in keeping succeeding generations of girls out of school. The World Bank estimated in 1998 that fewer than one-third of Indian females were enrolled in schools at any level. Only 40 percent of girls between the ages of seven and nine, 37 percent of the ten to fourteen year olds, and 15 percent of fifteen to nineteen year olds were attending classes. Dropout rates for girls were also high (World Bank 1999).

Satyen Gangaram Pitroda—an Indian-born entrepreneur in the high-technology industry who gave up his U.S. citizenship to return to his birthplace in the 1980s to serve the government—has a theory about why India had allowed so much illiteracy and disregard for education to grow. Pitroda, who became science adviser to then prime minister Rajiv Gandhi, considered the most modernizing of contemporary Indian politicians, said that after independence, India's first prime minister, Jawaharlal Nehru, and some of his most influential advisers opted for steel mills and other industries to produce substitutes for imported goods, at the expense of education and family planning programs. "If we had concentrated more on the software, the human resources—female literacy, education—in the 1950s and 60s," Pitroda, who was known as Sam, said in an interview in 1989, "we would have a population of about 600 million now." The population by then was climbing toward 900 million, a third larger than Pitroda thought it should have been. A smaller Indian population would more than likely also be better educated (Crossette 1989). And women would not be competing with as many unemployed men for jobs.

At independence in 1947, India had about 340 million people, among them a significant number of those well-educated women who had become active in politics, the economy, academic life, the arts, and public affairs. Like Sarojini Naidu, some of them had come of age as colleagues of Mohandas Karamchand Gandhi as he led his nonviolent struggle against British colonialism. Gandhi—called "Mahatma," a title bestowed by his followers that means "great soul"—advocated a grassroots development philosophy that encouraged people to be self-reliant, thus preparing them for sustainable growth after independence. "In this period there emerged many women activists and leaders who were committed to and pursued these development ideals," Ponna Wignaraja wrote in *Women, Poverty and Resources*. "They also agitated for equality between men and women as essential to the building of a new nation, a principle which was embodied in the Indian Constitution" (Wignaraja 1990: 65).

But for many who were working to aid the poor and improve the lives and well-being of all women, the 1950s and 1960s brought disappointments, in part for the reasons Sam Pitroda suggested. In addition, rural development programs, including the Green Revolution in agriculture, often turned out to benefit the better-off farming communities, not the poorest villages. Trickle-down policies did not deliver, often because bureaucracies stood in the way of progress or politicians interceded and enriched themselves on development aid. "The poorest and among these the poor women were further marginalized," Wignaraja wrote (1990: 66). Women began to feel that their place in society was not improving, perhaps even slipping, as the freedom and democracy they had won peacefully did not deliver the promised equality and old social patterns proved to be resistant to change. In China, meanwhile, centuries of tradition were being overturned radically, even violently, as women were mobilized by a new Communist government with slogans of equality like "Women hold up half the sky."

■ The Dispiriting Dynasties

To consider women in political life in India, it is necessary to set aside some mythology about South Asia in general. It is often said that India, Bangladesh, Sri Lanka, and even Pakistan had women as heads of government, while most western industrial nations did not. But these Asian women, however much they may have served later as unwitting role models, were not propelled into high office entirely or even largely by their own efforts. Prime Minister Indira Gandhi, who had no brothers as rivals, succeeded her father, Jawaharlal Nehru, first as leader of India's Congress Party and then (after a brief period) as prime minister. The story continues. In recent years, the party, in disarray and defeat, turned to Sonia Gandhi, the widow of Rajiv Gandhi, Indira's son, who was assassinated in 1991 on his way to a political comeback. Sonia Gandhi is an Italian-born woman with no independent political experience, but she is a Gandhi now, and the party faithful follow her. In Bangladesh, two women who served as prime ministers—Sheikh Hasina Wazed and Khaleda Zia—inherited their mantles from assassinated men, Sheikh Hasina's father, Mujibur Rahman, and Zia's husband, General Zia Rahman. In Sri Lanka, Srimavo Bandaranaike survived a murdered husband, S. W. R. D. Bandaranaike, and took up his political reins. Their daughter, Chandrika Kumaratunga, whose husband also died in a political assassination, was ultimately elected president after great hesitation about joining politics and an extended period of reflection while living safely in Europe, outside her ethnically torn country. Pakistan's Benazir Bhutto, who was twice prime minister, very consciously portrayed herself to voters before her election in 1988 as the daughter of Zulfikar Ali Bhutto, a former head of government convicted and hanged for murder under a military ruler, General Mohammad Zia-ul-Haq. Her election posters bore both her image and her father's. After she was twice dismissed from the prime ministership on charges of corruption and mismanagement, many Pakistanis held her husband, Asif Ali Zardari, a businessman, responsible for having led her into unethical territory for his own gain.

A number of prominent Indian women are looking more critically at Indira Gandhi's legacy, too. Nehru's daughter and political heir dominated both the Congress Party and Indian politics in general for nearly two decades until her assassination in 1984. As prime minister, Gandhi, who was not related to Mahatma Gandhi, never named a woman to her cabinet, though she had close female advisers and friends. One of her closest friends, Pupul Jayakar, told the Women's Feature Service in an interview that "Indira Gandhi never really took up issues which related to the socio-economic specificity of women's lives" (Women's Feature Service, September 3, 1997).

One lesson that many contemporary women in Indian politics have drawn from Indira Gandhi's tenure as prime minister is that they will have to demand by law a certain percentage of parliamentary seats—or state assembly seats or seats on local councils or village governing bodies called *panchayats*—if they ever want a fair representation in the corridors of power. The system of saving seats for women, now in effect at local levels but still being debated in Parliament, has its outspoken opponents, since many other women in politics fear that parties would merely assign the reserved places to slates of their most faithful followers—perhaps even the female relatives of politicians already in power—who would not buck their "business as usual" agendas.

Some women in politics have chafed at keeping quiet when decisions were made that they could not easily accept. Margaret Alva, another colleague of Indira Gandhi, had to bear the brunt of widespread criticism in the 1980s as a loyal Congress Party minister under Indira's son, Prime Minister Rajiv Gandhi, when he forced a law through Parliament denying Muslim women the right to alimony. Rajiv Gandhi, who had a European wife and a passion for modernization, would have been expected to be more sympathetic to women's rights. Nevertheless, he did not want to risk opposition from male Muslim voters, who supported his party, after the Supreme Court of India ruled in favor of a deserted Muslim wife, Shah Bano, and ordered her ex-husband to support her. Gandhi's law overturned that legal decision, to the consternation of many Indian women of all religions. "Very often, the dilemma between our opinion as women activists and our commitment to the larger interest of the party does create situations," Alva was quoted as saying (Women's Feature Service, September 3, 1997).

Opponents of reserved seats for female candidates argue that it would be better for women to break into politics under their own steam, not beholden to the very groups that have excluded them for so long. A few strong-willed women have proved this can be done, among them Mamata Banerjee, a feisty and controversial politician who built herself a base—and her own political party—in Calcutta and used it to maneuver her way into a leading role in the state of West Bengal as well as in national politics. Like Banerjee, other women coming into politics in India now are also beginning to fall into that category of nondynastic politicians, closer to their counterparts in industrialized democracies than to the famous women who have populated their nations' recent histories, inheriting at local as well as national levels the political fealty and patronage systems of male relatives. The new, independent women in Indian politics have some of the same problems as women everywhere, however. Most critical is the shortage of money to mount effective campaigns.

■ Investing in Women

The early disappointments and failures felt by Indian women in the decades after independence had some salutary effects. Self-propelled, independent women's movements began to appear. In 1975, the year of the first UN-sponsored International Conference on Women, a milestone document appeared: *The Report of the Commission on the Status of Women in India.* It acknowledged that Indian women faced cultural and political biases that defied quick fixes. By then, however, some determined women were beginning to take matters into their own hands. In the southern state of Tamil Nadu, the Working Women's Forum was taking shape by the late 1970s to help city women, many of them street merchants. In 1981 this nongovernmental organization established its own bank, the Working Women's Credit Society, with seed money from a U.S. donor, Appropriate Technology International (now renamed EnterpriseWorks Worldwide). That organization had been chartered by the U.S. Congress in the 1970s, when there was considerably more enthusiasm in Washington for aiding the developing world. Through neighborhood branches, the Working Women's Forum helped poor urban women economically while teaching them to make the best use of social services for themselves and their children.

Across India in the northwestern state of Gujarat, the Self-Employed Women's Association, now known worldwide as SEWA, was founded even earlier, in 1972, as an outgrowth of the labor movement among textile workers in Ahmadabad, historically the creative and productive heartland of Indian textiles. Fabric from Ahmadabad was known for its quality and artistry before colonial times. The city's Calico Museum is one of India's most captivating craft galleries. Ahmadabad was also Mahatma Gandhi's base for many years; there he built the Sabarmati ashram, a commune for his followers. But in Ahmadabad, as in other cities, women often found themselves on the fringes of the organized labor movement. SEWA was soon helping women struggling to survive in a variety of trades and occupations, from ragpickers to petty shopkeepers, through its network of local branches. It also opened its own small-scale credit bank.

Ela Bhatt, a middle-class English teacher still in her thirties, was the force behind SEWA's founding in the 1970s, and she was still at its

Rekha Datta

Members of a SEWA video cooperative

helm in the 1990s. An example for women in self-help projects around the world, Bhatt later served as chairwoman of the International Coalition on Women and Credit. In that capacity, she told the World Summit for Social Development in Copenhagen in March 1995 that "poverty will not disappear through charity." Access to finance was the best hope of the poor, she argued. Later that year, Bhatt introduced Hillary Rodham Clinton to the SEWA project in Gujarat. The U.S. first lady became a strong advocate of the SEWA approach to microcredit.

The changes in women's lives in India since independence have been uneven from region to region, sometimes because there was no Ela Bhatt to light a spark or no environment to support an independent working women's movement. More generally, there was the influence of history. In West Bengal—and its vibrant capital, Calcutta, the intellectual pulse and once the administrative center of the British Empire in India—families were more apt to educate their girls than might have been the case in the nearby, more agrarian states of Bihar or Uttar Pradesh, where women are still least likely to go to school and most likely to meet death by violence in the home. Calcutta's early flowering as a cultural, business, and corporate center opened jobs to women in new areas like public relations and marketing; this process also took place in Bombay (now Mumbai). Both cities were entertainment and film centers, creating careers in acting and writing. Later, the advent of high technology in cities like Mumbai and Bangalore, India's electronics hub, expanded opportunities for women again, although women's magazines argue that the culture of the high-technology world is still geared toward men, especially at the upper levels. Women all over the world might agree; many North American and European women have reached similar conclusions.

In south India, particularly the often-studied state of Kerala, a number of influences combined to raise the status of all women—not just those in professions—to a higher plane than in any other region of the country. K. E. Eapen, who was head of Kerala University's Mass Communications Department when the state began moving toward a goal of 100 percent literacy, says that several historical characteristics of Kerala life were important to women. First, there were enlightened local kings, the maharajas of Cochin and Travancore, who over the years supported girls' education and other social developments that benefited women. Second, there was a long history of indigenous Christian-run schools since some influential high castes in Kerala had adopted Christianity and its dedication to teaching in the first century C.E., directly from the Middle East and 1,500 years before European missionaries arrived in South Asia on the heels of mercantile adventurers. Education for both sexes remained a central mandate for the otherwise ultimately diversified churches of Kerala. Finally, voters in the state elected a Communist-led government with a strong social agenda soon after Indian independence. Over the years, the political left played a large role in providing easy access to basic health care, usually within walking distance of most families, as well as equality of schools and other public services for girls. The left also advanced the social status of women, as well as men of the lowest castes, and opened jobs for them in government and politics. Whole families were then elevated and fundamentally transformed. Many also raised their living standards substantially by sending family members to work in the Arabian/Persian Gulf area and other countries in the Middle East during oil boom years, where they were valued for their high level of educational attainment.

In the desert state of Rajasthan, women traditionally decorate mud houses with intricate patterns in whitewash or paint

Barbara Crossette

Women have fared far less well in other regions of India, particularly in the "cow belt" of the north and in the desert state of Rajasthan, where rigid caste codes and warrior traditions have dominated social life to the frequent detriment of women and girls. In parts of Rajasthan, literacy for women drops to 10 percent or lower. In regions like these, social statistics are warning signals to those who believe that an upwardly mobile middle class of even 200 million people—the high estimate—allows Indians to somehow negate or gloss over the reality of hundreds of millions of others living in poverty and illiteracy. Some regional differences have receded to a degree because of the unifying role of television, which can afford glimpses of life outside the neighborhood and give women encouragement from the examples of what other Indian women have accomplished. In middle-class families across the country, women may travel away from home for jobs or education and then marry men from other states, increasingly by choice rather than by arrangement. These and other hallmarks of a new mobility have freed those women, although still a relatively small number, from the often claustrophobic, possibly constrained, or sometimes physically perilous life within an extended family of in-laws.

■ Learning About Life and Love

In their personal lives, Indian women have often been without the kind of information about their bodies and their rights that women elsewhere can find readily in newspapers and magazines or on frank television talks shows and even sitcoms. For those unable to read, any useful knowledge available to the well-educated minority was always beyond their grasp, and government-controlled television and radio shied away from topics like sex and personal relationships. For those girls who went to school, sex education was a rarity. Women who were able to read newspapers and magazines could find a few frank columns on health and human behavior but virtually nothing written about homosexuality, certainly not as an accepted lifestyle. As late as 1998, politicians in New Delhi tried to storm a movie theater showing *Fire,* a film about a lesbian relationship, still a taboo subject in most Indian homes.

There was also scant helpful, encouraging, informative material for women who might want to try living alone, however difficult it would be. Women who wanted to know more than they could glean from friends about sexuality in marriage were often without sources of professional advice. Many brides went ignorant and frightened into their wedding nights. "In India, almost every marriage starts with rape," a woman who assisted battered brides said bitterly in an interview in New Delhi. Much unnecessary unhappiness was born of misunderstanding because men were also uneducated in comprehending women and their feelings and needs. In many Indian cities, where often poorly qualified doctors hang out signs offering help in sexual matters, "sex counseling" still means no more than enhancing male performance or pleasure, not improving relationships.

Changes in public opinion are coming, though not always rapidly or universally. In young middle-class families, where access to information of all kinds has vastly expanded and foreign travel is becoming possible, there is more openness about sex and reproduction. "Men are more commonly interested in reproductive health than is commonly believed," Anu Radha wrote in a survey of what social scientists have been learning about sexuality in India in recent years (Women's Feature Service, September 2, 1998). "Social researches based on community surveys have shown that men know little about contraception, do not want their partners to use it, and are not interested in planning their families. [But] Individual attitudes and behavior among men vary enormously, and notwithstanding these researches, on balance the evidence suggests that many more men would participate if they had the right opportunity to do so. . . . It's only in recent years that many programs are being organized involving men."

The fear of an epidemic of HIV/AIDS in India has focused more attention on sex education, since India now has the world's second-largest number of HIV-positive people, according to UN estimates. Radha found that the 1994 United Nations International Conference on Population and Development in Cairo, which ended with a strong challenge to women to take charge of their own reproductive health—not only family planning but also their general physical, emotional, and social well-being—played a significant part in mobilizing women in India. Many women also got a boost in confidence from the Fourth World Conference on Women held in Beijing a year later. But the Cairo conference in particular, Radha wrote, "reminded the world audience that good reproductive health is the right of all people, men and women alike, and that together they share responsibility for these matters. Neither men or women are likely to enjoy good reproductive health until couples are able to discuss sexual matters and make reproductive decisions together" (Women's Feature Service, September 2, 1998).

Changes in popular culture have an impact on women's lives almost everywhere in India. The once-limited, government-controlled television and radio broadcasts that stayed away from any controversial subject, high among them strong social issues like women's rights, have been sidelined by a plethora of cable and satellite programs that bring, for good or evil, bold and racy topics and behavior into full view even in distant villages. A vibrant collection of new novelists—many but not all writing in English, which has a limited readership—craft earthy, even scandalous stories. Shobha De, for example, has become a best-selling author of what her critics call trashy novels, but her writing has thrown the underside of life in Bombay, India's entertainment and business capital, into a new kind of spotlight. Her stories are antidotes to the treacly romantic or gratuitously violent films Bombay produces for mass consumption. De lampoons the pretentious and satirizes the famous while pouring into her tales gritty details of sexual liaisons that break all taboos. Arundhati Roy, a prize-winning novelist, probed a southern Indian family's deepest, most personal secrets boldly in her universally acclaimed novel, *The God of Small Things*. Both foreigners and Indians learned new things about themselves.

This new frankness is not limited to literature. In Bangalore in the mid-1990s, a major survey asked college students for the first time about their childhood sexual experiences and found that one-third of the young women and a number of young men reported having been sexually abused as children, usually by relatives (Women's Feature Service, February 1, 1996). Community leaders, shocked by the findings, set up a hotline for victims, created workshops at which parents and students could discuss the issue, and began training counselors. Once again, it was a grassroots movement that demanded action and change.

"Most women in India are poor, but with remarkable resilience organize food, water and homes for their families," said Anita Anand, who manages the Women's Feature Service from her base in New Delhi and spends all her time surveying Indian womanhood and women everywhere in the world, in a 1999 interview.

> All this, while fighting off rape and assault and putting up with drunken husbands and fathers. Working at several jobs to put children through school, they neglect themselves, especially their health. But they are now supported by middle-class women, by their families, by women's organizations, by development agencies and by the government. Over the years, there has been a realization that giving women political, economic and social choices means a better India for all. Women, individually and in groups, are doing remarkable things. Can these transformations come together in an institutionalized way so that they can become more effective? This is the challenge.

■ Bibliography

Baria, Farah. 1998. "Girls Just Wanna Have Fun." *India Today*, October 19, pp. 32–33.

Basu, Srimati. 1999. *She Comes to Take Her Rights: Indian Women, Property, and Propriety.* Albany: State University of New York Press.

Bhattacharji, Sukumari. 1994. *Women and Society in Ancient India.* Calcutta: Basumati.

Bumiller, Elisabeth. 1990. *May You Be the Mother of a Hundred Sons: A Journey Among the Women of India.* New York: Ballantine Books.

Burton, Antoinette M. 1994. *Burdens of History: British Feminists, Indian Women, and Imperial Culture, 1865–1915.* Chapel Hill: University of North Carolina Press.

Chaudhary, Pratima K. 1995. *Women's Education in India: Myth and Reality.* New Delhi: Har-Anand Publications.

Choudhury, Arundhati Roy. 1998. *Uniform Civil Code: Social Change and Gender Justice.* New Delhi: Indian Social Institute.

Crossette, Barbara. 1989. "Why India Is Still Failing to Stop Its Population Surge." *New York Times*, July 9, p. 4.

———. 2000. *India: Old Civilization in a New World.* New York: Foreign Policy Association.

Dutt, Ela. 1998. "Focus on Poverty and Hunger, Sen Tells the B.J.P." *India Abroad*, October 23.

Giri, V. Mohini. 1998. *Emancipation and Empowerment of Women.* New Delhi: Gyan Publishing House.

Government of India. 1995. *Ministry National Crimes Bureau Report on Geographical Distribution of Dowry Deaths in India.* New Delhi: Government of India.

Kudchedkar, Shirin, and Sabiha Al-Issa, eds. 1998. *Violence Against Women, Women Against Violence.* Delhi: Pencraft International.

Landes, David S. 1998. *The Wealth and Poverty of Nations: Why Some Are So Rich and Some So Poor.* New York: W. W. Norton.

Mittal, Mukta, ed. 1995. *Women in India: Today and Tomorrow.* New Delhi: Anmol Publications.

Narasimhan, Sakuntala. 1999. *Empowering Women: An Alternative Strategy from Rural India.* New Delhi: Sage Publications.

Pande, Mrinal. 1991. *The Subject Is Woman.* New Delhi: Sanchar Publishing House.

Poonacha, Veena. 1997. *Women's Empowerment and Political Participation.* Mumbai: Research Center for Women's Studies.

Rani, D. Lalitha. 1996. *Women Entrepreneurs.* New Delhi: A. P. H. Publishing.

Sankaran, Kamala, ed. 1992. *Women in Politics: Forms and Processes.* New Delhi: Friedrich Ebert Stiftung.

Sheel, Ranjana. 1999. *The Political Economy of Dowry: Institutionalization and Expansion in North India.* New Delhi: Manohar.

Spear, Sir Percival. 1978. *The Oxford History of Modern India, 1740–1975.* 2nd ed. Oxford: Clarendon Press.

Subbamma, Malladi. 1994. *Women and Social Reform.* M. V. Rama Murty, trans. Hyderabad: Booklinks.

Unnithan-Kumar, Maya. 1997. *Identity, Gender, and Poverty: New Perspectives on Caste and Tribe in Rajasthan.* Providence, R.I.: Berghahn Books.

Usha Roa, N. J. 1983. *Women in a Developing Society.* New Delhi: Ashish.

Venkateswaran, Sandhya. 1992. *Living on the Edge: Women, Environment, and Development.* New Delhi: Friedrich Ebert Stiftung.

Visaria, Pravin. 1997. *Women in the Indian Work Force: Trends and Differentials.* Pune: Gokhale Institute of Politics and Economics.

Wignaraja, Ponna. 1990. *Women, Poverty, and Resources.* New Delhi: Sage Publications for UNICEF.

Women's Feature Service dispatches from New Delhi, 1996–1999.

World Bank. 1999. *India Country Gender Profile.* See online at www.worldbank.org.

9

Population, Urbanization, and the Environment

Holly Sims

Although India occupies just 2.4 percent of the world's surface area, its dazzling mosaic of people and cultures, wildlife, vegetation, and landscapes make it the most diverse and complex country on the planet. India's territory is framed by towering snow-capped mountain ranges in the north and languid emerald lagoons in the south that ultimately yield to unspoiled beaches facing the Indian Ocean and the Arabian Sea. Yet India also is home to some of the world's most crowded and polluted cities.

India is one of a very few countries whose constitution enjoins citizens to protect the environment. Yet economic growth has been the overriding priority of successive governments, and the environment has borne heavy costs. According to the World Bank, a conservative estimate of India's annual losses from sickness and death caused by air and water pollution and the economic costs attributable to resource degradation exceeds $20 billion (World Bank 1998).[1]

Despite the marked disparity between Indian constitutional designers' hopes and disquieting indicators of actual performance, Indian commentators and activists have contributed more to the development of international consciousness and thought about humankind's place in the universe than have citizens from any other country apart from the United States.

One of India's most famous citizens, Mohandas Karamchand Gandhi, called "Mahatma" (great soul), was perhaps the first world leader to publicly question modern societies' reckless pursuit of eco-

157

nomic growth in the name of "progress." Asked in 1947 whether newly independent India would emulate Britain's development experience, Gandhi was reputed to have responded, "It took Britain half the resources of the planet to achieve this prosperity; how many planets would a country like India require?"

The varied ways in which contemporary Indians have shaped international environmental consciousness will be briefly considered following discussion of the main question at hand: How does one assess the state of India's environment? A diverse group of experts would disagree both on major contributing factors to environmental degradation and on possible remedies. They would offer a variety of conceptual lenses designed to bring factors potentially responsible for environmental debasement into focus while relegating other possible causes to the background.[2] The choice of a specific focus or lens is conditioned by a person's values, views on the world, and perspectives on cause-and-effect relationships, which in turn may be influenced by specialized training.

For many western observers, the most salient characteristic of India's environment is the sheer size of its population. A conceptual lens trained to focus on demographics generally implies that population pressure is the major environmental problem and population control is the obvious solution. Other experts contend that poverty rather than population pressure is the most critical factor ravaging India's environment and prescribe economic growth as a solution. Still others identify hazardous modern technology as the world's greatest threat.

During the 1960s and 1970s, the same three factors—population growth and demographic pressure, poverty, and hazardous technology—emerged as the prime suspects in global environmental degradation. Commentators disputed which factor held overriding importance, but many later realized that they are interrelated. Just as serious scholars and practitioners developed a more sophisticated appreciation of the environment's complexity and the dynamic and sometimes unpredictable interaction of its component elements, a fourth potential degradation suspect—governments—claimed center stage.

Advocates of market-based approaches blamed governments for wasteful resource use and advocated reliance on market forces to determine the prices of water and energy, for example. The most extreme proponents of a conceptual lens focused on markets and governments urged the privatization of all public goods, such as national parks, in hopes of promoting greater responsibility for resource management (see Anderson and Leal 1991). The ensuing pages offer a view through each of the four conceptual lenses.

A conceptual lens is a simplified view of a more complicated reality (Hempel 1996: 89). In this chapter, I do not "sell" any of the four conceptual lenses. The first two—population pressures and poverty—receive more attention because many Indian and western observers believe that they reflect the two key problems facing India's environment. Proponents of each lens debate their relative significance, however.

■ The Population Lens

Scholarly debates are cast into the background as advocates of the population lens offer readers a particular view, in hopes of persuading them that the major problem facing both the world and India's estimated 1 billion residents is the one proposed in 1789 by Thomas Robert Malthus, an English economist and clergyman. Malthus foresaw exponentially increasing human populations outgrowing food supplies. Ultimately, he predicted, they will succumb to starvation, disease, and war.

It is easy to understand why the population lens is so often trained on the country expected to overtake China as the world's most populous nation by the middle of the twenty-first century. One in every six people on the planet lives in India. By 2050, India may need to accommodate an additional 700 million people—equivalent to Africa's entire population. Since almost all the newcomers will settle in cities, increasing their size from today's 250 million to 750 million by 2050, the population lens often darts from burgeoning aggregate growth statistics to the overflowing cities that may become potential flashpoints of environmental degradation (Sampat 1998: 38).

Before considering the impact of rapidly growing cities and mounting pressures on such critical resources as water, two salient facts about India's population dynamics deserve note. First, generalizations have limited utility. India's diversity and complexity are reflected in striking regional variations in family size, infant mortality rates, and other key demographic variables. In some Indian states, particularly in the south, population growth is slow. The small southern state of Kerala is famous for population growth rates, life expectancies, and infant mortality rates that compare favorably with those in much richer nations. The discouragingly high birth, death, and infant mortality rates visible from the population "lens" are heavily concentrated in four sprawling states in India's Hindi-speaking belt—Bihar, Madhya Pradesh, Rajasthan, and Uttar Pradesh.

Second, India's birth and death rates are not static. They reflect considerable change since the beginning of the twentieth century, when birth rates were high but population growth was held in check by poor health facilities and recurrent epidemics. India's average annual rate of population increase was about 2.2 percent from 1951 to 1991, nearly double the growth rate of the three decades from 1891 to 1921. For some, the growth in population from about 361 million in 1951 to more than 846 million people in 1991 is frightening; for others, it is a heartening reflection of improved nutrition and access to health care. Today's galloping urbanization nevertheless raises the specter of old and new health threats and severe environmental challenges for local communities, the wider society, and the world beyond India (Sims 1992: 118–119; Cohen 1995).

▓ Indian Governments and Population Growth

No one could say that India's leaders have ignored population growth. India inaugurated the world's first national family planning program, in 1952, when its population was nearly 400 million. In the years since then, India's leaders have invested more than $3 billion in programs to curb fertility, but the country's population has more than doubled.

Indian officials have adopted an exhaustive list of strategies to slow population growth. They have spent more money on family planning than leaders in any other country. Each official five-year plan has stressed the urgency of family planning. Agencies have been created and ministers assigned and reshuffled at the highest level. About 15,000 family planning service centers disseminate information and supplies to the country's remotest areas. Government services are complemented by private-sector efforts, in factories and many villages and small towns.

Crude images of a two-child family adorn city buses and village walls throughout India, relentlessly proclaiming that "A Small Family Is a Happy Family." New ways of reinforcing that message are sought in every international conference and seminar on population and related issues. A plethora of institutes conduct research and training on demography, family planning, communications, and reproductive biology. India's family planning programs have received extensive advice and financial support from international agencies and experts (Bose 1988: 33–34).

Government leaders have tried to ensure that contraceptive supplies are adequate. To further reduce unwanted pregnancies, officials have tried particularly hard to encourage sterilization. Large numbers of clients for this procedure are sought in sterilization "camps," which spring up on desolate landscapes like traveling circuses. Demographic trends nevertheless have remained far out of line with official goals (Sims 1992: 122–123).

■ The Government and Population Control

Often observers mindful of India's mounting numbers will wonder why India does not control its population. An answer might have at least three parts, touching on "India," "control," and "population." First, India is not a unitary actor. Like the United States, it is a federal system that thwarts unilateral action by even the most determined chief executive based in New Delhi or Washington, D.C. In recent years, the directive capacity of India's central leadership has been limited by political decentralization, fragmentation, and economic liberalization.

Government family planning notices can be seen on many billboards. This one (in Hindi) advises parents to delay in arranging their children's marriages.

Frequent turnover of India's recent fragile coalition governments would deter almost any would-be leader from focusing on an issue like population limitation, which does not offer tangible short-term payoffs. There is no unitary leadership claiming to embody the national interest beyond the political lifespan of those whose tenuous hold on power is subject to challenge.

Second, control is problematic in a democratic context. An authoritarian political system's leaders can exert control over their subjects, but a democratic system is necessarily responsive and accountable to its constituents' preferences. India's leaders and its public learned that lesson the hard way after former prime minister Indira Gandhi declared an "emergency" and suspended civil liberties in 1975. Her younger son, Sanjay Gandhi, launched a frenzied drive to limit population growth through coercion rather than persuasion and incentives. The government thereby alienated millions of voters and was swept from power in elections held in 1977. The experience cast a lingering pall on India's family planning programs and made successive leaders wary of drastic action to slow population growth (Sims 1992: 125–126).[3]

Third, looking beyond population subject to control by people with a legitimate say in public affairs, a broad consensus favoring social change led by local communities and households has displaced earlier proposed solutions that empowered external actors to exercise control (Bose 1988; Staudt 1997). Two factors often cited as critical to demographic change are the position of females vis-à-vis males in a given society and female literacy. In patriarchal societies such as India, many women have little say in such vital questions as family size. Women's lowly position in society is indicated by early marriage, the dowry system, preference for sons, and discrimination against widows. Literacy is often associated with relatively low infant mortality, high contraceptive use, and later marriage. In combination, these factors lower both mortality and fertility rates. Broader social changes may be needed to help females make critical decisions regarding family size and health care. Such changes are not easily effected through legislation, and they will not occur overnight. In countries lacking social security systems, children offer the best hope of financial security for the aged; thus many poor people view large families as a blessing rather than a curse.

Perspectives on India's Expanding Cities

Cities in today's industrialized countries were catalysts for economic growth and social change, for they offered jobs; higher incomes;

A crowded Delhi neighborhood

access to health care and information; and exposure to a world more cosmopolitan than the villages where elites and traditions held sway. In modern India, the persistent lure of cities is suggested by statistics showing that the proportion of Indians living in absolute poverty in urban India may be lower than the corresponding figure for rural India.

In the twenty-first century, a majority of the world's population will live in cities, which the *International Geographic Encyclopedia and Atlas* (1979: 162) defines as a "densely populated urban center, larger than a village or town, whose inhabitants are engaged primarily in commerce and industry." A commonly used measure of urban growth is the "megacity," or a city with a population exceeding 8 million. In 1950, there were just two megacities—New York City, whose population was 12.3 million, and London, which then had 8.7 million residents. In 2015, there will be thirty-three megacities, twenty-seven in low-income countries (World Resources Institute 1996: 8).

India's megacities include Mumbai (formerly Bombay), with a 2001 population of 11.9 million, and Delhi, with 9.8 million residents. Delhi is gaining on Mumbai, with a population growth rate between 1995 and 2000 of 3.2 percent each year, compared with the latter's rate of 3.5 percent (*World Almanac Books* 2002). In both cities, 17 percent

Multistoried apartment buildings in South Calcutta

of residents were reportedly below the official poverty line. The actual figure may be far higher (World Resources Institute 1996: 154–155).

Rapidly growing but deteriorating cities and urban poverty signal global environmental stress and potential health hazards and mount a full-scale assault on the senses of visitors and residents alike. In a landmark decision on December 7, 2000, India's Supreme Court directed the Delhi government to relocate or shut down all industrial units in the capital that do not conform to pollution norms set by civic authorities. The judgment could affect as many as 1.5 million workers. During 1998, the court prodded city officials to ban taxies, buses, and motorized rickshaws more than fifteen years old and to replace leaded gasoline with unleaded fuel. Enforcement of these regulations will be difficult; meanwhile, cities' expansion across the globe generates industrial wastes and fossil fuel–based pollution that produces greenhouse gas emissions linked to global climate change. Thus far, the major contributors to emerging global problems are cities in the industrialized world, not their counterparts in India and other low-income countries (World Resources Institute 1996: 2). The latter's share will increase as their cities expand.

Automobile and
bus traffic jams the
streets of Calcutta

Ashok K. Dutt

Public Health Hazards

Environmental health threats combine the dark dregs of history with a fearsome new Technicolor world of bacteria and communicable disease (Garrett 1995). In September 1994, the highly contagious pneumonic plague, considered more devastating than the bubonic plague that ravaged medieval Europe, broke out in Surat, a city in the western state of Gujarat. By year's end, fifty-six people had died of pneumonic plague nationwide. The pestilence cost India dearly in economic terms. Many visits to the country were canceled amid widespread anxiety linking the local congestion and poor sanitation that fosters epidemics to the global integration that facilitates travel for both people and disease vectors (World Resources Institute 1996: 1, 42).

■ A View from the Ground

On the new frontier of human settlement on Earth, urban slums offer glimpses of humankind's tenacity amid adversity. Consider challenges facing India's capital city, Delhi. More than 1 million of its residents live in *jhuggi* shelters, temporary structures made of mud, thatch, plastic, and other discarded objects. While the model U.S. home expands in size and in the inefficient use of low-priced energy (Meyerson 1998: 1, C6), *jhuggis* are invariably small and offer dust, smoke, and noise pollution instead of ventilation or light. Many *jhuggis* are located near garbage dumps, power plants, and roads, exposing residents to chemical residues, toxic wastes, and car exhaust fumes. Congested roads and alleys thickly lined with settlers in degraded shelters concentrate the impact of vehicle and household pollution from "dirty" energy sources, including oil, wood, and coal.

Some blighted neighborhoods have launched inspiring initiatives to improve community health, nutritional intake, and environmental conditions. A local nongovernmental organization based in Delhi, Action for Security Health for All (its acronym, ASHA, is the Hindi word for "hope"), offers just one example. ASHA began in 1988 as an emergency health clinic to quell a cholera epidemic in a Delhi slum. Its staff quickly concluded that community health problems were linked to poverty, pollution, and environmental degradation; thus ASHA's approach to health care went beyond the relatively costly curative services offered by conventional health delivery systems that often are beyond poor people's reach.

Just as many population experts found that women's active participation is critical to demographic change, ASHA's staff concluded that women play a potentially pivotal role in community health. ASHA therefore trained local women in basic health care so that they could provide readily accessible services and in environmental education so that they could help safeguard their communities from respiratory and waterborne diseases (World Resources Institute 1996: 38–39).

■ Pressure on Natural Resources

Problems of resource depletion, such as water shortages, are less easily resolved, especially in a country where rain falls mainly during four months of the year. Because migrants to cities drain water and firewood from sprawling urban hinterlands, the urban poor often are blamed for enervating water shortages. The urban poor are not entirely at fault, however, since many factors involved are beyond their control. For example, farmers' profligate use of subsurface water for irrigation has caused alarming depletion of water supplies in at least six Indian states, thereby threatening future food production and supply within the countryside and to cities (Brown 1998).[4] Equitable water distribution to poor neighborhoods is thwarted by prosperous and politically powerful residents and enterprises that serve such constituencies as well as tourists.

In past centuries, many Indians routinely collected and stored water. India's landscape was dotted by lakes and tanks that served as reservoirs. Tank construction offered religious merit to indigenous rulers and security to the settlements that spread across India's vast plains. Wetlands provided refuge for humans, animals, and plants.

British colonists shifted priority attention to resource extraction. Tanks were allowed to decay, and urban lakes that once lent calm and serenity to Indian cities became repositories of green algae and garbage. Some Indian critics charge that contemporary planners mesmerized by a chimera of development have forsaken ancient traditions that served India well for centuries in favor of imported, modern elab-

Lake Pichola in Udaipur, Rajasthan. The marble palace in the center is one of several island palaces built there in the sixteenth to eighteenth centuries.

orate schemes to transport water across great distances at enormous cost (Chakraborty 1995: 27–31). Sadly, as experience in the United States and other societies suggests, extreme shortsightedness often governs water use, resulting in a need to pursue technically complex water delivery projects (Reisner 1993; Postel 1997).

■ Reflections on the Population Lens

The view that population growth, particularly in such low-income countries as India, is the world's overriding concern has drawn fire from many quarters as simplistic and ethnically biased. Proponents of the population lens often borrow the biological concept of "carrying capacity," which may usefully index the number of fruit flies a petri dish can support. But if the question is, how many people can the Earth support? the answer is, we do not know. That was demographer Joel Cohen's conclusion after several years of study. As Cohen observed,

> The Earth's capacity to support people is determined partly by processes that the human and natural sciences have yet to understand, and partly by choices that we and our descendants have yet to make. A numerical estimate of how many people the Earth can support may be a useful index of present human activities and of present understanding of how to live on the Earth; it cannot predict the constraints or possibilities that lie in the future. (Cohen 1995: 10–11)

In short, even the rapid growth of populations in recent decades does not predict the global environment's health. Those whose sights remain fixed on the population lens often are criticized for diverting attention from questions that may have more direct bearing on environmental carrying capacity, particularly issues of resource use.

The latter concerns were raised by Mahatma Gandhi in 1947 and echoed by contemporary Indian writers,[5] as well as the noted U.S. environmental writer Bill McKibben. According to McKibben, the United States "is in a real sense the most populous nation on Earth" (1998: 108) because its 281 million people consume three times the amount of resources used by India's 1 billion inhabitants. Since the average American will consume forty to fifty times as much as the average Indian, McKibben urged Americans to curb their own population growth in order to slow the planet's implosion from overconsumption.

Americans consume fifty-two times more meat per capita than do Indians, suggesting that the effective population of the United States with respect to meat consumption is more than 13 billion, compared to

1 billion for India. Supporting the world's current population on a U.S.-style diet would require as much energy as the planet now uses for all purposes, along with two and a half times as much grain as all its farmers produce (Durning 1991: 17; Ehrlich and Ehrlich 1990).

It is reasonable to ask how many people the Earth can support, but the question needs qualification: Given what kinds of economics and technologies? At what levels of material well-being? Living in what physical, chemical, and biological environments? And with what cultural values, what social, political, and legal institutions? Natural constraints on population size are not well understood, but neither are people's decisions about lifestyle and food, which in turn affect natural constraints. Such decisions are subject to change (Cohen 1995: 236–296).

During the 1960s, the population lens's stark vision of impending catastrophe led the United States to spend millions of dollars each year on population control programs in India and other poor countries. In the 1970s and 1980s, as public concern in the United States about global population growth diminished, a rival lens highlighting global problems and proposed solutions gained increasing support. Through a second conceptual lens, poor people in India and other low-income countries appear as a major cause of environmental degradation. The implied course of action centers on economic growth and its associated development rather than birth control.

■ The Poverty Lens

When Indian prime minister Indira Gandhi proclaimed in 1972 that poverty was the worst form of pollution, she dropped a metaphorical brick onto the burnished table facing delegates to the first international conference on the human environment, held in Stockholm by the United Nations. Many participants from the United States and other industrialized countries hoped that a new set of environmental ethics could emerge through education and transcend the "North-South divide," the differences between capitalist democracies and less prosperous countries that were aggravated by Cold War rivalries of the United States and former Soviet Union. The Indian prime minister's declaration resonated with residents of poor countries who were skeptical about narrowly focused strategies promising to control the demographic growth—and also, some suspected, economic growth—of nonwestern countries.[6]

Poverty's ill effects on the global environment claimed center stage in international meetings as the Cold War sputtered to an end in the late 1980s. *Our Common Future,* a famous study by the World Commission on Environment and Development, which was headed by a former prime minister of Norway, Gro Harlem Brundtland, helped shift attention to a second conceptual lens and to the catchy but ambiguous term, *sustainable development.* By the Brundtland Commission's definition, that would "meet the needs of the present without compromising the ability of future generations to meet their own needs" (World Commission on Environment and Development 1987: 8).

As the commission observed, poverty compels desperate people to strive to meet their present needs. As a result, it said, the poor may deplete dwindling stocks of fish and encroach on endangered species. The world's shrinking forest cover attests to pressures exerted by growing numbers of people too poor to afford commercial sources of energy, as do barren hillsides subject to erosion and flooding that wreak devastation on lands ravaged by rivers and streams swollen with displaced topsoil. Against a countryside drained of natural resources, the poverty lens highlights a view of city slums that collect people suddenly made surplus, just as flood-swept rivers gather soils detached from their erstwhile moorings. The global environmental impact is suggested by figures indicating that about 4.4 billion people in the world live in low-income countries like India. Among them, three-fifths live in communities without basic sanitation, one-third lack safe drinking water, and a quarter lack proper housing. One-fifth of children do not reach grade five in school; an equal percentage are undernourished (UNDP 1998).

India has the largest number of people in those dismal categories. According to the United Nations Development Programme (UNDP), more than 500 million Indians earn less than $1 a day. Why wouldn't such hard-pressed people put the search for fuel and their families' next meal before the long-term sustainability of the planet?

■ The Indian Government and Poverty

Since independence, economic growth has been an overriding priority for successive Indian leaders. It has proved enormously difficult to extricate India's poor from dire poverty. Beginning in 1960, state leaders sought to do exactly that. Indian leaders' famous official "poverty line" denoted access to a minimum amount of food and consumption items such as clothing. It helped to chart governmental goals and to measure subsequent improvements in living standards.

Certainly, there have been encouraging developments. Gross domestic product (GDP) per capita has more than doubled since 1960, from $206 to $425 in 1995. In 1960, the average person could expect to die at age forty-four; by 1995, average life expectancy was 61.6 years. Trends in infant mortality also showed marked improvement. In 1960, for every 1,000 live births, 165 infants died; by 1996, the figure had dropped to seventy-three (UNDP 1998: 142, 149).

Although GDP per capita remains the gold standard for measuring economies, many development experts say such statistics may obscure more than they reveal about the overall quality of life. A newer measure developed by the UNDP has sought to assess human development with respect to longevity, literacy, and command over resources needed for a decent living standard. The Human Development Index (HDI) measures improvement in the community or country as a whole. It is supplemented by the UNDP's Human Poverty Index (HPI), which assesses the extent of deprivation, or the proportion of people in the community who are left behind. Those measures show both India's achievements and the persistent gaps in its population's welfare.

India's HDI ranks 139th among 174 countries, led by Canada, whose HDI placed first, ahead of the fourth-ranked United States. In a field of seventy-seven countries loosely classified as "developing," with comparable data for 1995, India ranks forty-seventh in terms of HPI, which indicates that more than a third of its people—35.9 percent—live in poverty. UNDP figures show that nearly 20 percent of India's population lacked access to safe water in 1990–1996, 15 percent lacked access to health services, and 71 percent had no access to sanitation (UNDP 1998: 21, 26, 147).

▓ Reflections on the Poverty Lens

The Brundtland Commission's proposed solution for environmental degradation caused by the world's poor was sustainable development, which it believed would permit a five- to tenfold increase in global industrial production (World Commission on Environment and Development 1987: 213). But the argument that poverty is the cause of environmental destruction, expressed by the Brundtland Commission, Indira Gandhi, and many other policymakers and mainstream economists, faces at least three major criticisms. The first questions ambiguous terms like *poverty* and *development*. A second criticism challenges the suggestion that the poor are a prime cause of environmental degradation and need to learn from the presumably environmentally conscious well-to-do. A third rejoinder focuses attention on environmental fallout from consumption associated with affluence and development.

Poverty and development. What is poverty? Conventional economic statistics such as GDP or gross national product (GNP) are narrow and incapable of measuring transactions or circumstances beyond the cash-based economy. GDP measures of poverty suggest that people who wear handmade clothes rather than factory-made garments are poor. By Mahatma Gandhi's definition, however, handloomed cloth was a symbol of self-sufficiency and national pride. Some contemporary Indians used to a life enriched by social ties would agree with a view from traditional African society that poverty denotes a lack of family and friends.

The United Nations developed HDI and HPI to broaden conventional understandings of poverty and human development. The concepts behind HDI reflect extensive contributions from South Asians, including former Pakistani economist Mahbub ul-Haq and India's Nobel Prize–winning economist, Amartya Sen. In sharp contrast to many mainstream economists, Sen draws attention to social circumstances affecting people's access to such critical resources as food, instead of upholding income as a measure of poverty. His research suggests that several major famines reflected vulnerable people's lost "social safety nets" and not simply economic poverty (Sen 1981).

Although Sen's research garnered one of the world's highest honors, some Indian environmentalists criticize him for disregarding ecological dimensions of poverty. One leading environmental activist, Anil Agarwal, contended that for the millions of Indians who still live within a biomass-based economy, the immediate environment's yields—the "Gross Nature Product"—count far more than the GDP measured by economists (Agarwal 1998: 56–57).

If poverty is difficult to measure, then what is *development?* Some define it in terms of financial security and others in terms of consumer goods; still others place top priority on quality of life. Although scholars have debated the term and its implications for decades, often *development* and the equally vague *sustainable development* are used carelessly.

That was not the problem of concern to Agarwal and two other Indian environmentalists, Madhav Gadgil and Ramachandra Guha. In an important book, Gadgil and Guha characterize economic development as "growth of the artificial at the cost of the natural" (Gadgil and Guha 1995: 4). All three agree that views of development imported to the Indian subcontinent by British colonialists bent on resource extraction and the establishment of private property rights over lands traditionally held in common prevailed because ancient wisdom could not compete in a world increasingly dominated by glitzy "artifacts."

Views of the poor. The three environmentalists take issue with the poverty lens's focus on what they believe to be symptoms, rather than on the underlying problems compelling the poor to wrest fledgling trees and grasses from land subject to erosion and then sap its remaining life through inefficient cultivation and voracious livestock. Roughly half of India's population—about 465 million people—maintain a precarious hold on the natural environment that provides their livelihood. These "ecosystem people" include subsistence farmers, herders, fisherfolk, artisans, and members of indigenous communities. "Ecosystem people" are aware of the meteor showers of consumer goods that have reached Indian shores since the national economy turned outward toward the global marketplace, but "for the many who earn barely enough to fill their bellies, there is little left over to acquire the new goods on the market, be they soaps or blenders, mopeds or TV sets, apples flown in from the Himalayas or flats in high-rise buildings" (Gadgil and Guha 1995: 3).

A second category of poor people is even more disadvantaged. "Ecological refugees" comprise perhaps one-third of India's population, about 310 million people. They include the Indians tourists see near *jhuggis* in the shadow of high-rise buildings under construction in New Delhi and other cities and the gaunt men in search of daily wage labor perched on the rooftop of a train or bus traveling to or from prosperous farming areas such as Punjab during peak times of the agricultural cycle (Gadgil and Guha 1995: 3–4). Their transient existence is buffeted by uneven capitalist "development," whose pace quickens when resources are used in construction of dams and mines, for example. As a result of such construction, millions of people become ecological refugees in the name of progress.

"Ecosystem people" and "ecological refugees" may have few options. Environmental education delivered by people with less direct ties to the earth probably is not a priority need. No learned scholar could have made that point more effectively than the Bishnois, members of a Hindu sect that primarily live near the harsh expanses of the Thar Desert in the central Indian state of Rajasthan.

The Bishnois have militantly protected wildlife and plants as part of their sacred traditions for centuries. Parts of arid Rajasthan bear witness to 500 years of Bishnoi beliefs and knowledge of nature, in green oasislike dots that contrast sharply with the dusty surrounding landscape. For Salman Khan, a dashing young actor frequently featured in action-packed Hindi movies, the Bishnois' homeland offered an ideal setting for a shooting expedition. Unfortunately, the shooting was not for a film but for endangered blackbuck deer. Khan's party killed two of the graceful animals and was then beset by irate Bishnois. Since the poachers escaped before the Bishnois could administer their own frontier-style justice, the Bishnois resorted to a legal system often bent to serve celebrities and the rich. Salman Khan was the first person to be arrested in the state and kept in the state forest department's custody since the Wildlife Protection Act came into force in 1972.

Ironically, the celluloid hero, Salman Khan, was to be featured in the World Wide Fund for Nature–India (WWF)'s 1999 calendar. Instead, the previously little-known Bishnois provoked considerable thought in India about endangered wildlife and natural resources such as forests, which the WWF reports have declined globally by a third since the 1970s (Verma 1998b: 15–16).

Whose development? For Agarwal, Guha, and Gadgil, such incidents show that the poverty lens is aimed in the wrong direction. In their view, the rich and aspiring rich are the major cause of India's environmental degradation, not the poor who often are displaced in the name of development. The poor cannot buy vehicles whose pollution blights congested urban neighborhoods. The energy-using gadgets increasingly displayed in Indian markets are beyond their reach.

Since 1991, India's economic liberalization has accelerated growth and has greatly expanded the availability of consumer goods. Signs of the "cola wars" familiar to U.S. consumers appear on biscuit-colored village walls throughout India, in sharp contrast to a previous era, when India was closed to multinational purveyors of fast food and beverages. Gadgil and Guha imply that for a widening sector of India's population, aggressively advertised consumer products have the mesmerizing effect of the snake charmers who are now nearly extinct. Their calculations suggest that perhaps one-sixth of India's people, roughly 155 million, have the resources sufficient to "devour everything produced all over the earth" (Gadgil and Guha 1995: 4). For many observers, such "omnivores" represent India's development because they are full-fledged participants in the cash economy. Their income levels range from the "superrich," who earn more than $500,000 a year in purchasing power terms, to various strata of the middle class. Since 1995, the numbers of superrich have quadrupled, from 10,000 to 39,000 (Sampat 1998: 37). The ranks of these "omnivores" include industrial entrepreneurs, urban professionals, and workers in the organized sector of the economy. In rural India, they are large or relatively large landowners with access to irrigation—the people many economists call "progressive farmers" because they can afford risks associated with innovation, such as new hybrid seeds and agrochemicals.

Environmentalists express three major concerns about capitalist development and poverty. First, equitable distribution of resources has lagged behind growth. For many ecosystem people and ecological refugees, India's increased productive capacity has not provided jobs or wages sufficient to offset inflation or unpredictable weather that toys with the lives of people whose survival largely depends on forces of nature. Second, because economic growth is a top priority for a poor country of India's size, environmental protection and regulations have

A vendor at the Howrah Railway Station,
one of the busiest in India

had limited impact. Also, Gadgil and Guha argue, government officials are themselves omnivores. (See the section titled "The Economic Rationalism Lens" for a discussion of government officials and poverty.) Third, although affluence itself is not inherently destructive, many environmentalists would agree that "achieving *material* affluence, in the context of industrial society, constitutes an inexorable assault on nature," marked by consumption of nonrenewable energy, beef, automobiles, land, and building materials (Hempel 1996: 7).

Estimates of India's annual environmental losses vary widely, from the World Bank's staggering figure of nearly $80 billion each year, adjusted for people's purchasing power, to an admittedly conservative estimate by the UNDP of more than $10 billion. A breakdown of the conservative estimates suggested that urban air pollution cost India $1.3 billion a year and that water degradation's health costs amounted to $5.7 billion each year, nearly three-fifths of the total environmental costs (UNDP 1998: 79).

While statisticians argue over numbers, few would deny that environmental degradation will intensify as India, China, and other low-income countries emulate the consumption patterns of industrial countries. The production of carbon dioxide associated with global climate change represents one of the gravest environmental threats facing the planet. It could disrupt the relatively stable climate that has prevailed since settled agriculture emerged some 10,000 years ago, thereby allowing the world's population to increase from a few million to well over 6 billion.

Although the industrialized world accounts for most of the emissions associated with global climate change, possible consequences threaten the entire globe. Poor people in poor countries—such as India's ecological refugees and ecosystem people—may be hit hardest by smaller harvests, growing water shortages, and rising seas.

In 1995, the United States produced the largest share of carbon dioxide emissions worldwide: 24 percent, or 20,500 metric tons per person. During the same year, the average Indian produced only 1 metric ton of carbon dioxide emissions. Yet according to the UNDP, recent research predicts that Indian and Pakistani harvests will decline by more than 30 percent by 2050 because of the vagaries of the weather (UNDP 1998). The threat of global climate change has helped focus attention on a third conceptual lens that pinpoints modern technology and its hazardous "externalities," or side-effects, as the major environmental scourge.

■ **The Technology Lens**

Nuclear tests by India and Pakistan during 1998 served to enhance the importance of arguments about technology's capacity to harm as well as benefit humankind and its surrounding natural world. Debates on that subject and on India's role in the world as an industrial and political heavyweight or as a modest champion of simplicity and peace have enlivened the nation's public discourse for decades.

During the 1940s, sharply contrasting views on humankind's relationship to technology were presented by the two giant figures of India's independence movement, Jawaharlal Nehru and Mahatma Gandhi. Gandhi hoped to promote grassroots democracy and local self-reliance, based on what later writers called "appropriate technology"— tools that increase workers' productivity but do not devalue or replace them (Sampat 1998: 31). The two leaders' differing priorities on the nation-state and economic prosperity versus the primacy of local communities and voluntary simplicity have echoed in countries throughout the world (Sampat 1998: 31).

Nuclear Dreams and Nightmares

Nuclear power's critics argue that it is costly, hazardous, and potentially devastating on a massive scale. Its supporters counter that unlike conventional fossil fuels, oil and the coal that India possesses in abundance, nuclear energy is a "clean" fuel source because it emits no polluting greenhouse gases.

India's nuclear pioneers saw nuclear power as an entry point into modern technology. India was the first Asian country to launch a nuclear program. For a brief period following World War II, before U.S. and Soviet Cold War rivalry drew nuclear research behind closely guarded doors, many Indian scientists visited the United States for training in nuclear physics. Early backers of nuclear technology dreamed of electricity "too cheap to meter" (Paccy 1993: 178). That was an appealing prospect in a country where energy was a massive stumbling block to rapid industrial growth.

In many of India's constituent states, postindependence governments made prodigious efforts to extend electricity to rural areas. Had the nuclear program succeeded in providing cheap and reliable electricity, it could have greatly enhanced the country's prosperity. Yet nuclear power's promise flickered to approximate the faint glow of a

20-watt lightbulb. By 1996, nuclear power provided only 2 percent of India's electricity (Chaudhuri: 126–129; Pacey 1993: 180). An early World Bank assessment still holds true today: "as in most other countries . . . performance of nuclear power stations in India has fallen below expectation" (Pacey 1993: 180). Development of India's nuclear potential has been slowed by managerial problems that plague many countries and by poor maintenance.

Long after the 1986 explosion of a nuclear power station in the former Soviet town of Chernobyl underscored the potential impact of unleashed radioactive wastes, a decline in the industrialized world's demand for nuclear power diminished the supply of staff qualified to work with such a complex technology. In India and most of its Asian neighbors, demand for nuclear power is growing because of problems with alternative fuel sources, but trained staff are relatively scarce (Takahashi and Lee 1995: 14).

The noted U.S. environmentalist Barry Commoner relentlessly proclaims that modern technology offers no free lunch (Commoner 1990: 57–58). The strongest reminder of the bill for a nuclear power lunch is radioactive wastes that may remain dangerous to humans for about 240,000 years (Gerstenzang 1998: 1). Storage of such wastes will tax scientists' ingenuity in India and throughout the world. Low literacy and inadequate information available to people who live near nuclear facilities increases the likelihood of their potential contact with nuclear wastes and leakages. Farmers, for example, have unwittingly used radioactive wastes to irrigate their fields.[7]

During the spring of 1998, Indian prime minister Atal Bihari Vajpayee sought to rekindle the excitement once associated with nuclear research by authorizing underground nuclear explosions that caused shock waves around the world, especially in countries that jealously guard their own potentially destructive technologies. The specific concerns of environmentalists were minor distractions on a global canvas dominated by images of war, but they nevertheless deserve attention—particularly so in a country that experienced the world's worst industrial accident, the disaster in Bhopal.

■ The Bhopal Tragedy

Early on the morning of December 3, 1984, methyl isocyanate, a toxic gas, leaked from a pesticide plant owned by Union Carbide, a U.S.-based multinational corporation, and billowed out into surrounding shanties and streets of the central Indian city of Bhopal. An estimated 10,000 people died following exposure to suffocating fumes; many others were severely disabled and died prematurely ("Bhopal's Second Tragedy" 1997).

Viewed through the poverty lens, the bleak prospects facing many of the victims, who were ecological refugees from the countryside, would hold overriding significance. Relatively few of them were plant employees; most maintained their decrepit shelters dangerously close to a chemical factory. It is a familiar problem in low-income countries.

The technology lens focuses less on the affected people—many of the survivors now battle health problems and vainly wait for compensation—and more on problems that are said to be inherent in chemical production technology.[8] For Commoner, the Bhopal disaster vividly illustrated an inevitable clash between the "ecosphere"—the cyclical natural world—and the linear, innovative, but ecologically disharmonious processes of the technosphere fashioned by ingenious but reckless humans. It was not coincidental, Commoner observes, that the Union Carbide plant manufactured another environmentally hazardous technology, chemical pesticides (Commoner 1990: 15).

■ Toxic Chemicals and Land Degradation

Farmers in parts of India have used chemical pesticides since the 1940s, but pesticide use soared in the mid-1960s, when national leaders launched the famous Green Revolution to make India self-sufficient in its staple food grains, wheat and rice. Officials promoted scientists' new high-yielding varieties of seed, using incentives such as price supports and subsidies on the chemicals and energy that the seeds required. Although food production increased dramatically, this newly intensive form of agriculture involved trade-offs and risks to the environment (Sims 1988).

Pesticide contamination is one of the most important. High-yielding varieties of seeds are less resistant to pests than traditional varieties, especially when farmers practice monoculture by limiting the number of plant varieties sown. Monoculture is associated with "modern" industrialized farming, but even though its efficiency may increase farmers' profits, it also increases the risks of pest attacks and adverse environmental consequences (Sims 2000b: 169; Shiva 1991).

The targets of pesticides have shown remarkable ability to develop resistance to even the most formidable weapons in chemical manufacturers' arsenals, leading farmers to use ever-increasing doses of more deadly and often more costly chemicals as they find themselves on a "pesticide treadmill" (Bull 1981; Dinham 1993). Since June 1997, more than 500 Indian farmers have dramatized the problem—and the financial difficulties facing small farmers—by committing suicide. Some have died following consumption of the pesticides that failed to protect their crops (Sharma 1998: 2; Verma 1998a).

Indian farmers use far less pesticides per acre than their North American counterparts, but potential hazards are compounded in South Asia by minimal safety precautions and equipment, uninformed users, the persistence of particularly toxic pesticides that are banned in the industrialized world, and concentrated pesticide use in regions where commercial agriculture prevails. Unscrupulous dealers may sell nasty concoctions to desperate farmers who incurred debts to purchase agro-chemicals, only to face hardy pests that devour their crops (Verma 1998a).

Although many Indians consume high levels of pesticide residues in their food, with uncertain consequences, the common belief that hazardous pesticides are a "necessary evil" that help to produce food for growing populations is questionable. Pesticide use in India and most low-income countries is linked more to such export crops as cotton, coffee, and tea than to food staples for poor domestic constituencies. Cotton is particularly vulnerable to pest outbreaks, which helps explain the preponderance of farmer suicides in 1997–1998 associated with crop failures in the cotton belt of the southern state of Andhra Pradesh (Dinham 1993; Verma 1998a).

■ "New and Improved" Technology?

The sharpest critics of pesticides that are easily misused when farmers lack information and manufacturers and dealers operate under lax regulation would advocate a version of cold-turkey withdrawal. In traditional agriculture, most farmers practiced what today is called "integrated pest management" (IPM), whereby farmers outwit pests with strategies to attract predators—for example, birds—that thrive on the pest in question. IPM would please those who view the industrialization of agriculture with alarm.

Observers who celebrate modern technology for its efficiency might favor genetic engineering to insert mechanisms into seeds to deter potential threats. Such techniques have become commonplace in the U.S. food industry, but environmentalists in India and some European countries worry that as traditional, time-tested plant varieties are replaced, dwindling biodiversity will promote a monoculture that is vulnerable to diseases and pests. Farmers in South India have taken direct action to head off a perceived threat to their traditional farming practices, which they say would force them to purchase seeds each year from multinational corporations such as Monsanto, a U.S.-based agribusiness firm. In late 1998, farmers' protests marred Monsanto's first field trials of cotton seeds implanted with bollworm-resistant genes. Under the leadership of M. D. Nanjundaswamy, head of a militant farmers' union based in the southern state of Karnataka, cultivators stormed onto trial plots in Andhra Pradesh and Karnataka, uprooted the transgenic cotton planted by Monsanto, and set it ablaze.

Monsanto maintains that the transgenic cotton would ward off bollworm attacks, which ideally could translate into lower doses of pesticide applications. Yet the company's experiments drew protests from farmers in the same part of Andhra Pradesh that had experienced the worst ravages of cotton crop failure and pesticide-related farmer suicides.

Monsanto's critics also charged that experiments were a devious cover-up to introduce a "terminator gene," a seed that may be used only once because its reproductive capacity is then eliminated.[9] Traditionally, farmers have traded seeds among themselves and saved their own seeds following a harvest, thereby avoiding the need to purchase new seeds each season ("Seeds" 1998: 18; Verma 1998a: 36).

■ Reflections on the Technology Lens

The technology lens draws attention to the need to consider the risks and possible costs of technological innovation. Yet its analytical utility is affected by a society's level of economic and technological development, the ambiguous nature of technology, and the lack of clear alternatives to technological society. The technology lens is more compelling in a society such as the United States than in India because the generally literate U.S. population has considerable access to information, including specifics on products' ingredients. Science is drawn into the public and political arenas, and litigation is prevalent. Such conditions do not apply in most poor countries. Instead, economic growth holds overriding priority, and often technology is accepted as a vital catalyst for change. In India, science is less politicized than in the United States, the regulatory system is far weaker, and prospects for citizens' redress through the judicial system are limited.

In addition, the pervasiveness of technology and the demand for it that is magnified by advertising makes it difficult to maintain a clear focus on technology as the prime cause of environmental degradation. Damage from modern technology may be tallied in the twenty-first century in terms of costs of climate change. Meanwhile, the technology lens is blurry. Some technologies minimize humankind's toll upon the Earth. For example, India has become the fourth-largest generator of wind power, which offers clean, renewable energy that capitalizes on the forces of nature.

Finally, now that Gandhi's once-influential voice is still, a viable large-scale alternative to modern society is hard to visualize. India offers an array of small-scale, environmentally conscious experiments, but their wholesale replication would be fraught with difficulties.

■ The Economic Rationalism Lens

The fourth and final conceptual lens, "economic rationalism," blames government for environmental degradation. Criticism of official environmental policies has centered on three points. First, many economists fault governments for placing a low value on critical resources, particularly water and energy. Second, business and industrial interests have deplored the loss of time and profits to cumbersome government regulations and corruption. A third criticism focuses on failures of implementation. Environmental regulations may be sporadically enforced or bent to give advantages to powerful interests.

In its most extreme form, "economic rationalism" urges privatization of all resources and strict observance of property rights. More commonly, market-based measures are preferred over governmental action (Dryzek 1997: 102–104). Until 1991, many economists criticized Indian central and state governments' pervasive roles in the economy, which they believed limited India's ability to compete in a global marketplace. Such critics welcomed Indian officials' initiatives to "liberalize" the economy by encouraging foreign investment, privatizing certain state enterprises, and dismantling trade barriers that protected domestic industry (Sampat 1998: 32).

Before considering policies that encourage the misuse of vital resources, it is essential to recall why the Indian government assumed a major role in the nation's economy after 1947. From the 1950s to about 1980, many development experts assigned governments major responsibility for expediting economic growth and social change in poor countries, particularly those emerging from colonial rule. Prime

Minister Nehru and his immediate successors endorsed that perspective and emphasized economic growth by subsidizing resources critical to industrialization, including energy and water. In retrospect, the government's dominant role in power generation and distribution is easily justified. The private sector was limited and weak in independent India's early years, and it was not inclined to serve a largely unprofitable rural clientele (Sims 2000a).

■ The Politics and Economics of Government Subsidies

Contemporary scholars are struck by the negative unanticipated consequences of subsidies on water and energy. Subsidies established powerful constituencies that actively resisted official attempts to allow prices to rise to market rates. Also, vital water and energy resources were mismanaged and overexploited. The agencies responsible for generating and distributing most of India's power—the state electricity boards (SEBs) run by constituent states—are notoriously inefficient. Their staggering annual financial losses rose to $1.7 million by 1995 (Salgo 1996; Sims 2000a). Since they are beyond the national government's direct control, state-level politicians can thwart central directives to raise energy prices for farmers, who are an important constituency. Other states have embarked on the politically charged path of SEB restructuring, however.

■ Implementation Failures

Many factors thwart effective policy design and implementation. They include proliferating laws and regulations that sometimes are contradictory and unenforceable. Deficient overall institutional capacity and poorly run state pollution control boards are others. Centralized policy processes and limited public involvement represent a vicious circle. Another recurrent criticism faults leaders for lacking "political will" (Sapru 1998: 170–176). Such problems bedevil environmental policy formulation and enforcement, not only in India but throughout a world more preoccupied with economic growth (Desai 1998).[10] One possible alternative force for environmental protection is the judiciary, but India's judiciary lacks the capacity to tackle environmental problems whose complexity daunts even experts with the mandates and resources to address them.

▨ Reflections on Economic Rationalism

The view that unleashed market forces constitute an effective alternative to government regulation has been hotly debated. Three considerations are important. First, government regulation emerged as a reaction to failures in the marketplace. Second, as U.S. energy expert Amory Lovins cautioned:

> We are making a mistake if we ask markets to do things they were not designed to do. Markets are only meant to allocate resources in the short-term, not to tell you how much is enough, or how to achieve integrity or justice. Markets are meant to be efficient, not sufficient; greedy, not fair. If they do something good for whales or wilderness or God or grandchildren, that's purely coincidental. (cited in Hempel 1996: 86)

Third, as the New Delhi–based Centre for Science and the Environment argued in a grim report on India's environmental pollution, "liberalization" has not visibly improved the nation's environment. Following liberalization, the report contended, India's traditional, often polluting industries lost resources that went instead to its rising electronic and software sectors. Older industries with obsolete technology could not compete for resources for pollution control; as a result, they polluted more than ever (Centre for Science and the Environment 1999).

■ India's Environmental Activists

To some extent, the gathering shroud of pollution is pierced by dedicated Indian citizens who tirelessly promote public awareness of the environment and mobilize initiatives for its protection. India has about 25,000 nongovernmental organizations and grassroots movements involved in environmental and social reform, so only a voluminous work could touch on the many ways in which Indian citizens have promoted environmental protection. Just four names are mentioned here: Anil Agarwal, Sunderlal Bahuguna, Medha Patkar, and Vandana Shiva (Sampat 1998: 31–38).

Anil Agarwal's campaigns against environmental degradation went far beyond the famous maxim, "Think globally; act locally." Agarwal thought and acted on international, national, state, regional, and local levels; in addition, he battled blood cancer, which he attributed to environmental pollution. Agarwal shaped dialogue in the international arena as a member of the World Commission on Water and as coauthor of *Global Warming in an Unequal World,* which enlivened global debates on climate change (Agarwal and Narain 1991). As founder and director of the New Delhi–based Centre for Science and the Environment and editor of its biweekly journal, *Down to Earth,* Agarwal is credited with promoting Indian environmentalism's scientific legitimacy (Kumar and Arora 1998: 28). He also founded a lively youth-oriented publication, the *Gobar Times* (*gobar* is the Hindi word for cowdung, a traditional fuel source). Agarwal died at fifty-four in 2002.

Sunderlal Bahuguna is associated with a grassroots movement known to environmental activists and scholars throughout the world: the Chipko movement. The movement grew from protests led by village women in the central Himalayas in 1973 against tree felling by urban industrial interests that was sanctioned by India's Forest Department. Since colonial days, the department saw its mission as protecting trees against local people and as transferring forest resources at throwaway prices to entrepreneurs. Bahuguna's involvement in the campaign helped provoke a reassessment of official policy and influenced international thinking about the nature of development.

Medha Patkar is another grassroots activist who has shaped both domestic and international environmental policy. Like Bahuguna, she has championed the interests of people whose livelihood is threatened by massive construction projects or external appropriation of forest resources. The slight social worker from Bombay became a revered leader of tens of thousands of subsistence farmers and tribal people threatened with displacement by the controversial Sardar Sarovar dam in the Narmada Valley of western and central India. Their nonviolent protests attested to a democratic political system's capacity to represent divergent perspectives. They also encouraged the World Bank to consider the projects' costs and benefits beyond economic and engineering criteria (Caulfield 1996).

Vandana Shiva, like Anil Agarwal, is well known to environmentalists in the industrialized world as an articulate commentator offering a perspective that does not reflect immersion in Washington, D.C., the headquarters of most U.S.-based environmental organizations. Trained as a physicist, Shiva's ideas about practical action were shaped by the Chipko movement. She is a longstanding critic of a narrowly based reductionist science that has promoted monoculture and stifled cultural diversity and of efforts to control genetic resources by multinational pharmaceutical and agribusiness enterprises.

The four activists illustrate that environmentalism is not simply the preserve of upper-middle-class people in rich countries, as some western scholars have claimed. Poor and socially disadvantaged people have actively participated in Indian environmental movements. Their leaders have shown great creativity in mobilizing support and media attention. Yet their impact is blunted by limited public awareness and by the failure of most political leaders to address environmental degradation (Gadgil and Guha 1995: 99).

■ Conclusion

In this chapter, I highlighted alternative perspectives on India's environment to draw attention to the multiple aspects of environmental degradation. A second objective was to illustrate the way in which proposed "solutions" to environmental problems often flow directly from the observer's own view of the problem, which reflects his or her values, worldview, and perhaps disciplinary training.

Any conceptual lens oversimplifies reality. Factors linked to environmental degradation—population pressure, resource use, affluence, harmful technology, and unsound public policies and management—are interrelated, but their interaction and dynamics are not well understood. The critical challenge is to understand their relationship rather than to focus narrowly upon specific component parts.

Mahatma Gandhi's question—how many planets would a country like India require?—draws attention to the larger context. India may be the world's most populous nation in terms of numbers of people, but the United States, as McKibben observed, is the most populous country on the planet in terms of resource use (McKibben 1998: 108). If India adopts a North American lifestyle and replaces all its bicycles and bullock carts with sports utility vehicles and its grain and vegetable-based diet with meat, the outlook for the twenty-first century is grim.

Gandhi's question still begs for an answer. The only possible response is that it depends partly on processes that human and natural sciences have yet to understand and partly on decisions we and our descendants have yet to make (Cohen 1995: 10–11).

■ Notes

I am grateful to Watson Sims for expert editing and multifaceted technical assistance.

1. Such estimates must be interpreted with caution, for they vary depending on the types of costs included in the calculations.

2. As Hempel observes in *Environmental Governance,* conceptual lenses shape perceptions just as the proverbial hammer leads the person who holds it to see everything as a nail that needs pounding.

3. Even the current Chinese leadership has found it difficult to control the most personal decisions in citizens' lives, although it is neither elected nor held accountable by the public.

4. Much of the semiarid United States, including California, has drawn extensive criticism for inefficient water use.

5. They include noted environmentalists Agarwal, Gadgil, and Guha. See Gadgil and Guha 1995: 177–178.

6. On the landmark Stockholm conference, see Caldwell 1990.

7. Interviews with two Punjab government officials and three environmental activists in Chandigarh, India, in August 1998.

8. Personal interview with Ward Morehouse, long a close observer of the Bhopal tragedy, in New Paltz, New York, on October 16, 1998; see also "Bhopal's Second Tragedy" 1997.

9. In the United States, the spread of genetically altered seeds has occurred with limited public attention. See Pollan 1998.

10. On the U.S. case, see Rosenbaum 1998.

■ Bibliography

Agarwal, Anil. 1998. "The Poverty of Amartya Sen." *Down to Earth* 7, no. 14: 56–57.

Agarwal, Anil, and Sunita Narain. 1991. *Global Warming in an Unequal World: A Case of Environmental Colonialism.* New Delhi: Centre for Science and the Environment.

Anderson, Terry, and Donald Leal. 1991. *Free Market Environmentalism.* San Francisco: Pacific Institute for Public Policy.

"Bhopal's Second Tragedy." 1997. *New York Times,* January 15, editorial.

Bose, Ashish. 1988. *From Population to People.* 2 vols. New Delhi: B. R. Publishing.

Brown, Lester. 1998. "The Future of Growth." In *State of the World,* Lester Brown et al., eds. New York: W. W. Norton, pp. 3–20.

Bull, David. 1981. *A Growing Problem: Pesticides and the Third World Poor.* London: Oxfam.

Caldwell, Lynton. 1990. *International Environmental Policy: Emergence and Dimensions.* 2nd ed. Durham: Duke University Press.

Caulfield, Catherine. 1996. *Masters of Illusion.* New York: Henry Holt.

Centre for Science and the Environment. 1999. "Unhealthy Growth." *Down to Earth* 7, no. 17: 32–50.

Chakraborty, Sujit. 1995. "Criminal Waste." *Down to Earth* 4, no. 11: 27–31.

Chaudhuri, Basudeb. 1996. "India's Energy Future May See Rise of Nuclear Power." *Forum for Applied Research and Public Policy* 11: 126–129.

Cohen, Joel. 1995. *How Many People Can the Earth Support?* New York: W. W. Norton.

Commoner, Barry. 1972. *Closing Circle*. New York: Bantam Books.

———. 1990. *Making Peace with the Planet*. New York: Pantheon.

Desai, Uday, ed. 1998. *Ecological Policy and Politics in Developing Countries*. Albany: State University of New York Press.

Dinham, Barbara. 1993. *The Pesticide Hazard*. London: Zed.

Dryzek, John. 1997. *The Politics of the Earth*. New York: Oxford University Press.

Durning, Alan. 1991. "Fat of the Land." *WorldWatch* 4, no. 3: 17.

Ehrlich, Paul, and Anne Ehrlich. 1990. *The Population Explosion*. New York: Simon and Schuster.

Fountain, Henry. 1998. "Observatory." *New York Times,* December 29, p. D5.

Gadgil, Madhav, and Ramachandra Guha. 1995. *Ecology and Equity*. New York: Routledge.

Garrett, Laurie. 1995. *The Coming Plague: Emerging Diseases in a World Out of Balance*. New York: Penguin.

Gerstenzang, James. 1998. "U.S. Approves First Permanent Tomb for Atomic Waste." *Los Angeles Times,* May 14, pp. 1, 8.

Goldsmith, Edward, Peter Bunyard, Nicholas Hildyard, and Patrick McCully. 1990. *Imperiled Planet*. Cambridge: MIT Press.

Gordon, Leonard, and Philip Oldenburg, eds. 1992. *India Briefing 1992*. Boulder, Colo.: Westview Press.

Hempel, Lamont. 1996. *Environmental Governance: The Global Challenge*. Washington, D.C.: Island Press.

International Geographic Encyclopedia and Atlas. 1979. Boston: Houghton Mifflin, p. 162.

Kumar, Amit, and Vassantha Arora. 1998. "Green Activist Carries on Crusade Despite Ailment." *India Abroad,* August 28, p. 28.

McKibben, Bill. 1998. *Maybe One*. New York: Simon and Schuster.

Meyerson, Allen. 1998. "U.S. Splurging on Energy After Falling Off Its Diet." *New York Times,* October 22, pp. 1, C6.

Pacey, Arnold. 1993. *Technology in World Civilization*. Cambridge: MIT Press.

Pollan, Michael. 1998. "Playing God in the Garden." *New York Times Magazine,* October 25, pp. 44–51, 62–63, 82, 92–93.

Postel, Sandra. 1997. *The Last Oasis*. 2nd ed. New York: W. W. Norton.

Reisner, Marc. 1993. *Cadillac Desert: The American West and Its Disappearing Water*. New York: Penguin.

Rosenbaum, Walter. 1998. *Environmental Politics and Policy*. 4th ed. Washington, D.C.: CQ Press.

Salgo, Harvey. 1996. "India Faces Restructuring: The Need Is with the States." *Electricity Journal* 9, no. 3: 56–62.

Sampat, Payal. 1998. "What Does India Want?" *Worldwatch* 11, no. 4: 31–38.

Sapru, R. K. 1998. "Environmental Policy and Politics in India." In *Ecological Policy and Politics in Developing Countries,* Uday Desai, ed. Albany: State University of New York Press, pp. 153–182.

"Seeds of Discontent." 1998. *Down to Earth* (December): 31.

Sen, Amartya. 1981. *Poverty and Famines.* Oxford: Clarendon Press.

Sharma, Devinder. 1998. "How Agriculture Has Suffered Under Liberalization." *India Abroad,* December 4, p. 2.

Shiva, Vandana. 1991. *Violence of the Green Revolution.* London: Zed.

Sims, Holly. 1988. *Political Regimes, Public Policies, and Economic Development.* New Delhi: Sage Publications.

———. 1992. "Malthusian Nightmare or Richest in Human Resources?" In *India Briefing 1992,* Leonard Gordon and Philip Oldenburg, eds. Boulder, Colo.: Westview Press, pp. 103–136.

———. 2000a. "States, Markets, and Energy Use in China and India." In *The United Nations and the Global Environment in the 21st Century,* Pamela Chasek, ed. Tokyo: United Nations University Press, pp. 140–160.

———. 2000b. "Political Economy of Environmental Degradation and Restoration in Two Punjabs." Unpublished paper.

Staudt, Kathleen, ed. 1997. *Women, International Development and Politics.* Philadelphia: Temple University Press.

Takahashi, T., and M. K. Lee. 1995. "The Present and Prospective Situation of Nuclear Energy in Asia." *Nuclear Energy Agency Newsletter* 2: 11–17.

UNDP (United Nations Development Programme). 1998. *Human Development Report.* New York: Oxford University Press.

Verma, Jitendra. 1998a. "Escape to Defeat." *Down to Earth* 6, no. 19 (February 28): 29–36.

———. 1998b. "Reel-heroes and Real Ones." *Down to Earth* 7, no. 12 (November 15): 15–16.

World Almanac Books. 2002. Ken Park, ed. New York: World Almanac Education.

World Bank. 1998. *Environment Matters.* Washington, D.C.: World Bank.

World Commission on Environment and Development. 1987. *Our Common Future.* New York: Oxford University Press.

World Resources Institute. 1996. *World Resources.* New York: Oxford University Press.

10

Religion

Ainslie T. Embree

oreigners often comment on the multiplicity of religions in India and the religiosity of its people, as Mark Twain did in his account of his travels around the world in the 1890s. As he entered Bombay harbor, he was aware, he wrote, that he had come at last to the land that everyone desires to see "and having seen once, by even a glimpse, would not give up that glimpse for all the shows of the world combined." India was the mother of history and the grandmother of tradition, but above all, it was "the home of a thousand religions and two million gods" (Twain 1989: 347–348). Twain's amused tolerance for India's multiplicity of religions and deities was not shared by all foreign visitors; many found its varieties of religious experiences repellent, "a tangled jungle of disorderly superstitions" (Lyall 1889: vol. 1: 2).

This seeming religiosity of the Indian people has also been frequently commented on within the Indian tradition itself. Swami Vivekananda, who first introduced many in the United States to Indian religion in the 1890s, became the great exponent of the theme that India stood for spirituality and the West for materialism. India, he declared, "is the land to which every soul that is wending its way Godward must come," for "it is above all the land of introspection and spirituality" (Embree 1989: 159). This idea of the spirituality of India in contrast to "the cursed modern civilization" of the West was a central theme in the thought of Mohandas Karamchand Gandhi (1927: 43–45), who was called "Mahatma" (great soul). But there was also harshly critical com-

ment from within the Indian tradition. Basavanna, a poet who lived in
south India in the twelfth century, complained that the people made
gods out of everything: "Gods, gods, there are so many, there's no place
left for a foot" (Ramanujan 1973: 84). In the fifteenth century, the poet
Kabir made a comment that is often echoed in India at the beginning of
the twenty-first century: "The Hindu says Ram is the Beloved, the Turk
[the Muslim] says Rahim is. Then they kill each other" (Kabir 1983: 4).

■ Lived Religions

In the nineteenth century, and still today to a considerable extent,
Hindu beliefs and practices became the standard explanation for almost
all aspects of Indian society, especially those that westerners found
strange or deplorable: poverty, illiteracy, poor treatment of women, the
caste system, the worship of idols, poverty, and sectarian violence. This
understanding of the role of religion in Indian society was not, however, confined to westerners—it was shared very widely by many
Indian nationalists, notably Jawaharlal Nehru, who saw religion in
India as characterized by obscurantism and bigotry, a reactionary force
preventing needed change or abolition. "Religion in India," he wrote,
"has not only broken our backs but stifled and killed all originality of
thought and mind" (Akbar 1988: 183).

All the writers, foreign and Indian, are referring to what is often
called *lived religion,* a term used to indicate contemporary beliefs and
practices rather than textual studies of the foundation documents of
religious systems. The writers were expressing, somewhat fancifully
perhaps, what they understood of the India of their time. In this chapter, I attempt to sketch, in a summary fashion, something of the nature
of these varied religious experiences and their influences. Those experiences are so embedded in the vocabulary of social and political discourse that some understanding of them is necessary for any exploration of contemporary India.

Having said that, it is obligatory to undertake that most difficult of
tasks, to indicate how the term *religion* is being used. Endless attempts
at definition have been made, but a simple one must suffice here to
delimit those aspects of human experience under discussion. Religion
is understood here as a fusing of memories and experiences around
symbols that are regarded as possessing powers that transcend ordinary
life, and these shared experiences unite people into a community. Such

a definition says nothing about the truth or falsity of religion, only that religious beliefs give, in the words of the anthropologist Clifford Geertz, "an aura of factuality" to moods and motivations so that they seem uniquely realistic (Banton 1968: 4). Religion is understood as a part of culture, that is, all those patterns of behavior and thought that are transmitted from one generation to another. Religion is not a self-sufficient entity but is embedded in the historical processes that shape and respond to all human creativity.

The Census of India confirms that India is a religiously pluralistic society, not just in terms of the many religious communities represented—that is true of any large nation, including the United States—but because of the very large numbers of people in the different religious groups and their presence in India for hundreds of years. According to estimates based on the last census in 1991, about 800 million people identified themselves as Hindus, about 135 million as Muslims, 20 million as Christians, 15 million as Sikhs, nearly 6 million as Buddhists, and 3 million as Jains. In addition, 3 million were designated as "other." These included such distinctive and ancient communities as Parsis or Zoroastrians, about 70,000, and Jews, then numbering only a few thousand, as well as adherents of tribal groups who denied they were Hindus. Although each of these religions of India is interesting in terms of its beliefs and location within Indian history, Hinduism and Islam command the most attention in social discourse because of the number of their adherents and the articulateness of their self-statements. In recent years, however, Christians have assumed a special importance because of alleged discrimination against them by Hindu groups.

The term *Indian religions* is frequently used to refer to those systems of beliefs and practices whose origins and development through the centuries has taken place within the Indian subcontinent, in contrast to those systems that have been brought to India from other areas. The four that are indigenous to the subcontinent are Hinduism, Buddhism, Jainism, and Sikhism. The systems thought of as non-Indian, having originated outside the subcontinent, are Islam; Christianity; Judaism, often contrasted with Indian religion as "Semitic" or "Abrahamic" because of common origins and belief patterns; and Zoroastrianism, which originated in Iran. All of them, however, have roots in India that go back at least 1,000 years, so they are in no sense "new" or "un-Indian." Furthermore, all these religions, indigenous and nonindigenous, originated in some part of the Asian continent.

■ Four Indigenous Religions

The four indigenous religions share, although with many variations, certain assumptions or aspects of a worldview, or "axioms of a system of meaning" (Keyes and Daniel 1983: 3), that are usually taken as distinguishing them from the nonindigenous groups. These ideas developed and took shape over very long periods of time, and it is little use to speak of them in terms of dates of origin. One of these assumptions is an acceptance of the idea of reincarnation, or samsara: that is, the idea that all living things will die but will be reborn again in some form. A second is a belief in karma, a word for which there is no real translation. It conveys the idea that all actions—mental, emotional, physical—must have consequences that lead to rebirth. A third assumption is embodied in another word for which there is no ready equivalent, dharma, which refers to the moral obligations that come with birth and that are not imposed by any deity but result from one's own actions in previous lives. Dharma is often used by Indians for what westerners would call religion, meaning the duties, obligations, and beliefs that life imposes on one. It is both the way things are and the way they should be. Good people, then, are those who fulfill their dharma. A fourth assumption is *moksha,* sometimes translated as "salvation," but "liberation" is better, carrying the sense of being freed from the cycle of birth and rebirth. These concepts are, it must be stressed, not at all religious beliefs in the sense of being creedal statements that an adherent accepts for inclusion with the group. They are part of a worldview that seems, from very ancient times, to have pervaded the subcontinent and that gives depth and meaning, not only to the adherents of the indigenous religions but often to members of all religions imbued with the Indian ethos.

▒ Hinduism

Westerners and some Indians often argue that Hinduism is not a religion but many forms of belief and practice loosely linked together. Hinduism has no single authoritative scripture but rather a multitude of sacred texts; it has no identifiable historical figure as a founder, no creedal statements to summarize its beliefs, and no institutional structure to guarantee conformity; and instead of insistence on one God, it permits belief in the existence of many or none. In contemporary discourse in India, however, *Hindu* and *Hinduism* are used by Hindus themselves, not only in English but also in Indian languages, to differentiate themselves from adherents of other religions. *Hindu* is used in the Indian constitution to refer not only to Hindus but also to Jains, Buddhists, and Sikhs, although this usage was later rejected by the Sikhs.

Many cultural streams contributed to the complex mosaic of the indigenous religious systems of contemporary India, as distinct from those, like Islam, that originated outside. All of these streams are readily identifiable in contemporary India and are in no sense merely historical artifacts. One is the Dravidian, relating to the culture and languages of south India; the other, the one best known and most studied as well as the most controversial, is the Indo-Aryan element.

In recent years, much emphasis has been placed on the Dravidian element in Indian religion, partly because of scholarly interpretations based on textual and archaeological evidence but also because of strong political movements in modern times that have stressed the cultural autonomy of the linguistic areas of south India. Languages belonging to the Dravidian language branch are distinct from and perhaps predate the Indo-Aryan languages of north India. The Dravidian languages are concentrated in the four states of Tamil Nadu, Andhra Pradesh, Karnataka, and Kerala, and scholarly research quite convincingly indicates patterns of religious practices and beliefs deeply rooted in these regions that have contributed greatly to Indian religions. The indigenous, or Dravidian, religions of south India seem not to have been so much concerned with extraterrestrial deities as with "the sacramental character of life: anything associated with the production or ending of life was felt to contain a potentially dangerous power" (Deshpande and Hook 1979: 11–13). Three agents were especially associated with this power: women, a source and symbol of fertility and life; low-caste persons in contact with death or dead substances; and the king, who controlled the prosperity of the kingdom and who possessed the power of life and death. But power was not only dangerous: it was also beneficent and life affirming. Relations to both aspects were managed through rituals, sacrifices, and gifts.

Scholars also place great emphasis on south Indian religion in the development of bhakti, which, as noted below, means complete devotion to a particular deity. The god is identified as king, lord, ruler, to whom utter obedience and loyalty are given as his due. Female deities received the same devotion, with the added characteristics of power associated with the title of mother. These aspects of religion have become part of an all-Indian religious inheritance.

The other cultural stream, the Indo-Aryan, was long regarded as the central component of Indian religions, but it is now deeply enmeshed in controversy over the nature and origin of the Indian tradi-

The magnificent temples of south India had pools
for bathing, emphasizing the importance of ritual
cleansing in Hindu worship

tion. In the nineteenth century, as the result of philological research into
and studies of the most ancient Indian texts, it was widely accepted that
around 2000 B.C.E., a people known as Aryans and speaking an Indo-
European language invaded north India through the western hills, conquered the areas now known as the Punjab, and gradually extended
their control over the whole subcontinent. Their language and their religion, enshrined in the great texts, the *Vedas,* became, it was believed,
the foundation of Indian culture, including the Hindu religion. Current
scholarship has modified the Aryan myth, as it has come to be known,
and Romila Thapar, the well-known historian of ancient India, has
summed up the view of most modern scholars by saying that the idea
of conquest should be replaced by considering "the possibility of
migrations and technological changes being responsible for the arrival
and dominance of the Aryan speakers" (Thapar 1994: 3). The languages and religious concepts associated with the migrant tribespeople
from outside the Indian subcontinent were fused through the centuries
with indigenous languages, religious ideas, and practices.

　　Out of this fusion, in the period from roughly 2000 to 600 B.C.E., a
vast literature was produced that became the charter documents of Hin-

Village children
in south India
celebrate a festival,
pulling a local deity
in a cart

Ainslie T. Embree

duism, the oldest of which was the *Rig Veda.* In this literature, the priests, or Brahmans, have a vital role as religious specialists, because they alone had the knowledge for the correct performance of the rituals that maintain the cosmic order through sacrifices to the gods. In the *Upanishads,* the last category of Vedic literature, a remarkable change is seen in religious and philosophical ideas. There is great attention to release from the unending cycle of birth and death, with liberation or *moksha* coming through knowledge, which is understood as a realization of the unity of all reality. In this abstruse speculation, the gods play little role; the emphasis is on the seeker after spiritual truths and their discovery.

Scholars use the term *Brahmanical Hinduism* for the developments that place an emphasis on the religious and legal importance in society of the role and ideas of the Brahmans, centering on the "mythic vision and ritual ideologies presented by the Vedas" (Heesterman 1987: vol. 15: 217). Their ideas and social values remain normative for many people in Indian society.

The central place of this Vedic literature and the peculiar role of the Brahmans is one of the aspects of thought that differentiate Brahmanical Hinduism from the other great movements, Buddhism and Jainism, and it is very much part of "lived religion" in contemporary India. The two great epics, the *Mahabharata* and the *Ramayana,* both of which center on dharma and the Brahmanical understanding of the good life, are still immensely influential. One evidence of this is that a section of the *Mahabharata,* the *Bhagavad Gita,* has achieved a popularity during the last two centuries that it seems not to have had before. It is partly due to the printing press, which has made millions of copies available in modern Indian languages, and also because it has been translated many times into English, making it readily accessible as a compendium of Hindu teachings. All things to all people, it was read by the great social reformer Bal Gangadhar Tilak (1856–1920) early in the twentieth century as a call to action, violent if necessary, against the foreign oppressor, and by Mahatma Gandhi as the gospel of nonviolent love. In recent years, both the *Mahabharata* and the *Ramayana* have been modernized into immensely popular television serials.

Two kinds of religious specialists are integral to Brahmanical Hinduism. One is the priest, who in the most ancient level of the tradition knew the sacred formulas used for approaching the deities in the great Vedic ceremonies. In everyday life, he was the individual with the special qualifications required to perform temple rituals as well as the rites of passage, such as birth, initiation, marriage, and death. A description of a modern Hindu priest by a U.S. scholar is probably fairly accurate for other times and places:

> [They] may find themselves jacks-of-all-trades, called upon to recite *mantras,* perform or advise on life-cycle rites, inaugurate a new house, provide horoscopes, sanction marital arrangements, advise on illness, counteract the evil eye, arbitrate disputes, perform accounting, or administer the age old ritual attention to the images of the household shrine. (Knipe 1987: vol. 11: 541)

The other type of religious specialist is the searcher after truth, the teacher, the mediator, the guru. He or she—for the guru can be either man or woman—is one of the most characteristic features of the Brahmanical tradition. The emphasis is on knowledge and on the recognition of the need for a spiritual guide, one who has found the way to

truth and is able to help others. Spiritual guides are numerous throughout all levels of Indian society, ministering to the spiritual needs of
ordinary folk in their own localities or at pilgrimage sites.

In modern India, the appeal to return to "Hindu values" usually
refers to the way of life that was articulated by Brahmanical Hinduism.
The ideal of the good society that emerges in the literature can be summarized under two grand concepts. The first of these is of society
divided into four great divisions, or *varnas,* with each class being
bound to the others by reciprocal duties, creating a harmonious society.
There is no historical evidence that such a society ever existed in reality, but the idea has had immense appeal through the ages, with
Mahatma Gandhi being an influential exponent of a modernized version. The other, closely related, is that the good person is one who finds
the meaning of life in following his or her dharma.

One of the most distinctive features of modern India is the development of the languages associated with particular regions. Many of
these languages are now closely identified with modern Indian states:
Tamil in Tamil Nadu, Marathi in Maharashtra, Bengali in West Bengal,
Punjabi in Punjab, with only the most widespread, Hindi, not having a
single homeland but remaining dominant in the great belt of northern
states. It was in these languages that many of the most distinctive religious movements found expression, adding to the great richness of the
Indian literary tradition. Of special significance for the history of religion was the emergence of many sects and cults, often regionally based
and expressing themselves in regional languages, not Sanskrit, the language of classical Brahmanical Hinduism. These various forces worked
together to create quite distinct regional characteristics, which provide
much of the social and political structure of modern India.

Two developments within Hinduism, however, cut across geographical, linguistic, and cultural boundaries. One was what has been
called Puranic religion, in reference to the *Purana,* the texts that tell in
great detail of the lives of the gods. The other development was bhakti,
the devotion to a particular deity, which became the most widespread
expression of religion everywhere in India.

The *Puranas* are woven into the everyday life of India, for
although they were written in Sanskrit, the myths and legends they
contain are known everywhere in all languages. In the words of a
believing Hindu scholar, the *Puranas* remind us "the Almighty is
alone worth seeking" as they "expatiated on the glories and exploits of
different forms of divinity, set forth the types of worship, and
described the sacred shrines in the different holy places to which pil-

grimages were made" (Raghavan 1988: 321). Three major forms of deity are celebrated in the Puranic literature—Vishnu, Shiva, and the Goddess—but all have many manifestations—the feminine power alone is given 1,008 names in one of the *Puranas.* Vishnu is worshiped through his avatars or incarnations, of which the most widely known and worshiped are Rama and Krishna, who has been especially celebrated in poetry and painting. Rama, as noted below and in other chapters, has assumed enormous political importance in contemporary India. Shiva is worshiped in various forms, but most commonly in the form of the lingam, an ancient phallic symbol of fertility that possibly dates back to the Indus culture or tribal beliefs. The third form of the deity widely worshiped throughout India is some form of the Goddess, the Great Mother. Although goddesses only become prominent in the Puranic literature, the worship of the divine feminine principle is surely part of the most ancient level of human existence in India. Puranic religion permitted the growth of many of the cults and sects of modern Hinduism.

Bhakti—intense, emotional devotion to a particular deity that is characterized as a relationship of love—is what many Hindus, both now and in the past, understand to be true religion. Although the word is used in many ancient texts, particularly in the *Bhagavad Gita,* the forms in which it was most widely expressed appear to have originated in south India. It found its most notable expression in the songs of poets in regional languages, those spoken by the masses, celebrating the deity they loved and worshiped, and from whom they received the joy of personal communion (Hawley and Juergensmeyer 1988). Many of these poet-saints, as they are often called, were women, one of whom, Mirabai, lived in Rajasthan in the sixteenth century. Her poetry exemplifies an important function of the bhakti tradition: through a devotion to one's lord that renounced all other loyalties, one could inwardly defy many of the conventions of caste, class, and gender while outwardly conforming to them. Some of the poet-saints were from the lowest castes, suggesting that bhakti provided a safety valve for the frustrations and restrictions society imposed.

The *Ramcaritmanas,* the story of Rama's life, composed in the sixteenth century in Hindi by Tulsidas (ca. 1532–1623), is perhaps the most influential of all the bhakti works. Mahatma Gandhi called it "the greatest book of all devotional literature," and western scholars have characterized it as the best and most trustworthy guide to the popular living faith of the ordinary people (Lutgendorf 1994: 1). In north India every year, thousands of performances are given of plays celebrating

Rama's story as told by Tulsidas. Bhakti by its very nature is constantly changing, and new forms of devotion appear continually. Rama has become extraordinarily important in recent times through his use as a potent symbol of Hindu unity against Muslims, as demonstrated by the fervor aroused in the 1990s by events leading to the destruction of the mosque known as the Babri Masjid (see below).

New gurus emerge and gather followers, giving Hindu religious life an appearance of spontaneity. To the outsider, observing Hinduism in contemporary India, it appears to be, as one writer puts it, "a sea of ever-shifting eddies and vortices that catch up individual believers in various aspects of their devotional lives" (Hawley 1988). Because of the nature of bhakti, new gods and goddesses can appear to answer new human needs in new circumstances, or old ones can take on new functions. A fascinating example of this is the goddess Shitala Mata, who protected against smallpox. With the disappearance of that disease, she has become the deity to appeal to against the current dreadful scourge of India, HIV/AIDS.

■ Jainism and Buddhism

Throughout history, the religious and social dominance of Brahmanical Hinduism was challenged by other systems, of which Jainism and Buddhism were the most influential. Both played significant roles in Indian history, with Buddhism becoming one of the three great world religions, along with Christianity and Islam, as it spread throughout Asia and now into many other part of the world, although it virtually disappeared from India itself. Although Buddhism and Jainism both shared general assumptions regarding karma, samsara, and dharma, they differed on their interpretations of the human condition and the methods for obtaining *moksha,* or liberation. They both differed from Brahmanical Hinduism on three important points: they rejected the authority of the *Vedas;* they allowed Brahmans no preordained hierarchical spiritual role; and they denied the importance of social obligations that separated groups or castes within society, arguing that they were not relevant to liberation. Jainism stresses nonviolence and the refusal to take life in any form as the absolute requirements for beginning the process of liberation from the cycle of rebirth. Although believing in great spiritual leaders who offer guides and inspiration, it rejects belief in deities. Perhaps because of its rejection of any occupations that required the taking of life, in modern India the Jains became bankers and merchants.

The Jains built hilltop temple-cities that became centers of pilgrimage. This one, Sitrunjaya, near the town of Palitana in Gujarat is a fantastic complex of temples dating from 1616 in their present form, but on a much older site.

Ainslie T. Embree

Buddhism's disappearance from India itself can probably be explained by its absorption into the mainstream of Hindu culture as well as by the aggressive counterattacks by Brahmanical Hinduism. A curious reversal has taken place in modern India, however, where since 1954, the census figures show a thousandfold increase in the number of Buddhists in India. It is due to the social reform movement initiated in the 1930s by Bhimrao Ramji Ambedkar, who was called "Babasaheb" by his followers and was the leader of the Untouchables or Dalits, the most socially oppressed of all classes in India. Believing that Hinduism was the cause of their condition, he decided to convert his followers to Buddhism, a religion older than Hinduism and free, in his view, from its degrading oppression. These new Buddhists now number over 4 million and are a very important element in the increasing refusal of the lowest groups to follow the political leadership of the upper castes and classes.

▣ Sikhism

At the beginning of this chapter, four forms of Indian religion were mentioned that shared some common assumptions but differed greatly in others, three of them being Hinduism, Jainism, and Buddhism. The fourth is Sikhism, which developed in the fifteenth century. Older books often suggest that Sikhism was a synthesis of Islam and Hinduism, but current western scholarship tends to argue that there is little evidence of this and that the origins of Sikhism can be found within the Indian tradition of bhakti as transformed by Guru Nanak (1469–1539), whom his followers regard as the founder of the new religion. Out of his teachings came one of the most distinctive of religious communities, which though relatively small in number has had a memorable impact on India, as well as any country to which it has gone. Three elements define Sikhism as a faith and a community. One is the teachings of Guru Nanak, as preserved in the Sikh scripture, the *Adi Granth.* Another is the institution of the guru, or teacher, who is in some sense the voice of God; there were ten gurus, with Nanak being the first and Gobind Singh (1675–1708) the last. The third distinctive element of Sikhism is the *khalsa,* which according to Sikh tradition was formed by Gobind Singh into a militant community to defend the faith and was given visible symbols, of which the most obvious is the uncut hair and beard of the men. Insofar as the core of a faith can be stated, for Sikhs the summary of their faith is found at the beginning of the *Adi Granth:* "One, True Name, Creator, Without Fear, Without Hate, Beyond Time, Unborn, Self-existent, the Guru's Gift of Grace" (Embree 1988: 491–510).

■ Two Indigenous Religions

▣ Islam as an Indian Religion

The heading asserts the theme of this section: that Islam is firmly rooted in Indian civilization, despite its frequent characterization as alien to the Indian cultural ethos. Three major interpretations have distorted the history of Islam in India. One that often finds expression in

popular writing by both Indians and foreigners is that there is a legacy
of 1,000 years of hatred between Hinduism and Islam. Hatred does not
endure for 1,000 years—it must be nurtured in specific contexts, and
that is what one sees in modern India. Another error, egregiously common even in scholarly writing, is that the Muslim conquerors offered
the defeated peoples the choice of conversion or the sword. There is little evidence for large-scale forced conversions, and the continuing
presence of an immense Hindu population suggests that such a policy
was never systematic: the Muslim rulers were interested in collecting
revenue from the people, not alienating them. Another frequent assertion is that there was widespread destruction of Hindu temples by the
Muslim rulers. Certainly there was some such destruction, but it was
not wholesale, as witnessed by the many Hindu temples that survived
the Turkish conquests. One has to bear in mind that conquerors frequently destroy the symbols of the power of conquered rulers, and temples and churches and religious sanctuaries are very often statements of
political power. The reading of history that sees Hindus and Muslims in
a state of enmity throughout history assumes that "Hindu" and "Muslim" were dominant forms of self-identity, with the two groups self-
conscious of themselves in broad religious categories. Until the late
eighteenth century, however, it seems clear that the signs or symbols by
which groups identified themselves had to do with castes; religious
sects, whether Hindu or Muslim; region; and, above all, the possession
of political and economic power. What seems indisputable is that two
great cultures and religious systems, the Hindu and the Islamic, while
borrowing much from each other along the social margins of their existence, retained their separate core identities for 1,000 years. Coexis-
tence, not assimilation, was the characteristic behavior of both communities, and it was made possible by the nature of Hindu society as
well as the political policies of the Muslim rulers.

In north India, from the eighth century on, the political landscape
was dominated by numerous small kingdoms, and it was their rulers
who faced the intrusion of foreign elements, first in Sind by Arabs in
the early eighth century and then in Punjab by Turkic groups from central Asia beginning in the eleventh century. Since these invaders were
adherents of Islam, it is tempting, in the light of modern understanding
of religion, social identity, and Muslim-Hindu relations in contemporary India, to view these incursions as clashes between religions, but
that view is surely an anachronism. The Arabs came to Sind as traders
and then, as so often has happened in history, sought to improve their
position by military conquest. The conquest of Sind, part of modern

Pakistan, began in 711, and the Muslim rulers apparently gave their Hindu and Buddhist subjects the status of *dhimmis,* as they did elsewhere to Christians and Jews on payment of the special tax known as *jiziya.* This seemed a sensible accommodation to rulers primarily interested in realizing revenue from their subjects, not in forcing them to convert to Islam. This practice was generally followed during later conquests by Muslim rulers in India proper, although the ulema (the community of Islamic religious leaders) often denounced it as a failure of the ruler to enforce Islamic law.

The major thrust of Islam into the Indian heartland came not from the traditional homelands of Islam in the Middle East but from the Afghan plateau, where Turks from Central Asia had established themselves. In 1192 the ruler of the principality of Ghor defeated the ruler of Delhi, which marked the beginning of the long process of subjugation of the rest of India. Since the new rulers took the title of sultan, the period from the beginning of the thirteenth century to 1526, when a new conqueror appeared, is referred to as the Delhi Sultanate. During these three centuries, much of Indian life was unchanged: the majority of the people remained Hindu, agricultural life went on as before, and patterns of trade seemed not to have changed very much. But something new had certainly been added: the political power that came into India embedded in its own political and social culture, with Islam as a well-defined, articulate creed, henceforth was a profoundly important element in Indian social and cultural life.

The political problem that the Muslim rulers faced in India, stated in the broadest terms, was how cultures and religions can coexist. That they coexisted for more than 600 years when the rulers were Muslims says much about the nature of Islam in India, as well as of Hinduism.

There are no truly reliable statistics, but by the middle of the eighteenth century, about one-fifth of the people of the subcontinent were probably Muslims. Little is known with certainty about how this large Muslim population came into existence. As noted above, there is no evidence of forced conversion on a large scale, but the Muslim population had a composition that reflects its history. A large number of the upper classes claim descent from immigrants from the older Islamic regions—central Asia, Iran, Arabia—who came as soldiers, scholars, or administrators seeking opportunities under the new Muslim rulers, but they are a relatively small part of the total. In the urban areas, lower castes might have seen advantages in adopting the religion of the rulers, and the same may have been true in the rural areas in relation to landlords. It is possible that the lives of the Sufis, the members of orders of mystics, may have attracted followers from the same groups. Islam made itself accessible to the people of India by using the regional languages, and it is certain that the shift to Islam was very gradual—a movement for which the western term *conversion* is inappropriate. The fact that the largest concentration of Muslims are on the western and eastern margins of the main centers of Hindu culture—in what is now Pakistan and Bangladesh—suggests that possibly the population of these areas had not really come under the strong influences of Brahmanical Hinduism.

Within this Muslim population were found all the schools and sects of Islam, including the two great divisions of Sunni and Shia. The Turks who came to north India from the northwest were Sunni, and their learned men, the ulema, brought with them the rich cultures of Iran and the rest of the Islamic world, so that Delhi became one of the great centers of Islam as well as a military power. In other areas, rulers with Iranian connections had established their rule, and they gave their patronage to Shia scholars. The result was that all the many divergent schools of Islam flourished in India.

Orthodox Muslim scholars were always aware of the dangers from the tendency toward syncretism, or accommodation with Hinduism, and one of their abiding concerns was to work for a purified Islam. Almost inevitably, this emphasis on ridding Islam of any accretions from without led to drawing a line between Muslims and non-Muslims and seeking to use political power to defend Islam. One of the causes of conflict in modern times between the two communities is almost certainly the attempts by religious leaders of both Hindus and Muslims to "purify" their respective religions.

By the end of the eighteenth century, Islam in India had undergone a dramatic change, for everywhere the Muslim rulers were being replaced by non-Muslims. In addition to the indigenous powers, the Marathas and the Sikhs, the British East India Company was rapidly becoming the major actor on the Indian scene, bringing with it elements of a new and threatening civilization. To come to terms with it would be one of the great tasks of Indian Islam in the nineteenth and twentieth centuries.

■ Christianity as an Indian Religion

There are three quite distinct phases of the history of Christianity in India. The first one dates from very ancient times, for according to the traditions of the Thomasite or Syrian churches of south India, Saint Thomas, one of the twelve apostles of Jesus, came to India and founded the church before he was martyred in 72 C.E. Although historical evidence for this tradition is lacking, it is fairly certain that there were churches in the fourth century, making Christianity in India older than Christianity in northern Europe. Cut off from western Christianity but in contact with the churches of the Middle East, the Christians in south India, principally in Kerala, were integrated into the wider Indian society. They seem to have made no attempt to seek converts outside their area, and there is little indication of interaction on a religious or philosophical level with either Hindus or Muslims. The second phase of Christian history began with the establishment of Portuguese power at the beginning of the sixteenth century. The splendors of the great churches at Goa, their capital, bear witness to the Portuguese activity in spreading Christianity, often by force and compulsion. The large Roman Catholic population in Goa and elsewhere is also the result, however, of the work of missionaries, the most famous of whom was Saint Francis Xavier (1506–1552). The Roman Catholic missionaries traveled throughout India and were active in the Mughal courts, but they seem to have made little lasting impression there, although their letters to their superiors in Europe provide valuable information about Indian conditions.

The third phase of Christianity in India, which began with the establishment of British power by the British East India Company at the end of the eighteenth century, was marked by contradictions and ambiguities. In contrast to the Portuguese, the British East India Company forbade missionary activity in the territories it acquired in India until 1813, on the grounds that Christian proselytizing would cause resentment among the people and threaten British power. This attitude remained quite widespread among British officials throughout the modern period.

By the middle of the nineteenth century, representatives of the major European and North American churches became active in the founding of western-style institutions such as schools, colleges, hospitals, orphanages, and printing presses. It is fair to say that the number of converts made were small in proportion to the expenditure of human and material resources. Christian activity in all these areas had an important impact, and some facets of the work of the churches will be noted in the following section on interaction between the religious communities in India.

■ Religions in Interaction and Reinterpretation

Émile Durkheim's famous thesis that virtually all the great social institutions have been born of religions because the idea of society is the soul of religion, with religion attaching the individual to society (Durkheim 1995), receives considerable support from the history of modern India. Obviously, no date can be set for the beginning of modern India, but it is conventional to assign to it the period toward the middle of the eighteenth century, when the Mughal Empire, based in north India, lost effective control over the subcontinent to various contenders for power, including the Marathas and their own military commanders and finally the British, in the guise of the great trading institution, the British East India Company. Partly because of these political changes but more importantly because of internal forces long present in Indian religion itself, momentous changes can be traced in religious activities and their relation to the social and political order. Some of the most socially significant of these changes can be conveniently categorized as interactions between religious communities and reinterpretations of the essential meaning of the teachings and belief systems of the different communities.

The broad historical context of these changes is the slow military and political conquest of Indian powers by the British, beginning in the middle of the eighteenth century but not really coming to a conclusion until the middle of the nineteenth century. In this period, we see the intrusion of those institutions we have come to associate with modernity: the bureaucratic organization of the modern state, with its control of all military power; capitalism; industrialization; and a world trading system. In the first half of the nineteenth century came the new forms of communication that were the product of science and technology: steamships, railways, telegraphs, postal systems, and the printing press. The British were fond of saying that these artifacts of modernity were their gift to India, but of course they would have found their way to India without the British, just as they reached China and Japan, and the changes they brought about would have happened in some fashion in any case. Most of these aspects of modernity, it should be kept in mind, were not only new to India but were new to the rest of the world, and in a very real sense Britain itself was modernizing as it took control of India. What is problematic and has been the subject of vigorous if inconclusive debate since the very beginning of that control is how many of the changes that took place in the nineteenth century were due to western intrusion. This argument is particularly vehement in the religious sphere, but the argument made here is that there were indeed changes in Indian religion and habits of thought, but the causes and consequences were embedded in patterns of thought and behavior that far preceded the coming of the West. The contribution of the West was probably to give new directions or a new vocabulary, literally in the case of the English language but also in terms of intellectual conceptual structures, and to speed the process of change.

In this chapter's surveys of earlier periods, it was emphasized that change and development have taken place at all times in religious expression in India. Furthermore, throughout history there have been protests of many kinds—against idolatry, caste, and the domination of temple priests. New groups have also formed, many of them associated with the bhakti movement, of which the origin and growth of Sikhism is the most dramatic example. The vital forces that made possible the changes in habits of thought and religious ideas came from within both Hinduism and Islam, and it was because of the ability of these religions to reinterpret themselves that religion was able to play the role it did in modern India. It is hard to think of any other country where religion was as intimately related to the acceptance and encouragement of the forces of nationalism, social reform, democracy, and the findings of modern science as India. That this is so is surely because religious reform movements did not go against the grain of Indian culture.

■ Western Criticism of Indian Religions

In these reform movements, Christianity, one of the non-Indian religions mentioned above, contributed to the movements of interaction and reinterpretation within the major religious communities. For good or ill, one of the significant features of Christian activity in India was a bitter and forceful denunciation of Hinduism and Islam that has become part of the historical imaginations of both India and the West. It must be remembered, however, that the harsh criticism did not come only from Christian sources but from the West in general. Karl Marx, for example, made many of the same criticisms of Hinduism as Christian leaders, getting some of his opinions from the irreligious James Mill who, without having seen India, declared Hinduism to be all "disorder, caprice, passion, contest, portents, prodigies, violence, and deformity" (Mill 1826: vol. 1: 330). The reaction of the both Hindu and Muslim leaders and intellectuals to the verbal assaults from the West is an essential element in the intellectual history of India.

Long lists were compiled of what were regarded as the barbarous and degrading superstitions of Hinduism: idolatry, animals worshiped as deities, scandalous stories of the private lives of the gods, human sacrifice, polygamy, female infanticide, and child marriage. Islam was especially excoriated for its treatment of women, the cruelty of Muslim rulers, and their commitment to wage holy war. From within both Hinduism and Islam, these charges were rebutted in a variety of ways, but there can be no doubt that these criticisms, harsh and wrongheaded as they were, were a major element in preventing religious dialogue.

Another challenge from the forces of Christianity was somewhat different: Christian mission societies introduced institutional patterns that were part of nineteenth-century western society. They included educational institutions of all kinds, orphanages, hospitals, and social service centers. The churches in the West were persuaded to support these institutions on the grounds that they could be the means for conversion through example and precept. They were, at the same time, expressions of the humanitarian and philanthropic movements characteristic of the nineteenth-century western world, particularly of Great Britain and North America. Colleges for women were a special innovation and were largely the work of U.S. churches. There were remarkably few conversions in any of the many colleges and schools founded by the western churches, no more than a half dozen in any one of them over a 100-year period. If, as their critics charge, they were instruments of conversion to Christianity, the church colleges in India must be counted the least cost-effective mechanisms for religious propaganda in history. There were, however, many conversions to western science, philosophy, and literature. As one well-known Indian Communist leader put it in his farewell to a missionary teacher in a Christian college, it was in his philosophy classes that he had realized that all religions were fraudulent superstitions and that dialectical materialism was true.

Both Christians and non-Christians have often lauded the contribution that the missionary schools, colleges, and hospitals made to India, but it is only fair to note an overall assessment of the effect of these institutions on Indian life by a knowledgeable, if hostile critic, Arun Shourie, a prominent Hindu nationalist politician. He acknowledges that generations of young men and women, including himself and his family, received modern education at the educational institutions and that hundreds of thousands of people had received medical treatment at the hospitals, but he concludes: "While they introduced us to a smattering of western learning, they led us to completely forget and—with no knowledge of it at all—feel ashamed of our tradition. . . . Where they established modern hospitals . . . they made us completely oblivious of the vast medical knowledge that had been accumulated over the centuries here" (Shourie 1994: 6–7). Shourie could have gone to an institution in India, of which there are many, where he would have received teaching only in Indian science, but it is a part of modernity that he chose not to do so. Although Shourie's view is an exaggeration, it undoubtedly represents an important aspect of the interaction of religions in their cultural manifestations.

▓ Movements Within Hinduism

Commentators on religion in modern India sometimes give the name "neo-Hinduism," or new Hinduism, to the interpretations of the traditional faith that emerged in the nineteenth and twentieth centuries, and there is some justification in that, but it tends to obscure how much of core beliefs and practices remained even in the most radical innovations. Most of the leaders noted here helped define what it meant to be a Hindu Indian.

Interaction and reinterpretation as modes of change are represented at the beginning of the nineteenth century in the career of Rammohun Roy (ca. 1772–1833), for he enunciated positions in regard to religion that have become part of the intellectual inheritance of India. Personal experience had made him bitterly critical of certain aspects of his society, especially idol worship and the treatment of women, made famous by the practice known as sati, in which widows immolated themselves on their husbands' funeral pyres. Roy's criticism of these social practices was sharpened by the beginning of the outpouring of western criticism of Indian society. His response was not to deny the existence of such practices nor to defend them, but to formulate a new apologetic. None of these things were, he insisted, derived from the foundation texts of Hinduism. Idolatry, for example, was found not in the Vedic literature but in the much later Puranic texts. They were corruptions that had crept in through ignorance of the original texts of Hinduism, the *Vedas*. If they were swept away, what was left was a pure monotheism, and, he argued, the same was true of all religions, including Christianity and Islam. True religion, he insisted, was belief in the "almighty superintendent of the universe" (Jones 1989: 31). This conclusion led Roy to what was perhaps his most influential argument: since there was one common truth for all humankind, then Indians should be willing to adopt whatever was useful to them in western civilization, ending what he said was the age-old habit of Indian religion turning in on itself and refusing to learn from others. On this ground, he made a passionate plea for the introduction of education in English into India so that Indians could learn "mathematics, natural philosophy, chemistry and anatomy and other useful sciences" (Roy 1988: vol. 2: 33).

Roy's reading of the ancient texts caught the imagination of a generation of young Indians, particularly those in Bengal, who were anxious to come to terms with the West without denying the validity of their own culture. To a quite remarkable degree, Indians have proved their ability to accept whatever they found valuable in the West while maintaining their standing in their own religion and culture. One important aid in doing so was the remarkable society Roy helped to found, the Brahmo Samaj, which was strengthened by the famous Tagore family. Although frowned upon by the orthodox, the Brahmo Samaj provided a spiritual center for many Bengali Hindu intellectuals, and from its membership came an astonishing galaxy of scholars, scientists, artists, and writers.

Interaction and reinterpretation could take varied forms, as was shown in the work of another remarkable religious reformer, Dayananda Sarasvati (1824–1883). His condemnation of many Hindu practices, such as idolatry, child marriage, and the treatment of women, was similar to Roy's, but his conclusions about interaction and reinterpretation were radically different. After a long spiritual pilgrimage in search of truth, he believed he had found it in the *Vedas*. Hinduism had been corrupted by the *Puranas* and bhakti, and all truth, he insisted, was to be found in the Vedic texts. There was no need to accept anything from the West. He mounted a very strenuous attack on false religions, in which he included much of the Hinduism of his day, including Sikhism, Christianity, and Islam. He founded an organization, the Arya Samaj, which won a wide following, probably partly because its declaration that India did not need to look outside itself for truth was appealing to nationalist sentiment but also because of his vigorous counterattacks on Christianity and Islam.

The Arya Samaj undoubtedly contributed to the increasing tension between Hindus and Muslims, especially in Punjab, but at the same time it instilled a new sense of pride in being Indian, and many of the best-known leaders in the nationalist movement in Punjab came from its ranks. Whereas the Brahmo Samaj had appealed to upper-class intellectuals, especially Brahmans, the Arya Samaj attracted many of its members from the urban middle classes and castes. Its great emphasis on education, especially on the education of girls as necessary for building a strong nation, gave it a firm base for leadership in postindependence India.

Another religious movement that made a strong appeal to many intellectuals involved in the nationalist movement is associated with Shri Ramakrishna (1836–1886), a Hindu mystic firmly in the traditional mold, and his disciple, Swami Vivekananda (1863–1902). Ramakrishna's special devotion was to the Divine Mother, and his devotees saw in him one who had achieved the ancient ideal of unity with the divine. His mingling of what has been called "the complexity of the secret and the dialectic of the erotic" brought into prominence elements of Indian religion that had been played down in the other reform movements (Kripal 1994: xv). His disciple, Vivekananda, translated his message to mean that God is in everyone and everything, which led him to his distinctive conclusion that all religions are true. Furthermore, he implied, those reformers like Rammohun Roy and Dayananda who denounced idol worship were wrong: one should worship the form of the divine that answers one's own personal needs. Western materialism may have conquered India, but India's spirituality would conquer the world. It could only be done, however, if India had a vigorous, robust national life. That this message caught the imagination of the college students whom he frequently addressed is not surprising. Making use of moderns means of communication and a modern vocabulary, Vivekananda carried his message throughout India, Europe, and the United States.

To a remarkable degree, the understanding of Hinduism or neo-Hinduism by contemporary Indians, perhaps even when they are not aware of it, draws heavily upon the reinterpretations of Roy, Dayananda, Ramakrishna, and Vivekananda. That is also true to a considerable extent of a far more famous thinker and activist, Mahatma Gandhi (1869–1948), who brought religion to the center of Indian political and social discourse. A political leader of consummate skill who personified the Indian national movement from 1920 to 1947, Gandhi always insisted that his religion informed his political activities, and although admittedly reinterpreting many aspects of traditional Hinduism, he insisted that his beliefs were consonant with true Hinduism. He summarized his religious and political philosophy in such words as ahimsa and satyagraha, which he translated as love, truth, nonviolence, and God. Gandhi acknowledged his debts to Henry David Thoreau, Leo Tolstoy, John Ruskin, and the New Testament, but the appeal he made to the people of India was successful because it touched deep religious beliefs from their own traditions. In practical action, such religious appeals could be baffling to those who did not share them, but Gandhi's religious commitment shaped Indian political developments. Although some Indians, both Hindu and Muslim, regretted Gandhi giving religion a central role in defining Indian nationalism, it is possible that there was no other way to appeal to the Hindu masses.

▓ Movements Within Islam

The interactions and reinterpretations within Hinduism throughout the nineteenth and twentieth centuries had counterparts within Islam, but the social and political position of the Islamic communities during that time gave very different impetus to reform movements in Islam. Within the Hindu community, leaders quickly saw the possibility of using the British conquest to reassert a place in society that had long been denied them, whereas Muslim leaders saw a drastic decline from 700 years of Muslim rule. They were also aware of the threat to their own positions from the newly assertive spirit within Hinduism. Some Muslim leaders talked of a jihad, a holy war against the British, but they lacked the resources and the following for such a move. Other leaders, notably those associated with the theological seminary at Deoband in north India, took the course of withdrawal from contact with the social and political changes that were taking place, seeking to preserve the traditional teachings and institutions of Islam. Through a network of schools, they sought, as a scholar of their movement put it, "self-conscious reassessment of what was deemed authentic religion," but unlike some Hindu movements, it did not involve acculturation to western patterns (Metcalf 1982: 348).

There were, however, Muslim spokesmen for accommodation with western learning and science, the most effective of whom was Sayyid Ahmad Khan (1817–1898). He insisted that the Quran was the authority for belief and practices, not the customs that had accumulated through the years. He argued that the findings of modern science could be accepted, and where they seemed to conflict with the Quran, the quranic passages must be interpreted allegorically, since science, founded on the law of nature, was also God's word, and therefore there could be no conflict between the two. The teaching of the Quran is validated, he argued, not by miracles but by its inherent truth as shown by reason. The college he founded at Aligarh, now Aligarh Muslim University, became the great center for Muslims wanting to come to terms with British power and western learning. Ahmad Khan opposed the Indian nationalist movement on the ground that India needed British rule to keep peace between Hindus and Muslims (Lelyveld 1977).

In contrast to the modernism of Sayyid Ahmad Khan and his followers, the most powerful defenders of traditional Islam in India came from two movements, the Jama'at-i-Islami and the Tablighi Jama'at, which went to the masses, calling for a revival of Islam. The founder of the Jama'at-i-Islami was Maulana Maududi (1903–1979). For Maududi, there could be no distinction between Islam as a religious faith and politics, and more than anyone else, he gave Islam in India and later in Pakistan a political vocabulary. Terms and phrases first used by Maududi, such as *the Islamic system of life, the Islamic constitution, the economic system of Islam,* and *the political system of Islam,* have now become accepted usage for Muslim writers and political activists throughout South Asia (Ahmed 1991: 464). The Tablighi Jama'at does not, by way of contrast, seek political power but stresses the necessity of the individual's acceptance of the basic teachings and practices of Islam. It works by isolating individuals from their family and everyday life, forming them into small temporary communities for religious teaching and devotions, and then sending them out to win others.

■ Communal Tensions and Secularism

▨ The Politicization of Religion

No discussion of Islam and Hinduism in the modern period can avoid consideration of the growth of tensions between Muslims and Hindus from the 1920s, which led to frequent riots with much loss of life and culminated in the partition of the Indian subcontinent into two states, India and Pakistan, in 1947. It is now conventional to argue that religion was not the cause of violence or of partition, but rather social and economic causes that expressed themselves in religious terms. It is true that partition in 1947 had to do, in the end, with complex quarrels over a unitary state versus a loose federation, but religion was used in India, as it has been used elsewhere, to define differences, legitimize hostility, and appeal to people who were not moved by arguments about constitutional niceties. *Communalism* became the widely used term in India to denote an emphasis on group identity and group behavior, not upon the individual, with that behavior—social, economic, and political—attributed to adherence to a particular religion. Real differences in behavior may not in fact exist, or they may belong to individuals, but as with anti-Semitism in the West, the attribution of group identity smothers individuality. Among the most common causes of riots were such incidents as Hindus organizing processions and marching through streets, playing music in front of mosques, or, on the other side, Muslims killing cows.

The communal riots that were such a common feature of Indian life in the 1920s and 1930s, that marked the partition of India in 1947, and that have continued to take their toll in human lives, have, of course, more complex causes than music before mosques. One was the rise of modern politics, when opportunities to gain political power through voting became possible and politicians appealed to communal identities for votes. As a Hindu politician said in 1926, "Unless I call the other community names and damn them before my electorate, I have absolutely no chance of being elected" (Thursby 1975: 76). Muslim politicians made the same sorts of appeals.

The other great actor in the communal antagonisms was the British, and a frequent charge was that they had created the antagonism between the two communities in following a policy of "divide and rule." This crudely put, the statement is implausible, but many British politicians were convinced, as one of them put it, that "between the two communities lies a chasm which cannot be crossed by the resources of modern political engineering," so that the increasing hostility and violence made the continuance of their rule necessary and possible. In India itself, however, the governor-general was aware how dangerous the Hindu-Muslim divide was for both India and Great Britain (Thursby 1975: 173).

The revivalist and reform movements were also very important factors in making religious identity a primary component of social and political life, thus leading to communal tension. Within Hinduism, there were many such movements, but three were especially significant in creating a sense of Hindu identity and a corresponding unease in Muslims. One was the *shuddhi* (purification) movement led by a dynamic Arya Samaj figure, Swami Shraddhanand (1856–1926), which aimed to reconvert Muslims to Hinduism on the grounds that they had once been Hindus. This activity aroused intense opposition among Muslims, especially from the Tablighi Jama'at movement. The bitterness caused by the *shuddhi* movement culminated in the murder of Shraddhanand in 1926 by a Muslim.

Two other movements that date from the 1920s illustrate the difficulty in separating religion from politics. One was the Hindu Mahasabha, which although a political party, had as a central concern the strengthening of Hindu self-confidence. It always denied that it was anti-Muslim, but its definition of who was a Hindu was significant: "A Hindu is one who regards India as his motherland and the most sacred spot on earth" (Thursby 1975: 168). The Mahasabha did not attract a large formal membership, but statements like this one became well known and were widely accepted, even by many leaders of the Indian National Congress party. Muslim leaders read them as exclusionary, that is, meaning that being Indian was synonymous with being Hindu. Nationalism was being equated with Hinduism and Hinduism with communalism. One of the most perplexing issues of modern democratic politics, the role of the religious allegiances of large groups of the population, was being made part of political discourse.

Another movement founded in 1925, the Rashtriya Swayamsevak Sangh (RSS), makes an even more vociferous and ultimately successful claim for the recognition that India was a Hindu nation. In doing so, the RSS denies that it is either a religious or political organization, claiming to be only a cultural one. Its stated function is defining and defending the Hindu nation, a role summed up later in its constitution, which indicates how thin the dividing line is between religion, culture, and politics: "To eradicate difference among Hindus; to make them realize the greatness of their past; to inculcate in them a spirit of self-sacrifice and selfless devotion to Hindu society as a whole; to build up an organized and well-disciplined corporate life; and to bring about the regeneration of Hindu society" (Embree 1994: 619).

Its critics allege that it encourages violence and terrorism and that its antagonism to Christians and Muslims has created hatred and suspicion among religious communities. The RSS made little impact before independence, but since then it has emerged as the most vocal opponent of the idea, enshrined in the constitution, that India was a secular state, that is, one where all religions had equality before the law and none had any special legal standing. The electoral successes of the Bharatiya Janata Party (BJP),with its leadership drawn from RSS cadres, exemplifies the depth of the appeal of Hindu nationalism.

The coming of independence to India in 1947 did not signify any very perceptible change in the inward religious life of the people, for all the variegated forms of faith and practice that for so long had been integral to the culture continued their immemorial functions of providing meanings for existence and structures for daily life. Worship at a family shrine, observances of religious holidays, participation in rites of passage, and pilgrimages to holy places continued as they had for centuries. Also as in the past, new expressions of the divine, or charismatic leaders, continued to draw followers.

Some have achieved more fame outside India, like Rajneesh, whereas others have great followings in India as well as in the West. Of these, perhaps Satya Sai Baba is the most famous, with many followers among prominent politicians, judges, and businesspeople. Two hundred thousand devotees attended his seventy-fifth-birthday celebrations in December 2000 in the small south India town, Puttaparthi, where his main center is located ("Test of Faith" 2000: 26–31). Satya Sai Baba has been called "a jet-age holy man" because of his following among the rich and influential in India, but at a deeper level, he is a familiar figure through the ages. As one scholar put it, "He does the things a deity should: he receives the homage and the devotion of his devotees, and he reciprocates with love and boons. And, above all, he performs miracles" (Babb 1986: 160–161). A revered female guru, Sri Mata Amritanand-mati, or "Amma," made a touching plea for peace and social justice at the Millennium World Peace Summit at the United Nations in September 2000, and she frequently visits her large overseas following. A feature of her teaching that appeals to many, both in India and abroad, is her insistence that it is harmful to think of religions as having different understandings of truth ("Destroy" 2000: 15). Although this religious activity does not seem to have much social content, it undoubtedly gives to many of the Hindu population a sense of being masters in their own house, of having access to what is most profound in their religious tradition, the means of liberation.

For Indian Muslims, independence from the British brought new problems, although they welcomed it as much as any group in India. Many of the best-known Islamic leaders, both in politics and religion, had gone to Pakistan, leaving them without spokespeople in a vulnerable position. The majority who stayed were among the poorest people in India and also the least educated. They also carried the stigma of belonging to the community whose leaders had divided India, and Hindu communalists were quick to charge them with sympathy for Pakistan.

There were, however, opportunities for Muslims in India to express their obedience to their God. There were no legal restraints on religious practices, and the mosque remained central to their lives. Muslim personal law governing marriage, inheritance, divorce, and adoption, as codified by the British in the nineteenth century, was retained by the new Indian government. Preindependence movements, such as the Jama'at-i-Islami and Tablighi Jama'at, continued but served different purposes. The Jama'at-i-Islami has stressed preserving the rights of Muslims against what it regards as the attempts by Hindu communalists to weaken them by withdrawing the special provisions of Muslim personal law and by discriminating against them in public employment. The Jama'at-i-Islami's political activities have led some of its critics to charge it with encouraging violence against Hindus. The Tablighi Jama'at movement, however, does not encourage political involvement, for they are concerned not to remake the world but "to remake

Reading the Quran in the Jami Mosque, built in 1424, in Ahmadabad

individual lives, to create faithful Muslims who undertake action in this life only because of the hope and promise of sure reward in the next" (Metcalf 1994: 710).

Although many continuities exist within the religious communities, a new political role became possible for them in the new liberal democratic society. The issue in broad terms was familiar in many countries, both now and in the past: What role should religion have in society, and what should be the relationship of the state to religion?

Before independence, there had been persistent demands from groups like Mahasabha and the RSS for a recognition of a special place for Hindu culture as representing the birthright of the majority of the citizens. Coupled with this demand was criticism of Islam and Christianity as alien ideologies that weakened Hindu society. Such attitudes had been rigorously denounced by the leaders of the Indian National

Congress party, most notably by Jawaharlal Nehru, who became prime
minister of India in 1947 amid the carnage and bloodshed of the riots
that accompanied partition.

▨ The Challenge of Secularism to Religion

The answer that Nehru and almost all the leaders of India gave to
the question of how the different religions could live in harmony was
that India should be a secular state. In 1947, probably the majority of
opinionmakers in India—journalists, academics, politicians, and businesspeople—would have given assent to Nehru's proposition that "the
cardinal doctrine of modern democratic practice is the separation of the
state from religion" and that the idea of a religious state "has no place
in the mind of the modern man" (Smith 1963: 155). This emphatic
rejection of religion as a determining factor in the life of the state contrasts with the widespread view, noted at the beginning of the chapter,
that the people of India are peculiarly religious, but Nehru and those
who agreed with him would have answered that it was precisely the
religiosity of Indians that made the secular state necessary. It seemed to
be the only barrier against the violence so often associated with religious communities seeking, at times, to safeguard themselves from
what they perceive as threats or, at other times, to rid the world of evil
personified by other religious groups. The term *secularism* as used in
India differs from its usage in the West, for it does not imply any hostility to religion or a denial of its importance. Nor does it have quite the
meaning of the U.S. phrase, *separation of church and state,* which
arose in the context of denying that there should an established church,
as in most European countries, notably England. Presumably the
Founding Fathers were thinking of a multichurch society, not a multireligious society of the kind that exists in India. Although India was
not defined as a "secular state" until a constitutional amendment was
passed in 1976, the concept was at the forefront of discussion after
1947. Perhaps the most succinct definition of what was meant comes
from a U.S. scholar, Donald Smith, who, after an exhaustive study of
the issue, concluded: "The secular state is a state which guarantees
individual and corporate freedom of religion, deals with the individual
as a citizen irrespective of religion, is not constitutionally connected to
a particular religion nor does it seek to promote or interfere with religion" (Smith 1963: 4).

Years before, in 1926, Nehru had written of his hope that the passage of time would "scotch our so-called religion and secularize our

own intelligentsia" and that, just as in Europe, mass education had weakened the power of religion, so the process "was bound to be repeated in India." Sixty-five years later, surveying what had happened in between, a commentator wryly observed, "Noble thought, yes, but quite out of tune with the realities of Indian social and political life" (Hasan 1991: 285).

An indication of what some of those realities were in the relationship of religion to the state and society came in the constitutional debates in 1948–1949. The advocates of a secular state found themselves in a dilemma that has remained central for India. As a secular state, the government could not in any way favor Hinduism, but as a nation-state it had the right and duty to promote Indian culture. This culture, however—its art, literature, music—is saturated and colored by Hinduism, as the European Middle Ages were by Christianity. What was to be the place of other religions with different and, at times, conflicting cultures?

In a study whose title indicates its thesis, *The New Cold War? Religious Nationalism Confronts the Secular State*, Mark Juergensmeyer argues that what we are witnessing in India, as elsewhere, is a challenge by indigenous religious forces to modern liberal democracy that attempts to ignore religion. The religious forces at times see violence as necessary in defense of religion, and, in Juergensmeyer's words, the "great encounter between cosmic forces—an ultimate good and evil, a divine truth and falsehood—is a war that worldly forces only mimic" (Juergensmeyer 1995: 155).

Four incidents can illustrate such a confrontation. One, the Babri Masjid incident, represented Hindu nationalism, whose standard-bearer is the RSS and whose ideology had gained considerable support in the general population. Another is the violence created by a group of Sikhs in Punjab in what they regarded as the defense of their religion. A third is the uprising by Muslims in Kashmir, and a fourth is the violence against Christians that erupted in various parts of India after 1998. All are very complex issues and can be only mentioned here in briefest outline.

It was suggested above that the most pervasive expression of Hinduism is bhakti, the way of devotion to a deity, but this form of piety does not seem to receive much emphasis in Hindu nationalism, being replaced by a perhaps more ancient path, *karmayoga,* a discipline that emphasizes the central Hindu construct, dharma, the path of duty and right action. Such a path of action was the demand in the 1980s for the destruction of the Babri Masjid, a mosque in Ayodhya supposedly built after the Mughal emperor Babur had destroyed a temple that Hindus believed marked the birthplace of the god Rama. In its place, the temple of Rama was to be rebuilt. Eminent Indian historians, many of them Hindus, pointed out that there was no real evidence for any of this story and that, in any case, Rama was a mythical character. But as one of their number remarked, it is not possible to dispose so easily of religious belief. "We cannot counterpoise history to myth as truth to falsehood. These are different modes of knowledge, varying ways of understanding the world, ordering one's life and defining one's actions" (Gopal 1991: 122). Demand for destruction of the mosque built up, summarized in the slogan popular at the time, "God must be liberated." For many Hindus, the mosque became a symbol of the defeat of Hindu India by Muslim Turks; for Muslims, the agitation was a reminder of how precarious their position would be in modern India if militant Hindus should gain power. In December 1992, thousands of young men destroyed the mosque, cheered on by a woman orator who said that Hindu men who would not shed their blood for Hindu India had water, not blood, in their veins. As the 400-year-old building collapsed, a holy man exclaimed, "The sun sets on Babur at last. The taint has been removed forever" (Embree 1994: 647–648). In the next few days after the destruction of the mosque, a wave of violence swept north India, with at least 1,000 people killed, mainly Muslims. Many supporters of the concept of the secular state were in despair, feeling that the religious violence had signaled a shift away from their vision of a religiously neutral state toward a Hindu nation, which was the vision of the RSS and like-minded groups. The secularists may have been too pessimistic, but there is no doubt that at the end of the twentieth century, the demand for a defining role for Hinduism in national life had been placed on the national agenda, and it is most unlikely that it will be removed in the near future.

The violent confrontation in Punjab in the 1980s dramatized another position: the demand for autonomy by leaders of a regional nationalism defined largely in religious terms. This demand brought a religious group, the Sikhs, into conflict with both the secular state and Hindu nationalism. According to the government, the violence was due to terrorist groups, who were motivated by the desire to create a separate Sikh state and were funded by India's enemy, Pakistan. The militant Sikhs argued that they were driven to violence in defense of their religion against the violence of the state, which in their eyes was controlled by the Hindu majority that denied their rights.

In Sikhism, martyrdom does not just mean dying for the faith but fighting to the death against its enemies. When asked why they fought so bitterly and with such violence, the young Sikhs would answer that they fought for the truth as embodied in their religion. When one leader was asked why he mixed religion and politics, he answered, "Religion and politics go together in Sikhism and cannot be separated" (Embree 1989: 129). It is possible to argue that the frustrations of the young men who took to violence were rooted in economics and social problems, but it was the vision of the good society that they saw in Sikhism that offered them a solution "by legitimizing the violence that is born of hatred and despair" (Embree 1989: 132). The government of India succeeded in crushing the uprising that cost many hundreds of lives, but it left a residue of distrust and suspicion between the Hindus and the Sikhs that will not be easily healed.

Kashmir, famous for the beauty of its towering mountain ranges surrounding a fertile valley of lakes and streams, was the cause of two wars between India and Pakistan between 1947 and 1965 over conflicting territorial claims. After 1989, however, the situation changed from just rivalry between the two nations to what amounts to a civil war of militant insurgents in Kashmir against Indian rule. Police documents report that 33,854 people were killed, of whom 19,781 were civilians, 11,757 were militants, and 2,316 were members of the Indian security forces (Bearak 2000). These tabulations are, however, too precisely bureaucratic to be readily accepted by peace groups in either India or Kashmir, who believe that probably twice as many were killed and that many of those listed as "militants" were often innocent people killed by the security forces. In addition to the killing, thousands of refugees have fled from their homes for fear of the militant groups, who are referred to as terrorists by the Indian government but as freedom fighters by their partisans. The uprising has led to a breakdown of much of the normal civil structures of the area, including educational institutions, medical services, and the legal system.

How does religion enter this depressing picture? Unhappily, it informs all the three major components of the Kashmir situation. One of the components is, on the surface, the political rivalries of the two neighboring states, India and Pakistan, that were created from the decolonization process of Great Britain's Indian empire. Their wars and the rancor that has continued since they gained their independence in 1947 can be understood as the rivalries engendered by national interests, but underlying the political factors is the second component, religious antagonism. For Hindu nationalists, Pakistan represents, in the rhetoric they often use, the vivisection of the Motherland, and Pakistan's support of the militants in Kashmir is a continuation of this process.

Pakistan's claim for involvement in the bitter, brutal war in Kashmir is that as an Islamic nation, it is helping its Muslim brethren win their freedom. For Pakistan, the militants in Kashmir are engaged in a jihad, a holy war, in defense of Muslims who are oppressed by Hindu India. For Muslims, force is a god-given gift to be used against unbelievers, and it is a deadly sin to yield to a tyrant without fighting (Qureshi 1989: 162).

The fourth incident, the attacks on Christians that began to be reported with startling frequency in 1998, illustrates how violent confrontations can be seen from within a religion as defense of truth. Churches were burned, clergy were murdered, nuns were allegedly raped, and Christian schools attacked, mainly in isolated communities where the Christians were poor and few in number (Chenoy 1999). These attacks were new and puzzling phenomena, distressing to many Hindus as well as to Christians in India and abroad. The basic explanation for the attacks, which appear to have come from Hindu nationalist groups affiliated with the RSS, was that the Christians were an alien element, detrimental to Hindu civilization because of their proselytizing activity.

This charge that Christians seek to convert people from their ancestral faith to Christianity is a position held not just by hard-line Hindu nationalists but also by many Indians who would normally support secular, liberal positions. To westerners, who have grown accustomed to people changing their religion in much the same way as they do their political allegiances, this attitude may seem in contradiction to secularism, but it is congruent with deeply embedded cultural values. In effect, it asserts the primacy of the family over the individual, of the obligations rooted in the pervasive concept of dharma, and the sense that India, although permitting full freedom of worship, is ultimately a nation where Hindu culture—of which religion is an important component—is dominant. Gaining acceptance of the idea that religious adherence is a matter of individual preference was a long and bitter battle in the West, and the idea has not by any means become part of the way of thinking of even many modern Indian intellectuals.

Article 25:1 of the Indian Constitution, which guarantees individual religious freedom, states that "all persons are equally entitled to the freedom of conscience and the right freely to profess, practise and propagate religion." There was little objection to guaranteeing freedom of worship, but there was very strenuous objection from many Hindu groups and individuals to the right to *propagate* religion, and it was inserted after much argument. Christians and Muslims just as strenuously demanded such a right, arguing that propagation of their faiths was essential to the very nature of their religion. From a secular point of view, a well-known Indian historian has supported this right by arguing that the freedom of conscience guaranteed by the constitution "surely includes the right to change one's religion, and a curbing of that right can lead to restrictions on freedom of choice in general" (Sarkar 1999).

The opposition by many Hindus to conversion has three main strands. One is that the idea of conversion to another faith through proselytization is repellent; Hinduism is, as it were, genetically acquired through birth, and one should remain in the religion in which one is born. Closely related to this is another strand: that conversion to another religion is socially destructive, breaking the bonds of social relationships, the cement that holds society together. Islam and Christianity, it is alleged, introduce alien customs, beliefs, and practices that corrupt Indian civilization. That this criticism was widespread is suggested by Mahatma Gandhi's allegation that Christian converts tended to become denationalized, giving up not only their ancestral faith but also their national culture (Smith 1963: 165). Although this assertion would be challenged by Christians, it points to the almost ineradicable link between religion and culture in modern India. Through the years, this argument has become a potent weapon for the RSS and other Hindu nationalist groups against the place of Islam and Christianity in India and against Indian Muslims and Christians, introducing bitterness and fear into their lives. Ultimately, the real target of Hindu nationalist groups however, is not just the other religious groups but the secular state as enshrined in the Indian Constitution, for it is the secular state, they argue, that by giving equal status to all religions denies the legitimate place of Hinduism as the expression of Indian culture in India.

The third strand of Hindu opposition to conversion involves that most difficult of modern social and political concepts, the belief in toleration. Hindus correctly stress that Hindu society is remarkably tolerant of a wide variety of belief patterns and practices. There is, however, an aspect of this emphasis on Hindu toleration that is deeply divisive, and that is the insistence by Hindu intellectuals and spiritual leaders that all religious are true. This understanding of truth in modern Hinduism has been well summed up by Arvind Sharma: "All the various religious forms represent diverse paths to the one Truth, paths that are all in some degree valid" (Johnston and Sampson 1994: 270). Although this conciliatory reading is intended to be a meeting place with the other religious traditions that constitute India's diversity, in fact it is working out very differently at the present time. The declaration that all religions are true has become a dogmatic statement that condemns as bigots those religions of India, notably Islam and Christianity, that make universal claims for what they regard as their core truth. Clearly, much hard thinking must be done on the meaning of toleration before any meaningful dialogue can take place between religions in the Indian context.

■ Conclusion

To conclude a survey of "lived religion" in India on a note of violence and confrontation may seem perverse, but it is done deliberately as a reminder that religion, as it was defined at the beginning of this chapter, is woven inextricably into the tapestry of Indian history. Mahatma Gandhi used to say that when people argued that religion should be kept out of politics, this only showed that they knew nothing of either religion or politics. That is true, for good or ill, because of what historians call "historical consciousness," that is, those memories of the past that a civilization preserves to provide guidelines for behavior, to tell us who we are and where we came from. Historical consciousness does not refer simply to knowledge of the past but, as one historian expressed it, "hearing the past," listening to "the distilled memories of others, the stories of things we never experienced first hand. It means learning to make these things our own, learning to look at the world through their filter, learning to feel the living presence of the past inhering in the seeming inertness of the world as given to us" (National Council 1996).

Jawaharlal Nehru has often been quoted for his harsh judgments of the role of religion in India, yet few have spoken more movingly of the enduring gift of religion to India's historical consciousness. Brought up in a family of wealth and educated in England's most famous schools, he traveled throughout India as a young man and was depressed by the poverty and misery of the people. Then he discovered that India had a deep well of strength that gave the country the vitality to renew itself throughout the ages: "She was like some ancient palimpsest on which layer upon layer of thought and reverie had been inscribed. . . . All these existed in our conscious or subconscious self . . . and they have gone to build up the complex and mysterious personality of India. [Her] essential unity had been so powerful that no political division, no disaster or catastrophe, had been able to overcome it" (Nehru 1956: 42–46). Nehru refused to give the name of religion to that source of vitality, and yet at the end, it is hard to escape the claims of religion as the vitalizing force, for good or ill, in contemporary India as it has been in the past.

■ Bibliography

Ahmed, Rafiuddin. 1991. "Islamic Fundamentalism in South Asia." In *Fundamentalisms Observed,* Martin E. Marty and R. Scott Appleby, eds. Chicago: University of Chicago Press.

Akbar, M. J. 1988. *Nehru: The Making of India.* New York: Viking.

Babb, Lawrence E. 1986. *Redemptive Encounters: Three Modern Styles in the Hindu Tradition.* Delhi: Oxford University Press.

Banton, Michael P. 1968. *Anthropological Approaches to the Study of Religion.* London: Tavistock.

Bearak, Barry. 2000. "Kashmir: Lethal Decade." *New York Times,* September 7.

Chenoy, Kamal Mitra, ed. 1999. *Violence in Gujarat: Test Case for a Fundamentalist Agenda.* Private circulation. New Delhi: National Alliance of Women.

Deshpande, Madhav, and Peter Edwin Hook, eds. 1979. *Aryan and Non-Aryan in India.* Ann Arbor: Center for South and Southeast Asian Studies, University of Michigan.

"Destroy the Mind's Nuclear Weapons." 2000. *New India Times,* August 29.

Durkheim, Émile. 1995. *The Elementary Forms of the Religious Life: A Study in Religious Sociology.* Karen E. Fields, trans. New York: Free Press.

Embree, Ainslie T. 1988. "Sikhism." In *Sources of Indian Tradition,* vol. 2, Stephen Hay, ed. New York: Columbia University Press.

———. 1989. *Utopias in Conflict.* New Delhi: Oxford University Press.

———. 1994. "The Function of the Rashtriya Swayamsevak Sangh: To Define the Hindu Nation." In *Accounting for Fundamentalisms,* Martin E. Marty and R. Scott Appleby, eds. Chicago: University of Chicago Press.

Gandhi, M. K. 1927. *Hind Swaraj.* Ahmadabad· Navajivan.

Ganguly, Sumit. 1997. *The Crisis in Kashmir: Portents of War, Hopes of Peace.* Cambridge: Cambridge University Press.

Gopal, S., ed. 1991. *Anatomy of a Confrontation: The Babri Masjid–Ramjanmabhumi Issue.* Delhi: Penguin.

Hasan, Mushirul. 1991. *Nationalism and Communal Politics in India, 1885–1930.* New Delhi: Manohar.

Hawley, John Stratton. 1988. "Bhakti." In *Encyclopedia of Asian History,* Ainslie T. Embree, ed. New York: Scribner's.

Hawley, John Stratton, and Mark Juergensmeyer, trans. 1988. *Songs of the Saints of India.* New York: Oxford University Press.

Hay, Stephen, ed. 1988. *Sources of Indian Tradition.* Vol. 2. New York: Columbia University Press.

Heesterman, Jan C. 1987. "Vedism and Brahmanism." In *Encyclopedia of Religion,* Mircea Eliade, ed. New York: Macmillan.

Johnston, Douglas, and Cynthia Sampson, eds. 1994. *Religion: The Missing Dimension of Statecraft.* New York: Oxford University Press.

Jones, Kenneth W. 1989. *Socio-religious Reform Movements in British India.* Cambridge: Cambridge University Press.

Juergensmeyer, Mark. 1993. *The New Cold War? Religious Nationalism Confronts the Secular State.* Berkeley: University of California Press.

Kabir. 1983. *The Bijak of Kabir.* Linda Hess and Shukdev Singh, trans. Berkeley: North Point Press.

Keyes, Charles F., and E. Valentine Daniel, eds. 1983. *Karma: An Anthropological Inquiry.* Berkeley: University of California Press.

Knipe, David. 1987. "Hindu Priesthood." In *Encyclopedia of Religion,* Mircea Eliade, ed. New York: Macmillan.

Kripal, Jeffrey J. 1994. *Kali's Child: The Mystical and Erotic in the Life and Teachings of Ramakrishna.* Chicago: University of Chicago Press.

Lelyveld, David. 1977. *Aligarh's First Generation: Muslim Solidarity and British Education in Northern India.* Princeton: Princeton University Press.

Lutgendorf, Philip. 1994. *The Life of a Text: Performing the Ramacaritmanasa of Tulsidas.* Delhi: Oxford University Press.

Lyall, Sir Alfred. 1889. *Asiatic Studies: Religious and Social.* London: John Murray.

Marty, Martin E., and R. Scott Appleby, eds. 1991. *Fundamentalisms Observed.* Chicago: University of Chicago Press.

———. 1994. *Accounting for Fundamentalisms.* Chicago: University of Chicago Press.

Metcalf, Barbara Daly. 1982. *Islamic Revival in British India: Deoband, 1860–1900.* Princeton: Princeton University Press.

———. 1994. "Remaking Ourselves: Islamic Self-Fashioning in a Global Movement of Spiritual Renewal." In *Accounting for Fundamentalisms,* Martin E. Marty and R. Scott Appleby, eds. Chicago: University of Chicago Press.

Mill, James. 1826. *The History of British India.* London: Baldwin.

National Council for History Education. 1996. "The Mystic Chords of Memory." *Ideas, Notes, and News About History* 9, no. 2.

Nehru, Jawaharlal. 1956. *The Discovery of India.* London: Meridian Books.

Qureshi, Ishtiaq Husain. 1989. *The Religion of Peace.* Karachi: Royal Book Company.

Raghavan, V. 1988. "Puranic Theism: The Way of Devotion." In *Sources of Indian Tradition,* vol. 1, Ainslie T. Embree, ed. New York: Columbia University Press.

Ramanujan, A. K. 1973. *Speaking of Shiva.* Baltimore: Penguin.

Roy, Rammohun. 1988. "A Letter on Education." In *Sources of Indian Tradition,* vol. 2, Stephen Hay, ed. New York: Columbia University Press.

Sarkar, Sumit. 1999. "Conversion and the Sangh Parivar." *The Hindu,* November 9.

Shourie, Arun. 1994. *Missionaries in India: Continuities, Changes, and Dilemmas.* New Delhi: West End.

Smith, Donald E. 1963. *India as a Secular State.* Princeton: Princeton University Press.

"Test of Faith." 2000. *India Today,* December 4, pp. 26–31.

Thapar, Romila. 1994. *Interpreting Early India.* Delhi: Oxford University Press.

Thursby, G. R. 1975. *Hindu-Muslim Relations in British India: A Study of Controversy, Conflict, and Communal Movements in Northern India, 1923–1928.* Leiden: E. J. Brill.

Twain, Mark. 1989. *Following the Equator.* New York: Dover.

11

Caste

Vibha Pinglé

The caste system is a socially comprehensive, hierarchical system that stratifies Indian society. Drawing on Hindu scriptures, the caste system has influenced social, economic, political, ritual, and religious aspects of life in India for centuries. India's minority religious communities, such as Christians, Buddhists, and Muslims, have also been influenced by the caste system. Further, many of these religious communities have absorbed certain features of the caste system as well.

In the years since independence in 1947, the role of the caste system in India's social, economic, political, and ritual spheres has changed considerably. Although caste influences the economic and social spheres to a lesser extent than it did in the nineteenth century and the inequalities of the caste system have been significantly reduced, its role in India's politics has become important in recent years. Thus, Indian social structure today is marked by two trends: a movement toward greater social equality and a movement toward the increasing incorporation of caste identities in politics. Since the caste system is built upon inequalities, how can these two seemingly contradictory trends be explained? In this chapter, I address this question and in the process discuss the changes in Indian society, the factors underlying them, and some of the implications of these changes.

The character of the caste system through history has been the subject of much debate. There are scholars who argue that the caste system has maintained its hierarchical structure throughout most of India's history. Louis Dumont has argued that the caste system is basically static

231

and observes that there is an "indifference to time, to happening, to history, in the Indian civilization" (Dumont 1980: 195). For Dumont, this timeless quality is a consequence of a peculiar Hindu worldview, which he terms *Homo Hierarchicus*. Other scholars suggest that the view that the caste system has existed unchanged in India is mistaken. C. A. Bayly, D. A. Washbrook, and N. B. Dirks propose that the caste system, though it existed in India as a scriptural worldview, was consolidated and made into a rigid hierarchical system primarily by colonial rule and institutions (Bayly 1988; Washbrook 1988; Dirks 1992). Irrespective of one's position on the history of the caste system, there is little doubt that the caste system today is dramatically different from that which existed in the second half of the nineteenth and the first half of the twentieth centuries.

■ The Caste System

The caste system consists of four broad castes, or *varnas*—Brahman, Kshatriya, Vaishya, and Shudra—and hundreds of subcastes, or *jatis*. *Varnas* are primordial social categories derived from the Hindu scriptures. A *jati* is an endogamous hereditary social status group with a specific name and social, ritual, and economic attributes attached to it. Although *varnas* offer a scheme for locating *jati* categories in the social structure, the *jatis* are, in effect, the basic identity groupings.

Each *varna* has a specific economic position assigned to it. The Brahmans were the priests and the scholars of the society (the highest status), the Kshatriyas were the warriors and the rulers, the Vaishyas were the businesspeople, and the Shudras provided the manual labor (the lowest of the four *varnas*). Below the Shudras, in the lowest of social positions, were the so-called Untouchables. Known today as the Dalits, this status group was assigned the most menial of occupations in society. Dalits can be differentiated into more than 1,091 *jatis,* and together they constitute about 16.5 percent of the total population.

Each of the four *varnas* and the Dalits were thus assigned a specific economic function in the overall system of agricultural and craft production. The Brahmans, Kshatriyas, and Vaishyas were usually the landowners; the Shudras were peasants and small artisans; and the Dalits were landless laborers who worked for the upper-caste landowners. The *jati* categories define a person's occupation more specifically. The Shudra *varna,* for instance, is divided into a number of *jatis* such as Toddy-tappers, Carpenters, Blacksmiths, Potters, and Barbers.

Traditionally, the various castes came together symbiotically to grow crops and produce other necessary goods and services. Landowners paid for the goods and services required for agriculture that are provided by the other *jatis* (Blacksmiths, Carpenters, Potters, Laborers, etc.) with grain and other agricultural produce. These economic relations were long-lasting and usually hereditary. As Edmund Leach has noted,

> Caste society as a whole is, in Durkheim's sense, an organic system with each particular case and subcaste filling a distinctive functional role. It is a system of labour division from which the element of competition . . . has been largely excluded. The more conventional sociological analysis which finds an analogy between castes, status groups, and economic classes puts all the stress upon hierarchy and upon the exclusiveness of caste separation. Far more fundamental is the economic interdependence which stems from the patterning of the division of labour which is of a quite special type. (Leach 1960: 5)

This pattern of patron-client relations is referred to as the *jajmani* system, and it ensured cooperation between members of different *jatis* in a village. The *jajmani* relations refer to the vertical ties uniting members of the various social and economic groups in a particular village.

The role of the *jajmani* system in bringing together the different *jatis* is particularly important since *jatis* are endogamous and culturally distinct status groups. Nowhere is the cultural distinctiveness of the various *jatis* more visible than in the realm of religion and religious ritual. The various *varnas* and even *jatis* are all assigned specialized ritual and social positions, which are demarcated by notions of religious purity and pollution, creating rules regulating marriage, reciprocal relations between castes (commensality), religious worship, and social interaction.

A Brahman of a particular *jati* traditionally married only members of his or her group, not just any Brahman. All the other *jatis* also followed identical rules regarding marriage. A person belonging to the Lohar (Blacksmith) *jati* married only someone from the same *jati;* a Kumbhar (Potter) married someone from the Kumbhar *jati;* and a Yadav (Cowherder) married only another Yadav. This practice, called "endogamy," in conjunction with the economic, ritual, and social distinctions discussed below, maintained the distinctive quality of the various *varnas* and *jatis* for centuries.

Varnas, and in some instances even *jatis,* followed strict rules regarding commensality. Members of the various *jatis* would eat only with someone from their own or a higher *jati.* Traditionally, a Brahman would not eat with a member of the lower castes and would not eat food cooked (or even touched) by anyone other than a Brahman. Similar rules were followed by other *jatis* as well. In his analysis of a religious festival at the temple of Rama in the village of Rampura during the 1970s, M. N. Srinivas observed that the Brahmans were the temple priests; the Shudras cooked the sacred temple meal that was fed to people attending the festival; and the Dalits ran errands, cleaned the rice for the meal, beat the drums, and did the cleaning after the meal.[1] At religious feasts, the different castes ate separately. The Brahmans did not eat the meal prepared by the Shudras but were given only raw materials since their caste rules did not allow them to eat food cooked by a lower-caste person.

To take another example, at the funeral of an upper-caste person in some regions, members of the various caste groups performed specific ritual tasks: a Brahman officiated as the priest at the funeral pyre, a Shudra was assigned the task of cleaning the body, and the Dalits were the ones who cleaned up after the funeral. These tasks were a function of the extent to which each group was regarded as ritually pure or polluted. The Brahmans were the purest in ritual and social terms, the Shudras were the least pure of the four *varnas,* and the Dalits were regarded as being so ritually impure that they were untouchable. Such a ritual-social division of labor was present not only at funerals and religious festivals but at all social events. Social interaction between the various caste was thus defined by caste rules.

Members of the lower *jatis* and Dalit *jatis* were not allowed into many Hindu temples. In nearly all villages, each caste had its own well from which the caste members drew water. The lower castes and Dalits were not permitted to use the upper castes' wells and were often not allowed anywhere near the Brahman wells, for fear that their presence would "pollute" them. The various *jatis* also lived in separate parts of each village. In some regions, members of some low *jatis* were not allowed to walk on certain streets, and in yet other regions, upper-caste members regarded even the shadow of certain low *jatis* across their path as polluting. The fear of "pollution" and the search for "purity" guided almost all forms of social interaction in the village.

These ritual-social rules of the caste system were maintained not by legal sanctions but with the help of religious sanctions, economic threats, and on many an occasion physical force. Indeed, the social rules of caste were maintained even when the economic rules were not. For example, only a small percentage of Brahmans were priests, and not all cowherds were engaged in their traditional occupation. Traditionally, the flexibility regarding occupations was limited: a person belonging to the Shudra caste whose traditional occupation was tanning could work as a blacksmith but definitely not as a priest in a Brahman temple. Despite this limited flexibility in occupational caste rules, caste rules regarding social interaction and religious rituals were strictly maintained. A man belonging to the toddy-tapper *jati* (Nadar), for instance, was not allowed to enter major Hindu temples, even when he worked as a tradesman or businessman and not as a toddy-tapper. In other words, the polluting quality of his traditional caste occupation outweighed his involvement in the occupation itself.

For the most part, India's religious minorities have divided themselves into *jatis* and relate to the caste system as such. At the time of the most recent census in 1991, India's population was 846 million: 82 percent of the total population were Hindu, 12.12 percent Muslim, 2.34 percent Christian, 1.94 percent Sikh, 0.76 percent Buddhists, and 0.40 percent Jains. The social relations of Muslims in rural areas tend to mirror the relations of their Hindu counterparts. They have generally been treated in their villages as if they were a separate *jati*. Their participation in social events in the village or even in everyday social interaction, has thus been similar to that of Hindu *jatis*. Muslims generally tended to occupy a low position in the village's caste hierarchy and hence have normally been the target of considerable social restrictions. The precise position of the Muslim population in a village hierarchy varies from region to region and even from village to village. In most villages, however, upper castes have usually regarded them as "polluted" castes.

The Muslim population, like the Hindu population, is also internally divided into endogamous hereditary groups, which are placed in an intra-Muslim social status hierarchy. Each endogamous group is assigned a specific occupation and is traditionally linked to other Muslim groups and Hindu *jatis* in the village via *jajmani* relations. Unlike the Hindu caste system, however, the Muslim hierarchy is relatively looser. Rules regarding commensality and endogamy are more flexible in the Muslim community. In the Hindu community, rules of worship prevent certain *jatis* from entering the temple, whereas in the Muslim community, Muslims of all occupations and status worship in the same mosques (Mandelbaum 1972: 546).

Jati-like groups exist among Indian Christians as well. The first Christians, believed to have reached the southern shores of India in the first century C.E., are known as Syrian Christians. Most of them have traditionally been businesspeople or were employed as public servants. These occupations placed them in a status position considerably higher than that of artisans and laborers but below that of the priests. Economically prosperous Syrian Christians gradually became large landlords. Like the Muslims in India, the Syrian Christians also divided themselves internally into endogamous hierarchically placed groups. And as David Mandelbaum observes, their "way of life, except for religious practice, was not totally different from that of their [Hindu] neighbors of similar rank and occupation" (Mandelbaum 1972: 565).

Christianity was also brought to India during the colonial period via missionaries. Most of the Hindus who were converted to Christianity by the missionaries were from the lower castes. Most carried their prior *jati* ranking even after conversion. As a result, they have been incorporated into the caste system as lower- and, in some regions, middle-level *jatis*. Some, like the Nadars, however, have been relatively successful at hastening the pace of their social and economic mobility after converting to Christianity.

Two other religious groups in India, Jains and Sikhs, have been similarly incorporated within the caste system and have also absorbed aspects of the caste system into their communities to varying degrees. Jainism, one of India's oldest indigenous religions, emerged around 500 B.C.E. and is guided by the principles of nonviolence and social equality (relative to Hinduism). However, as Mandelbaum observes, "that social vision has yet to be realized among modern Jains. More than any other sect they have divided themselves into numerous jatis. A 1914 directory of one branch of Jains listed 87 jatis" (1972: 535). Most Jains are traders and businesspeople: the Jain community is internally divided into status groups based on the specific kind of trade or business in which a member engages. In south India, Jains are divided into four status groups. As in the Hindu community, the highest status group is that of the priests. As in the Christian and Muslim communities, rules regarding commensality and endogamy among the Jains are also much more flexible than those in the majority Hindu population.

Sikhism was founded in north India about 500 years ago, partly in response to the hierarchical nature of Hindu society. Like Christianity and Islam, Sikhism too has absorbed and been absorbed by the caste system. The *jatis* among the Sikhs include the highest, that of the Jats (who are primarily landowners), and various *jatis* of artisans, laborers, potters, and washermen. At the bottom of the Sikh hierarchy are the Mazhabi Sikhs, who perform the most menial tasks in the village. Although members of different Sikh *jatis* traditionally dine together and worship in the same Gurudwaras (place of worship), the *jatis* have tended to be endogamous.

In addition to religious minorities, about 8.1 percent of the Indian population has been classified as "tribal." Tribal groups are widely regarded as the original inhabitants of the Indian subcontinent. Traditionally living in remote hilly areas in central, west, and northeast India, tribal groups are among the poorest social groups in the country.[2] The tribal population is very diverse and ranges from groups that are small, numbering no more than a few thousand members, to groups with millions of members.

The traditional occupations of most tribal groups are hunting, gathering, and slash-and-burn agriculture. These tribal groups lie outside the caste system. First, in contrast to the *jatis,* the division of labor within the tribal group is low. The entire tribal group is traditionally more or less self-sufficient and is usually not involved in *jajmani* relations with members of other *jatis.* This characteristic, in particular, distinguishes them from *jatis* in the Hindu community. Second, unlike *jatis,* tribal groups see their fellow members as their kin. Interpersonal relations within the tribal group are egalitarian, in contrast to interpersonal relations within any *varna,* for example. Third, the religious practices of the tribal groups are less specialized than and often not significantly influenced by Hinduism. Anthropological accounts suggest that the religion followed by tribal groups is even more distant from scriptural Hinduism than the religion practiced by lower castes, the latter being less scriptural than that followed by the upper castes. And where certain features of Hinduism have been absorbed by a tribal group, they have tended not to replace their tribal religious beliefs.

■ Recent Changes in Indian Society

The transformation of the caste system described at the beginning of the chapter has been particularly rapid since India's independence in 1947. The very foundations of the caste system have been shaken. The Indian economy is no longer the village-based craft and agricultural economy it used to be a century ago. It is now an increasingly industrial economy that is integrated into the world system. Although the pace of Indian industrial development has been substantially below expectations, it is clear that industrial development has been widespread and significant enough to have eroded the traditional Indian village-based economic structure.

Modernization of the Indian economy has enabled members of
most castes to seek and find employment outside their traditional caste
occupation. New jobs in the manufacturing industry, service industry,
and bureaucracy have attracted members of virtually all castes. It is
easier than ever before for a person belonging to the lower castes to
find a job outside his or her traditionally assigned occupation. More
and more, Yadavs today are moving out of their traditional caste occupation of cowherding; and increasingly Chamars are not working as
cobblers. A growing number of lower-caste members and Dalits work
in modern occupations. The three upper castes—Brahmans, Kshatriyas,
and Vaishyas—no longer have the monopoly over these jobs that they
used to have. Because of economic development, the traditional link
between caste and occupation is being eroded. The material basis of the
caste system is gradually being undermined, and *jajmani* ties have
weakened. The *jajmani* system, where it exists today, regulates the
rural and agricultural economy, not the growing industrial and urban
economy.

A related factor that has contributed to the decline of the *jajmani*
system is urbanization. A predominantly rural society, India has undergone a profound transformation since independence with the rise of
metropolitan areas. According to the 1991 census, a little over one-
quarter of India's population lived in urban areas. At the time of independence, by contrast, only 12 percent of the population was urban.

Rural-urban migration has offered all castes the chance to break
free of the economic restrictions placed upon them by the caste structure in rural areas. Yadavs moving to a large metropolis or even to a
small town are unlikely to practice their traditional occupation of
cowherding. Although they still remain members of the Yadav caste
and may retain their Yadav identity, they do not relate to the Brahmans
who live next to them in the same way they might if both lived in the
same village and engaged in their traditional occupations.

In addition to economic development and urbanization, affirmative
action policies have also played a critical role in weakening the link
between the caste system and economic structure. Since independence,
the Indian government has implemented an affirmative action program
for Dalits, Shudras, and tribal groups. Affirmative action policies,
known in India as reservation policies, reserve a certain percentage of
government jobs for members of these castes. In addition, colleges and
universities are required to accept a certain number of lower-caste,
tribal, and Dalit students every year. In some Indian states, the percentage of university spots reserved for Dalits, Shudras, and tribal groups

is as high as 75 percent. Thus, economic development and urbanization have enticed members of the lower castes and Dalits to switch to occupations in the modern industrial economy, and affirmative action policies have offered lower-caste members an instrument by which to gain an entry into these nontraditional professions.

The political strength of the lower castes and Dalits is one reason that affirmative action policies in favor of the lower castes have been adopted and also expanded over time in India. Numbering more than 600 million, the lower castes, Dalits, and tribal groups together constituted two-thirds of the population in 2000. Using universal franchise as their political weapon, they are increasingly well organized, and consequently their electoral strength has been considerable in recent years. The upper castes, by contrast, make up only about 18 percent of the population. Not surprisingly, nearly all of India's political parties, including all large national parties (i.e., the Congress Party, the Janata family of parties, the Bharatiya Janata Party, and the Communist parties), support affirmative action policies for the lower castes.

Democracy has broken the traditional hegemony of the upper castes over politics. This process occurred in a number of stages. During the first stage, the Congress Party, the party that led the independence movement, maintained its position as India's leading party. The Congress Party's leadership was initially dominated by upper-caste and westernized politicians. The party's political strategy involved combining the lower-caste vote and the support of religious minorities and drew on the symbiotic relations between the castes to retain its power (Weiner 1962, 1967). The political arena was thus in the grasp of the entrenched upper castes.

In the second stage, the upper-caste politicians' use of traditional *jajmani* relations to garner electoral support gradually led to the emergence of an "ascendant" or "dominant" caste.[3] The economically and socially powerful *jatis* from among the lower (Shudra) castes began to resent the domination of the western-educated upper-caste politicians and to challenge the political system. These dominant castes (or powerful Shudra *jatis*) varied according to village, district and state. Political struggles between the upper castes and dominant castes gave rise to what Rajni Kothari refers to as "a bilateral structure of caste politics" (Kothari 1970: 14).

Leadership struggles and factional politics gave rise to multicaste political alignments. The competition for electoral support led factional leaders to seek the support of lower-caste community leaders. Political alliances thus became more complex, patronage grew, and its sphere expanded to include disadvantaged rural castes. Lower-caste leaders began to get an entrée into the electoral arena. The support of the lower-caste leaders could no longer be assumed by the upper castes but had to be worked for. The workings of the democratic system thus led upper-caste politicians to mobilize lower-caste leaders on a large scale—something their ancestors a few generations ago would not have considered.

This process came to be known as vertical mobilization. The lower-caste leaders who had been co-opted by upper-caste politicians had only limited power; they remained dependent upon the political needs and interests of these leaders. Nevertheless, a small lower-caste leadership emerged, especially among the dominant *jatis.*

There is another process of lower-caste mobilization that also resulted from democratic politics. It is referred to as horizontal mobilization, for it relies instead on leadership emerging within the lower castes (Rudolph and Rudolph 1967). Horizontal mobilization of the lower castes and Dalits occurred first in India's southern states (such as Tamil Nadu, Karnataka, Andhra Pradesh) and has recently emerged in the northern states (Bihar, Uttar Pradesh) as well. As a consequence, the Congress Party, which relied heavily on vertical mobilization, lost the lower-caste vote in the southern states in the 1960s and then in the northern states during the 1980s and 1990s.

In villages all over India, the hegemonic power of the upper-caste political leaders over the lower castes has declined. No longer can the village upper castes, or even the dominant castes, take for granted their control over local politics. They cannot always count on the election of their fellow caste members to governing bodies anymore. The lower castes and Dalits have gradually slipped away from the political and social grasp of the upper castes. Members of the Shudra *jatis* and even the Dalit *jatis* can today not only migrate to urban areas and find non-traditional jobs but also, thanks to a deepening of democratic politics, more successfully resist the domination of the upper-caste landlord, village priest, moneylender, and storekeeper, even if they stay on in their villages.

The entry of the dominant castes into the political arena paved the way for the entry of the Dalits. Periodic elections had by then gradually familiarized even the Dalits with the logic of democratic politics and strategy. Affirmative action policies had also begun to have an impact on the socioeconomic position of the most disadvantaged of castes. With greater access to schools and colleges, Dalits are growing increasingly resentful of the continued discrimination they face and are becoming conscious of the limited opportunities available to them in independent India. This realization is increasingly leading the Dalits to mobilize their fellow caste members into political parties. As a result, national parties such as the Congress Party can no longer take the support of even the Dalits for granted.

What has enabled the lower castes and Dalits to mobilize politically was the horizontal expansion of caste associations. Elaborating on the role that caste associations have played in modern Indian society, Lloyd and Susanne Rudolph observe that caste associations have, first, enabled "lower castes to establish the basis of self-esteem under circumstances in which they have begun to feel the inferiority rather than the necessity of their condition and to win social esteem, first from the state, then from the macrosociety, and last and most slowly from the microsociety of village and locality" (Rudolph and Rudolph 1967: 62–63). Caste associations have successfully done this by enabling the lower castes (and Dalits) to adopt the practices and norms and thus the social status of the upper castes. The Rudolphs observe that, as a result, the lower castes (and Dalits) have not only uplifted themselves but also have reduced the extent of social hierarchy in the society as a whole.

Caste associations have also helped in the establishment and maintenance of political democracy in India by mobilizing "similar but dispersed and isolated jatis of village and locality in horizontal organizations with common identities" (Rudolph and Rudolph 1967: 63–64). The electoral strength and political clout of the lower castes and Dalits grew substantially once they were mobilized.

The political and social rise of lower castes and Dalits has also been supported by political parties, both before and after independence. One of the stated goals of the leading parties during the nationalist movement was the abolition of the evils of the caste system. By this statement, they meant the elimination of caste restrictions and discriminatory practices. Much of this argument was rooted in the philosophy of Mahatma Gandhi and emphasized the unjust practices of the caste system and the need to create a more just society. Gandhi had proposed a new name for the Untouchables—Harijan (or the children of God).

Although his methods and strategies for eliminating untouchability have been critiqued by many political leaders and thinkers on the left and on the right, Gandhi's emphasis on the need to eliminate untouchability was absorbed into India's political and popular culture to the extent that it is difficult to find Indians who will today publicly speak in positive terms about untouchability or the injustices of the caste system. Andre Beteille has observed that "anyone who speaks against equality in public is bound to lose his audience" (Beteille 1991: 206).

Thus this ideological climate more or less eliminated the *old* caste-based discourse and arguments justifying inequality in the caste system, but it has led to the emergence of a discourse that pays lip service to caste equality while emphasizing caste distinctiveness. As C. J. Fuller notes, because "people cannot openly speak of castes as unequal, they describe them as [culturally] different" (Fuller 1997: 13). The lower castes and Dalits have increasingly adopted this view in their search for political and social power. The most ardent supporters of caste-based affirmative action policies are thus also the strongest critics of caste as a hierarchical system (Beteille 1997: 169).

The views of Bhimrao Ramji Ambedkar, called "Babasaheb" by his followers, have been especially important in raising social consciousness and self-esteem among the Dalits. Born a Dalit, Ambedkar went on to head India's Constituent Assembly, which wrote the nation's constitution. As mentioned in the previous chapter, Ambedkar converted to Buddhism and led large numbers of Dalits in his home state of Maharashtra to convert as well. For him, Gandhi's attempt at reforming the caste system was inadequate. Believing that the caste system could not be reformed and had to be eliminated entirely, Ambedkar argued for Dalit empowerment and consciousness raising so that the Dalits could overthrow the oppressive caste system.

Ambedkar's influence was first felt in Maharashtra, but of late, it has spread to north India as well. His ideology has helped bring rural Dalits together to form social and political associations. Festivals and social events celebrating Ambedkar's memory serve to cement intra-Dalit ties in villages. Moreover, affirmative action has enabled the rise of middle-class and professional Dalits. These Dalits are more aware of Ambedkar's views than the previous generation of Dalits and work to spread them among the poorer members of their community (Singh 1998: 2611–2618). In a study of Dalit political parties, Kanchan Chandra argues that these middle-class Dalits are now at the helm of Dalit political parties (Chandra 1998).

The three specific cases discussed below illustrate how the general process of change outlined above has unfolded. The first case examines social mobility among the Nadars. Because they were toddy-tappers, the Nadars were traditionally assigned a low position in the caste system. They have been successful at using caste associations to alter their traditional social status. The second case—that of the non-Brahman movement in Tamil Nadu—explores how democracy has enabled the lower castes to improve their social and political position. Third, changes in the relationship of the urban upper castes to the caste system are explored, and the implications of this new relationship for the caste system as a whole are discussed.

■ The Nadars and Caste Associations

The Nadars, known traditionally as the Shanans, were placed in the caste hierarchy somewhere between the Shudras and the Dalits. Their traditional occupation of toddy-tapping was considered polluting. As a result, Nadars were prevented from entering Hindu temples and forbidden to use upper-caste wells, carry an umbrella, wear shoes or gold jewelry, milk cows, and walk on specific village streets. Indeed, the social discrimination faced by the Nadars was so severe that they were required to get no closer to a Brahman than twenty-four paces (Hardgrave 1970: 105).

It is remarkable to observe the status of the community today. The Nadars have overcome all of the egregious social restrictions and ritual barriers noted above. They are no longer viewed as a polluting caste and have succeeded economically as well. The *jati* now includes some of the leading businesspeople, both of the southern region and the nation as a whole. They have also successfully asserted their power in the political arena.

Historical analyses suggest that this success is a result of social and political mobilization within the community and, in particular, of the influential role of the community association. The Nadar caste

> has transformed itself by creating new units of consciousness, organization and action. Today, by successfully changing their caste culture and having this change recognized by the state and by Madras society, the Nadars, like other castes which have participated in similar processes, occupy a new and higher place in a changed social order. (Rudolph and Rudolph 1967: 32–33)[4]

In the nineteenth century, the opening up of the economy during colonial rule had a dramatic effect on the Nadars. British rule helped to establish peace among the warring landlords in the region and improved roads. The Nadars traveled to local villages and town markets to sell their wares (toddy and jaggery, an unrefined brown sugar made from palm sap). With greater security, the Nadars began to trade across a wider area. They set up shops in regional towns, and Nadar families gradually migrated to these commercial areas.

The arrival of Christian missionaries during British rule also helped in transforming the Nadar community. Influenced by the Christian missionaries, many Nadars converted to Christianity, and many more took advantage of the schools established by the missionaries. Though Nadars continued to work as toddy-tappers, a significant number, helped by the Christian missionaries, began to acquire small parcels of land and engaged in cultivation. Education and the rise of successful Nadar businesses and landlords gave the community an increasing sense of self-respect, as well as a consciousness of the need to improve the social position of the community.

The Nadar Mahajan Sangam (Great Nadar Association) was formed to promote the interests of the Nadar community, meeting first in 1910 and again in 1917. Its general objectives included the promotion of the social and material welfare of the Nadar community and the protection of the rights and interests of the community, and its specific objectives included the establishment of (western-style) educational institutions, the provision of educational scholarships for economically disadvantaged Nadars, and the promotion of Nadar commerce and business. To meet its general objectives, the Nadar Mahajan Sangam pushed for official recognition of the community name of Nadar in place of the name Shanan and also the recognition of the community's Kshatriya (the warrior upper caste) status. The 1921 census was the first to record the name change to Nadar. The Nadar community association set up libraries and Nadar schools and colleges for men and women. It also established a cooperative bank that helped Nadars set up industries and other businesses.

Although members of the community in rural areas are still engaged in the traditional occupation of toddy-tapping, Nadars as a community "breached the pollution barrier, changed [its] rank within traditional society, and [came to] occupy an important place in the modern society of Madras and India" by the mid–twentieth century (Rudolph and Rudolph 1967: 44). Their successful political and social mobilization thus placed them on solid ground to pursue their political interests in a democratic India after independence.

■ Democracy and the Non-Brahman Movement in Tamil Nadu

If the caste association proved critical for the social mobility of the Nadars, democratic politics and universal franchise were the cornerstone of the successful non-Brahman movement that emerged in the southern Indian state of Tamil Nadu in 1916. Supported by the various non-Brahman castes and led by the dominant non-Brahman castes, the movement was very successful in hastening the pace of social and political mobility of the non-Brahman castes.[5]

Tamil society can be divided into three broad caste categories: Brahman, non-Brahman, and Dalit (or "Adi-Dravidas," as they are known in Tamil Nadu). Despite comprising only 3 percent of the total Tamil population, the Brahmans were active in politics and dominated local politics in Tamil Nadu (then known as the Madras Presidency) until the 1920s. Brahmans also dominated the professional and bureaucratic strata. Many of them were landowners, and as they started migrating to towns and cities in search of professional work, they became absentee landlords. The prevalence of western-style education among the Tamil Brahmans and their consequent entry in significant numbers into professional jobs exacerbated the social distance between them and the non-Brahman Tamil population and led to increasing resentment.

The non-Brahman movement was spearheaded initially by the Justice Party. Formed in 1916–1917, the leadership of the Justice Party consisted of urban-based prominent members of the non-Brahman dominant castes of the Madras Presidency. Most of the leaders came from the financially prosperous though ritually low castes of Chetty, Nair, and Mudaliar. As Robert Hardgrave observes, though these leaders professed to speak on behalf of the illiterate masses, they clearly did not represent them (Hardgrave 1965: 16). They were socially "low" but economically upwardly mobile.

During the 1920s and 1930s, the Justice Party had only limited success in improving the lot of the non-Brahman masses. Only with the introduction of universal franchise following independence did the non-Brahman movement become truly successful. The Justice Party nevertheless had prepared the ground for the entry of the non-Brahman community into the political arena.

The Justice Party was succeeded by the Self-Respect Movement and the Backward Classes League. The Self-Respect Movement claimed that the Justice Party was not adequately critical of the caste system. By 1944, the Self-Respect Movement merged with the Justice Party to form the Dravida Kazhagam (DK). The DK's stance against Brahman domination was more militant. The party demanded not merely the reform of the caste system but also the formation of a separate state without Brahman domination. After independence, the DK split to form the Dravida Munnetra Kazhagam (DMK).

The other major political party in Tamil Nadu was the all-India party, the Indian National Congress. The local branch of the Congress Party during the 1950s was headed by Kamaraj, a Nadar. Of course, leadership by a lower-caste person increased the appeal of the Congress

Party among the non-Brahman castes and especially within the Nadar community. Partly as a result of this competition, the DMK was compelled to look for ways to expand its appeal and came increasingly to identify its message of anti-Brahmanism and of social uplift with a promise to protect the poor. The DMK later divided into the DMK and the All-India Anna Dravida Munnetra Kazhagam (AIADMK). The AIADMK, which was in power in Tamil Nadu during various years in the 1980s and 1990s, instituted a large number of welfare policies aimed at the poor, especially poor women.

Thus, by the late 1970s, all the major political parties in Tamil Nadu claimed to represent the non-Brahman community and increasingly the "illiterate masses," a substantial number of whom were Adi-Dravidas. The anti-Brahman rhetoric and ideology has, consequently, died down since the 1940s and 1950s. The political struggle in Tamil Nadu is no longer between the Brahmans and the non-Brahmans but between the now politically powerful and competing non-Brahman castes, and increasingly the Adi-Dravidas and other non-Brahman dominant castes.

The non-Brahman leadership, in large measure, has ignored the interests of the Adi-Dravidas. The leadership of the Justice Party, the DK, DMK, and the AIADMK have all been dominated by non-Brahmans from the relatively successful non-Brahman dominant castes. Many are landowners who have exploited the Adi-Dravida agricultural laborers working on their lands just as the Brahman landowners did. Thus, although the non-Brahman movement successfully took on Brahmanism, it has tackled the interests of the Adi-Dravidas to a considerably lesser extent.

Change, however, is coming. Constitutional guarantees and new national laws promoting equality have increasingly made the Adi-Dravidas conscious of the social restrictions placed upon them, not just by the Brahmans but also by the economically prosperous and relatively socially advantaged non-Brahman castes. Adi-Dravidas are increasingly assertive in the political arena. As a result, there has been growing social and political conflict between the upper ranks of the non-Brahman castes and the Adi-Dravidas.

■ The Urban Upper Castes

If the social, political, and economic status of the lower castes and Dalits has changed considerably since the early twentieth century, then that of the upper castes has also been radically altered. The lower castes have indeed succeeded in leveling the ritual, social, and political playing fields to a significant extent, but it should also be noted that the entire caste system has been modified and the meaning of caste for the upper castes has changed as well.

Urban upper castes have been greatly influenced by western lifestyles. Adopting these practices has meant giving up a number of traditional caste-based rituals and behavior patterns regarding commensality and social interaction. Having a meal or a snack in a U.S.-style fast-food eatery or an up-market restaurant, for instance, is a fashionable thing to do for upper castes in the middle or upper middle classes. Doing so, however, requires giving up caste-based rituals and concerns about not eating with members of lower or Dalit castes or not eating food prepared by lower castes or Dalits. Laws against discrimination based on caste and religion and the difficulty of identifying a person's caste by his or her physical features make it impossible to judge the caste of the person sitting nearby in a restaurant, the chef, or his or her aides.

It is relatively easy for a person from a village to identify the caste of his or her fellow villagers by noting their traditional dress style, last names, and occupations. That is no longer possible in urban areas, where most men wear western-style clothes, women follow the dress style of the latest Indian film stars, and occupational mobility is increasingly easy. In addition, name does not always provide a clue to caste anymore since in urban areas, hundreds, if not thousands, of *jatis* coexist. An urban upper-caste person is likely to be conversant with *jati* names from his or her specific region, not from the entire country. All this makes it increasingly difficult, though not impossible, for people to discriminate on the basis of caste in the workplace or in the public space. Occupational mobility and modern lifestyles have put a damper on caste-based rituals and beliefs regarding commensality and social interaction more generally in urban areas.

If the caste system encouraged Brahmans to become priests, scholars, lawyers, doctors, engineers, or bureaucrats in the twentieth century, changes in modern India have altered this familiar professional route. Faced with affirmative action policies that benefited the lower castes and Dalits and restricted their ability to enter professional schools and occupations (especially in the state bureaucracy), Brahmans, who were traditionally discouraged from the business arena for ritual reasons, are opening businesses and industries, especially in urban areas. Until the mid–twentieth century, a Brahman who opened a leather factory was considered iconoclastic. Engaging in business was considered demeaning for a Brahman, and being involved in as polluting a product as leather was not easily accepted by the upper castes. Today, few young urban upper-caste members would even recognize that working with leather was considered polluting. Notions of pollution in work are changing.

In addition to changes in caste-based restrictions on occupational choice and on patterns of intercaste social interaction, rules regarding endogamy have changed as well. Until a few decades ago, a Brahman of a particular *jati* would have married only a Brahman of the same *jati*. Today, the endogamous group is widening to include neighboring *jatis* and *varnas*. Increasingly for the urban upper castes, the endogamous circle is defined more by a combination of class and caste (understood more in terms of *varna* than *jati*) than by caste alone.

Caste rules play a significant role in one other area of Indian life: rituals and religious ceremonies. The religious beliefs and ceremonies of urban upper castes remain governed by caste-based ritual rules. Members of different upper-caste *jatis* continue to retain their traditionally practiced rituals in religious ceremonies. The marriage ceremony of two Brahmans (even if they belong to different Brahman *jatis*) from a specific region is quite unlike the marriage ceremony of two Vaishyas from the same region. The manner in which the various upper castes celebrate Hindu religious festivals also varies. These variations are still largely maintained.

Thus, though caste-based ritual and religious differences are retained in urban areas, the urban environment has loosened caste-based social and economic rules and restrictions, not just for the urban upper castes but also for the urban lower castes and urban Dalits. One's *jati* defined one's lifestyle and worldview traditionally. But by the late 1990s, in urban India, one's lifestyle and worldview were influenced less by one's *jati* and more by one's income and class status, education, school, and occupation. In a recent survey, lower-caste, Dalit, upper-caste, and middle-caste members belonging to the middle class appeared to share social views more with each other than with lower-class members of their specific *jati* (Sheth 2000).

In short, for the vast majority of upper-caste members in urban areas, caste has come to play an increasingly limited role in the social sphere. It has a somewhat greater role in their personal lives: in decisions about whom they marry, and in their religious ceremonies.

■ Caste, Class, and Affirmative Action in India

The lower castes have used affirmative action policies and their increased political power to establish a significant presence in the middle class. In the mid-1970s, the middle class was composed almost exclusively of the three upper castes (Brahmans, Kshatriyas, and Vaishyas). Today, economically successful members of the lower castes, especially the dominant castes, are included in the middle class. Surveys indicate that despite consisting of almost two-thirds of the population, Dalits, tribal groups, lower castes, and religious minorities make up only about half of the middle class (Sheth 2000). Though the lower castes, Dalits, and tribals are not proportionately represented in the middle and upper class, their increasing presence in the middle class shows the distance covered during the twentieth century.

Affirmative action policies were introduced as early as 1870 in parts of south India. The princely state of Mysore was one of the first to adopt affirmative action policies favoring the backward castes. These policies spread throughout south India by 1920. North India, by contrast, introduced affirmative action policies only after independence. That south Indian lower castes and Dalits, who according to most historical accounts faced more egregious discrimination than their counterparts in the north, have risen—politically, socially, and economically—higher than north Indian lower castes and Dalits has been interpreted as evidence in favor of affirmative action.

However, despite their growing presence in the middle class and despite affirmative action policies, the socioeconomic conditions of the vast majority of the Dalits and the tribal population remain poor. They dominate the 36 percent of the Indian population that is below the poverty line. In India as a whole, a large proportion of Dalits and tribals are illiterate. Caste discrimination (especially in rural areas) and bureaucratic inefficiencies have ensured that the Indian government has done a rather dismal job of spreading literacy and providing basic social services, to the rural poor in particular (Dreze and Sen 1997; Weiner 1992). In 1991, only 52.3 percent of India's total population was literate; 37.4 percent of the Dalit population was literate, and this figure dropped down to 29.6 percent for the tribal population (Bose 1996: 99). If the statistics are disaggregated by state, there is a correlation between the states that had affirmative action policies for longer periods and had lower-caste parties in power since the 1950s and 1960s and the states that had relatively higher Dalit literacy rates. In fact, in

these states Dalit literacy rates were higher than the national average.
States where affirmative action did not have a long history and where
lower-caste and Dalit parties had only recently come to power had dismal Dalit literacy rates. In Bihar, for instance, where anti-Dalit sentiment runs high among the upper and the dominant castes, only 19.48
percent of all Dalits and 7.07 percent of Dalit women were literate
(Bose 1996).

■ Conclusion

This analysis of the changes in the caste system leads to a number
of conclusions about Indian society today. First, the traditional economic basis of the caste system has been deeply eroded. Economic and
industrial development has opened up new avenues for employment
and undermined the traditional *jajmani* relations. Occupational mobility is increasingly possible. Affirmative action has also increased
opportunities for the lower castes. Second, the logic of the democratic
system has weakened the power of the upper castes, made them
increasingly sensitive to demands from below, and provided not only
the dominant lower castes but also the Dalits with an entry into the
political arena. Nowhere has this been more visible than in the state-
level politics of Tamil Nadu. In addition, Dalits in the northern states
have begun to mobilize and organize in recent years.

The changes at the social level have been particularly dramatic in
urban areas. Social restrictions imposed by the caste system have substantially eroded. In Indian cities, rules regarding commensality are
ignored by members of nearly all castes, and rules regarding endogamy
have also weakened. Even in rural areas, endogamous groups are
expanding. But in urban areas, members of various *jatis* are likely to
marry not only members of their own *jatis* but also members of neighboring *jatis*. Caste-based restrictions concerning occupations have been
lost in the rush toward adopting a middle-class lifestyle. However, religious rituals continue to follow age-old norms. This tendency among
the urban middle class to be selective in retention of the caste system
has led scholars to argue that caste exists not as a complete system but
as a truncated one (Beteille 1997: 161). Sheth argues that castes continue to exist, but as sociocultural entities detached from the traditional
hierarchy of ritual statuses (Sheth 2000).

Thus caste identities remain strong, though not in the manner they
used to be a century or more ago. Caste has increasingly contributed to

people's political identities; lower castes have risen politically by using their caste identities. The relative success of affirmative action and the rise of Dalits and of the dominant lower castes have led to tension and frequently to violent clashes between them and the upper castes and between the dominant castes and the Dalits. In the southern states, the intercaste tension primarily takes the form of conflict between the successful lower-caste dominant *jatis* and the Dalits. In the northern states, where lower castes have risen to power only in recent years, the conflict tends to be between the upper castes and lower castes.

The rise of the Dalits and lower castes has direct implications for their status in the village and for the social structure of the village. Dalits and lower castes no longer accept easily demands placed upon them by the upper and dominant castes. Moreover, urban upper castes have been enticed by western values and modern lifestyles to give up their caste-based restrictions. The rural upper castes are finally being forced by the more powerful Dalits and lower castes to give up similar caste-based restrictions.

Traditionally, the caste system meant ritual purity, social power, and privileges for the upper castes. For the lower castes and Dalits, it implied gross social restrictions and a life of servitude. Today, for the former, the caste system shapes their marriage patterns, though to a declining extent, and provides only a set of inherited rituals and social customs that are increasingly dissociated from the caste system. For the lower castes and Dalits, caste is an instrument of social mobility. For this reason, a number of lower castes, even those who have succeeded socially, economically, and politically, choose to retain their caste identity or at least view their caste identity instrumentally. If *jati* is becoming increasingly irrelevant for the urban upper castes, it remains a powerful tool for achieving social, economic, and political power for the lower castes. Consequently, although politics increasingly draws on caste identities and uses a caste-based rhetoric, there is a leveling of Indian society in terms of social status and access to political power.

■ Notes

1. The Muslims in the village also participated in the festival: they were assigned the task of lighting the fireworks (Srinivas 1996: 29).

2. A handful of small tribal groups also live in south India.

3. Dominant castes are castes that (in a specific region) have a relatively high socioeconomic status despite having a low Shudra ritual status. Dominant castes include the Reddys, Marathas, Nairs, and Patels.

4. For a detailed discussion of the Nadar experience, see Hardgrave 1968, 1970.

5. For a detailed analysis of the non-Brahman movement in Tamil Nadu, see Hardgrave 1968; Swamy 1997; and Beteille 1991.

■ Bibliography

Bayly, C. A. 1988. *Indian Society and the Making of the British Empire.* Cambridge: Cambridge University Press.

Beteille, Andre. 1991. *Society and Politics in India: Essays in a Comparative Perspective.* London: Athlone Press.

———. 1997. *Caste in Contemporary India.* In *Caste Today*, C. J. Fuller, ed. Oxford: Oxford University Press.

Bose, Ashish. 1996. *India's Basic Demographic Statistics.* Delhi: B. R. Publishing.

Chandra, Kanchan. 1998. "The Transformation of Ethnic Politics in India: The Decline of Congress and the Rise of the Bahujan Samaj Party in Hoshiarpur." Paper presented at the meetings of the Association for Asian Studies, Washington, D.C.

Dirks, N. B. 1992. "Castes of Mind." *Representations* 37: 56–78.

Dreze, Jean, and Amartya Sen. 1997. *India: Economic Development and Social Opportunity.* Delhi: Oxford University Press.

Dumont, Louis.1980. *Homo Hierarchicus: The Caste System and Its Implications.* Chicago: University of Chicago Press.

Fuller, C. J. 1997. "Introduction." In *Caste Today*, C. J. Fuller, ed. Oxford: Oxford University Press.

Hardgrave Jr., Robert L. 1965. *Dravidian Movement.* Bombay: Popular Prakashan.

———. 1968. *The Nadars of Tamil Nadu: The Political Culture of a Community in Change.* Berkeley: University of California Press.

———. 1970. "Political Participation and Primordial Solidarity." In *Caste in Indian Politics*, Rajni Kothari, ed. New York: Gordon and Breach.

Kothari, Rajni. 1970. "Introduction: Caste in Indian Politics." In *Caste in Indian Politics*, Rajni Kothari, ed. New York: Gordon and Breach.

Leach, Edmund R. 1960. "Introduction: What Should We Mean by Caste?" In *Aspects of Caste in South India, Ceylon and North-West Pakistan*, Edmund R. Leach, ed. Cambridge: Cambridge University Press.

Mandelbaum, David G. 1972. *Society in India: Change and Continuity.* Vol. 2. Berkeley: University of California Press.

Rudolph, Lloyd, and Susanne Rudolph. 1967. *The Modernity of Tradition: Political Development in India.* Chicago: University of Chicago Press.

Sheth, D. L. 2000. "Society." In *India Briefing*, Philip Oldenburg and Marshall Bouton, eds. New York: M. E. Sharpe.

Singh, Jagpal. 1998. "Ambedkarisation and Assertion of Dalit Identity: Socio-Cultural Protest in Meerut District of Western Uttar Pradesh." *Economic and Political Weekly*, October 3, pp. 2611–2618.

Srinivas, M. N. 1996. *Village, Caste, Gender and Method: Essays in Indian Social Anthropology*. Delhi: Oxford University Press.

Swamy, Arun. 1997. "The Nation, the People and the Poor: Sandwich Tactics in Party Competition and Policy Formation in India, 1931–1996." Ph.D. diss., Department of Political Science, University of California at Berkeley.

Washbrook, D. A.. 1988. "Progress and Problems: South Asian Economic and Social History c. 1720-1860." *Modern Asian Studies* 22: 57–96.

Weiner, Myron. 1962. *The Politics of Scarcity*. Chicago: University of Chicago Press.

———. 1967. *Party Building in a New Nation*. Chicago: University of Chicago Press.

———. 1992. *The Child and the State*. Princeton: Princeton University Press.

12

The Arts

Ananda Lal

Since the breakup of the Soviet Union, India is the country with the largest number of ethnic, linguistic, and cultural groups in the world. In an area roughly one-third the size of the United States, it cradles more than three times the population of the United States, or one-fifth of the human race. Unlike the U.S. "melting pot," however, where a certain homogenization has occurred, India's diverse communities change markedly from state to state based on a number of factors, the most important being language. The Sahitya Akademi, or national academy of letters, recognizes and awards prizes to authors in twenty-two languages—nearly as many as the number of states. Most of these major literary languages count more than 20 million speakers each, and the country embraces hundreds of other languages and dialects.[1] To put it in the simplest terms, an Indian may not even be able to converse with a fellow Indian from the state adjoining his or her own.

The situation is made more complicated by the fact that within the same linguistic region, cultures may differ. Scattered across the country lie pockets—but not reservations—inhabited by about 300 mainly Australoid and Mongoloid tribes, who speak aboriginal tongues unrelated to the dominant languages in the states where they live. Furthermore, even in the same linguistic community, different religions have created distinctive cultural traditions: for example, there are Hindus, Muslims, and Christians who speak Malayalam or Bengali; Hindu and Sikh Punjabis; Muslim, Hindu, and Buddhist Kashmiris; Hindu and

Jain Rajasthanis; and Hindu and Parsi (Zoroastrian) Gujaratis. Natu-
rally, the variety of art forms in such a land multiplied exponentially.

Westernization in the nineteenth century brought with it new theories, ideologies, and practices, including the development of an artist's
identity into a concept of far-reaching import. In contrast, the traditional Indian artist underplays ego and even signature by effacing his or
her primary position as creator of an artwork. I use the present tense
because in villages the artists still follow this selfless habit of erasing
their names. Even now, thousands of their peers all over India make
handicrafts or act, sing, or dance professionally and with dedication but
go unheralded and unknown in books such as this one because commentators focus on modernist trends and fashionable stars instead.

These big names usually have very little to do with the rural and
semirural areas where three-fourths of Indians live. Virtually all the
great painters, authors, musicians, dancers, directors, and filmmakers
mentioned in this chapter come from towns and cities, went through
formal higher education, and (except classical performers) won appreciation from western-oriented critics and audiences. The rural, illiterate, nonwesternized majority may have difficulty comprehending their
works and their aesthetics. I do not mean to say that the average village
artist is backward or primitive, only that he or she has not received
enough research attention. Things may not improve drastically in the
twenty-first century because of the increasingly powerful media's constant itch for novelty and the money available to hype urban artists
beyond their true worth. We can only hope that the Internet and other
electronic media will help document the artists languishing in India's
villages.

Of course, one can argue that the urban-rural schism has always
existed, with city artists perennially commanding greater exposure,
whether in Renaissance Europe or in "Golden Age" India under the
Guptas (300–450 C.E.). The richly patronized classical works invariably
have been recorded more fully through the ages than the ill-preserved
folk styles. The point is, it need no longer remain this way. The
methodology for documentation only requires determination and concerted effort to do equal justice to India's folk masters.

One final general remark: despite the modernization that can be
seen in every art form, at a very basic level the Indian aesthetic experience continues to honor the ancient theory of *rasa*, in that the mood or
emotion of an artwork remains the central expressive concern of most
artists. Western readers, listeners, and viewers may feel that Indians
overdo the sentiments in their creations. They should bear in mind that

this feature is part of a 2,000-year history of giving *rasa* (variously translated as "taste," "flavor," or "essence" but commonly understood as "feeling") preeminence in art.

The various arts that I discuss in this chapter fall into two broad categories, the fixed and the fluid. By "fixed" I refer to those four disciplines—fine art (painting, sculpture), literature, cinema, and television—whose products we can return to repeatedly to view or read because their creators have eternalized them on canvas, page, film, or videotape. I classify the live performing arts—music, dance, theater—as "fluid" since these fleeting forms exist temporarily from performance to performance; try as we might, we cannot capture them on discs or cassettes because the aesthetic experience remains incomplete within those limits. This distinction between fixed and fluid genres is important to recognize in contemporary India for reasons that I raise later. One crucial difference, however, I must point out here: under western influence, the modern Indian fixed forms (in this case, literature and fine art) have departed radically from their classical forebears (such as religious verse, temple architecture, and miniature paintings), which have petered out, whereas in the fluid forms, classicism and modernism still coexist.

■ Fine Art

In many traditional Indian communities, fine art is part of daily life, not a self-consciously intellectual activity. In the eastern state of Manipur, for instance, the very acts of ritualistically eating a family meal, weaving handloom saris and cane basketry, and worshiping in the local temple incorporate elements of design, symbol, or motif that can only fall under the rubric of art. The cosmopolitan separation of art from life, as something to be exhibited and appreciated but unnecessary to day-to-day work, is an alien concept. Indeed, one wonders how many Indian villagers would understand the purpose or meaning of a framed painting on a gallery wall, especially since almost all contemporary Indian painters draw their inspiration from European artists.[2] Relatively few native forms of painting, such as Madhubani in Bihar state or Patachitra in Orissa state, exist in the Indian countryside.[3]

Prior to independence in 1947, although imitation of international movements had become firmly entrenched in the cities, some trailblazers in Calcutta and Bombay pioneered a revival of native styles. The Bengal school of art—originally nurtured by the Tagores and even-

Ashok K. Dutt

Madhubani folk art from northern Bihar: a painting depicting
a newly married bride and groom carried in a palanquin

tually finding a home at Visva-Bharati, the university set up by
Rabindranath Tagore—attempted to reconcile East and West.[4] Nandalal
Bose looked to the classical Buddhist frescoes at Ajanta for ideas;
Jamini Roy was the first Indian modernist to owe a debt to folk and
tribal art—in his case, the art of the Santals in Bengal. The dominance
of the Bombay and Bengal schools continued after 1947, the latter producing such acknowledged masters as the sculptor Ramkinker Baij and
the painters Gopal Ghosh, Paritosh Sen, Nirode Mazumdar, and now
Jogen Chowdhury. In Bombay, the Progressive Artists Group led by F.
N. Souza and M. F. Husain openly pledged allegiance to late European
expressionism (which "expressed" the artist's inner world rather than
external reality), whereas the simple joy of Indian landscapes and
nature appealed to apparently less radical artists, such as Akbar
Padamsee and K. K. Hebbar.

The debate over the derivative quality of Indian art persists. As art
institutions sprouted elsewhere in India during the 1950s, the Baroda
Group, centered round the newly founded M. S. University at Baroda
in Gujarat state, and the Group 1890 of Delhi, under its spokesman J.
Swaminathan, both faced allegations of excessive abstraction influ-

enced by western models. In the midst of these polemical disputes about the nature of original creativity, the figure of K. G. Subramanyan gradually rose to a powerful position of pan-Indian magnitude—as artist and educator, he worked at various times in Kerala (his home state), Santiniketan (the site of Visva-Bharati), Delhi, Baroda, Bombay, and London. Deeply interested in indigenous folk art and crafts, he borrowed techniques freely from all over India, such as the popular Kalighat *patuya* paintings of Calcutta or terracotta reliefs on temples.[5]

Perhaps the first full-scale excursion into native artistic traditions came from south India, in the 1960s. K. C. S. Paniker established the Cholamandal Artists' Village in the state of Tamil Nadu because of his realization of a pervasive Eurocentric impulse among urban Indian painters and their consequent lack of Indianness. Paniker visualized a commune influenced specifically by south Indian traditional handicrafts and by individual pathfinders like Jamini Roy. Largely unknown in its heyday, Cholamandal now receives due respect as a historic and farsighted enterprise.

Although painting has remained by far the most-practiced genre of fine art in India, there are a few leading artists in other media. Printmaking received a stimulus from the Graphics Department of Delhi College of Art under the leadership of Somnath Hore from 1958 to 1965 and the techniques invented by Krishna Reddy, who soon went abroad. Sculpture attracted some brilliant talent, like Meera Mukherjee of Calcutta. Prabhakar Barwe's experimentation with enamel paint in Bombay made fine use of an unusual medium.

By the 1970s, Indian art had moved into new directions. A growing circle of nativist painters began to study the representation and philosophy of Tantra (an esoteric branch of Hinduism and Buddhism dealing with ritualistic meditation and sexuality), resulting in a relatively large corpus of neo-Tantric works. The number of women artists increased to the point at which scholars could bunch them together for analysis as a movement. The Marxist ideology of many artists, often assumed, now evolved into a more explicit statement of social conscience among the younger generation, such as Sudhir Patwardhan and Vivan Sundaram.

A sea change occurred in the following decade. Suddenly, the upper class learned that artworks made excellent investments. Thus began the present upper-crust fad of collecting, which made the lives of proverbial starving artists much plusher but also automatically pushed prices beyond the reach of ordinary—often more discerning—buyers. Galleries and exhibitions arose to exploit the demand, and international interest in contemporary Indian art grew. It is difficult to tell how long this vogue will last.

As for content and method, the Indian-versus-western conflict still rages. Seniors like Ganesh Haloi in Calcutta continue to paint distinctive Indian landscapes without direct reference to foreign modes. However, hip celebrities like Vivan Sundaram of Delhi have shifted to installation art (exhibits constructed within galleries), the currently "in" thing—masterfully conceived and executed, no doubt, but conforming to international fashions. Commercialization and cosmopolitanism are the significant problems plaguing Indian art today.

■ Literature

At least art, theoretically, can be said to have a universal language. Not so with literature, whose readership is determined by the language of the text. Despite the national slogan that Indian literature is unified, though it is written in many tongues, over the years, by admitting more and more languages into the Eighth Schedule of the Indian Constitution, successive governments have only succeeded in proving Indians' plurality and dissimilarity. Even so, the number of languages in the Eighth Schedule falls short of the number recognized by the Sahitya Akademi. Regardless of such quibbles, India can boast of as many major living literatures as Europe. And, since nobody in his or her right mind would write a history of European literature in this day and age, it is equally futile for anyone to attempt a survey of contemporary Indian literature, for the simple reason that no person alive understands all the main Indian languages.[6]

Yet because of geopolitical factors, I must talk of "Indian literature"—though, funnily enough, there is not even any language called "Indian." I may mention the names of famous Indian painters, musicians or dancers, but I do not dare give names of writers in this chapter. I would need to think of the best authors writing since 1947 in more than twenty languages: not only a tall order but also a long-winded list. Rather, I propose to maintain perfect fairness by not naming anyone at all and, instead, discussing the broad sweep of currents in the Indian literatures during this period.[7]

Let us also not forget, as India's latest Nobel laureate, Amartya Sen, never tires of reminding us, the subject of literacy in the second most populous country on earth. Even at the beginning of the twenty-first century, the overwhelming majority of Indians remain illiterate.

Therefore, whose literature am I discussing, anyway? Evidently, that of university-trained, predominantly city-based authors. Whether anti-urban or pro-urban in their themes, they cannot be heard by their under-privileged fellow citizens deprived of primary education. However, the 30 percent who can read account for as many as 300 million people.

There lies strength in sheer numbers, for the chief linguistic phe-nomenon after independence has been the regional literature's quest for identity and equal rights. The continuing reorganization of states along linguistic boundaries satisfies these aspirations, and resistance against the perceived tyranny of a "superior" or dominant language has fired many literary rebellions. Of the states that refused to accept the central government's imposition of Hindi as the official national language, Tamil Nadu (formerly Madras) had the most volatile reaction, which was reflected in a pro-Dravida movement in Tamil literature of the 1960s that rejected words from Sanskrit in favor of pure Dravidian vocabulary.[8] A different example comes from Manipur, where the Manipuris, increasingly proud of their ethnic roots since the 1980s, banished the Bengali script in which they used to write and revived their ancient Tibeto-Burman characters in its place. They regarded the Bengali script as alien "Indian" cultural colonialism and their old alphabet as their "true" ancestral heritage. Popular protests against lan-guage policy have often caused riots.

To generalize, one may distinguish three broad periods of post-1947 Indian literature. For the first fifteen years or so, the unprece-dented violence that accompanied the partition of the country, culmi-nating in Mohandas Gandhi's assassination in 1948, found expression in the works of many a writer shattered by the sudden outburst of com-munal hatred and devastation. What became known as "partition liter-ature" emerged, its compass covering the riots, retaliation, the refugee exodus, resettlement, and even a darkly sardonic angle presenting the patent ridiculousness of the situation in which India and Pakistan, who should have celebrated their twin birth as free nations, fought a war with each other.

Four communities were particularly affected by their position along the new nations' shared borders: Kashmiris, Punjabis, Sindhis, and Bengalis. The transfer of Sind to Pakistan left Indian Sindhis with-out a homeland—a loss reflected in their literature by an intense nos-talgia. However, the divided lands of Punjab and Bengal, the two provinces dissected by partition, felt the brunt of Hindu-Muslim enmity as millions following their religion and escaping persecution migrated across both sides, leaving everything behind, often without anything awaiting them in their new homes. Contrasted to the Sindhi experience, the broken promises and ruthless killings of hundreds of thousands left Punjabi and Bengali literatures wounded by a deep sense of bitterness. And as a result of the Indo-Pakistani war in 1948, Kashmir became partitioned too, and it is still separated by the Line of Control demarcating the cease-fire. Not surprisingly, three of these states later went through insurrections caused by resentment of government treatment—the Naxalite uprising in Bengal, Sikh militancy in Punjab, and Kashmiri separatism—all leaving marks on their respective literatures. Now Sind in Pakistan faces a civil war; the recent histories of these four states may not be coincidental.

A general disenchantment among authors succeeded this period of literary trauma. Disillusionment with independence, observation of corruption in politics, criticism of administrative bureaucracy, and descriptions of declining morality became the new issues during the 1960s. Left-wing writing had existed prior to independence, but now it became a concerted movement. Leading literatures such as Bengali, Hindi, Malayalam, Marathi, and Telugu all passed through phases named by their literary historians as progressive, socialist, or Marxist. Emulating the modernist and realist styles and methods of the West, Indian authors abandoned their age-old mysticism and romanticism and turned contemptuous of "reactionary" native traditions. In the 1970s, for instance, the Bengali intelligentsia and ruling Communist Party denigrated the achievements of Rabindranath Tagore—showing disdain for his themes and class background that is still cultivated by "postmodern" Indians from different quarters, though Bengalis have wisely withdrawn their earlier objections. Along with dwindling idealism came a noticeable preoccupation with material matters, including greater frankness about sexuality.

Today, the third stage of Indian literature since independence may reflect a shift in focus from city and country to grassroots activism and a concern about people without a voice. Across languages, the deterioration in conditions of rural life has taken precedence over the romanticization of villagers so common in previous writing. Whether inspired by Marxist or Gandhian thought, contemporary Indian literatures privilege women (not only as subjects but as battlegrounds for feminism and gender studies); lower castes, or Dalits (Dalit literature is now an important nationwide phenomenon); tribals; and the poor (whose unjust suffering forms another significant topic of recent times).

One troublesome aspect of modern Indian literatures is their international presence and representation. The paucity of translations in general and the erratic quality of available translations make the awareness and reputation of Indian authors negligible outside India. Conversely, the easier accessibility of original Indian writing in English has given this particular literary tradition disproportionate visibility abroad, compared to its actual audience at home. Of late, the foreign press has lionized Indian-English novelists because they now command hefty advances from chiefly British publishing houses; in turn, the good publicity has led them to negotiate even larger deals with publishers. The multinational corporate backing that this group enjoys obscures not only the best writers in the regional tongues but also equally good Indian-English poets and translators published by small Indian imprints whose books do not reach the global market, not even through the Internet.

Often, we can even question the Indianness of some contemporary Indian-English authors, who are nominally Indians by birth but expatriates by choice, maintaining hardly any physical link with India today apart from hasty trips back to recharge their batteries for further inspiration. Although they continue to write about (and thus exploit the exotic appeal of) their former homeland, we can justifiably interrogate the authenticity of their "Indian" works. Sometimes a renowned figure like Salman Rushdie may even abuse his fame, pontificating about the stagnation of regional Indian literatures as opposed to the innovative strides taken by Indian English—although he is in no position to judge since he cannot read books in any of the regional languages (Rushdie 1997: 50–61). Foreigners interested in Indian literatures must not confine themselves to the shop windows of the West but undertake expeditions into the less glamorous alleys of Indian publications where the real treasures lie.

■ Cinema

In the late nineteenth and early twentieth centuries, Indians flocked to the theater for their evening's entertainment. Since the 1940s, until the very recent television boom, the cinema replaced theater as the object of popular audience attention. India is the world's largest producer of films with truly massive appeal and, next to Hollywood, has the most influential and independent movie industry. The export of Indian films is big business, too, not just to foreign nations with sizeable Indian populations but also to African, Middle Eastern, and former Soviet countries, where cinemagoers are avid fans of Hindi films.

The term *Hindi film* needs definition, for we must qualify the language and viewership of the "Indian" movie. As in the case of literature, Indian cinema exists in virtually every regional language, but unlike literature, it has come to be dominated by Hindi films. Yet this Hindi medium is really a curious patois liberally garnished with Urdu. In fact, although the official policy of national integration through propagation of Hindi as a common language has largely failed, this national cinema has succeeded in establishing a kind of mongrel Hindi as a common language of communication by the sheer popularity of the genre all over India. Moreover, regional film industries copied the mode, so that one can even argue that the genre turned into a national art form. However, in the past decade, many regional cinemas have faded, some becoming extinct under the monopolistic tyranny of the Bombay blockbuster.

Essentially, the commercial Hindi movie is escapist in purpose, catering to the fantasies of mainly the rootless unemployed and the mainstream middle class, both of whom want to be transported out of their depressing mundane reality to never-never land, where upper-class love stories occur in exotic landscapes and good vanquishes evil. True, its attraction cuts across class barriers, and the elite get drawn to its glitter too, but they are not crucial to its existence. Keeping in mind the morality of its customers and despite its obligatory erotic titillation, the Hindi film has conservative values and does not question the majority's social or community patterns. Critics suggest that these features are firmly based in the status quo, but this defense appears to come from those kindly disposed toward the genre.[9] Methodologically, these films make use of traditional performance techniques, featuring antirealistic songs and dances, and follow indigenous professional theater, which has always relied on melodrama for emotional impact. The trouble is, Hindi cinema corrupted even those methods. Producers now compose song-and-dance sequences first and then stitch an apology for a plot round them. Previously, Indian classical and folk music and dance used to supply films with inexhaustible noncopyrighted sources for soundtrack and choreography. Then, after a period of "borrowing" uncredited tunes, such as Tagore's, the producers began lifting western pop hits and music-video routines without any reference to their original context. Shameless plagiarism runs rampant in songs and dances as well as story lines; many new Hindi movies rip off Hollywood hits with no trace of acknowledgment. As for the melodramatic impulse, it has degenerated into a mere formula, whose simplistic narrative and stereo-typical characters have become completely predictable.

Yet, the commercial film was not always so bad. Immediately after independence, classics like Raj Kapoor's *Awara* (1951) and *Shri 420* (1955), Guru Dutt's *Pyasa* (1957), and Mehboob Khan's *Mother India* (1957) showed creativity and individualism, often spotlighting the rebel or outsider as hero. It helped that accomplished writers like K. A. Abbas, a leftist, scripted movies like *Awara* and *Shri 420*. The offbeat protago-nist stayed on but underwent a transformation with Ramesh Sippy's *Sholay* (1975), for a long time the industry's biggest box-office smash. In this vigilante vendetta, the renegades take justice into their own hands because the law no longer does (no doubt reflecting deteriorating admin-istrative conditions). The evolution of male leads from the lovable romantic Rajesh Khanna in the 1960s to the angry young man Amitabh Bachchan in the 1970s and the comparatively malevolent Shah Rukh Khan in the 1990s tells its own tale of the growing violence gratuitously used by Hindi directors. Crude handling of sex and bloodshed—the for-mula contains mandatory rape scenes—the typecasting of female roles into wife and vamp, and the objectification of women form disturbing trends in contemporary Hindi films.[10]

The art cinema in India arose unheralded in the 1950s and, since then, has managed to survive alongside the commercial industry. His-torians usually credit Satyajit Ray for starting this movement with *Pather Panchali* (1955), a Bengali film. It is an international classic that has been much analyzed and that, it is said, is screened somewhere in the world every day. Ray and his successors in different languages modeled their low-budget work consciously on European directors, as opposed to the U.S. school of spectacular extravaganzas followed by Bombay's Hindi filmmakers. Although Ray justly gained widespread foreign exposure, not merely on the festival circuit but thanks also to his appearance on university film studies' syllabi as the token Indian, other Bengali directors of his generation, such as Mrinal Sen and Ritwik Ghatak, made several excellent movies as well. On the whole, the practitioners of art film, whether in Bengali or other Indian lan-guages, jointly constitute the respectable face of Indian cinema.

The movement received impetus in the 1960s through the founding of the Film and Television Institute (FTII) of India at Pune (deliberately located outside yet close to Bombay) and government funding for new independent cinema. Many students of the FTII made a name with their nonconformist approach on projects supported by official grants: Mani Kaul's formalist *Uski Roti* (1969), Kumar Shahani's provocative *Maya*

Darpan (1972), and Ketan Mehta's folklike *Bhavni Bhavai* (1980). Meanwhile, Shyam Benegal in Hindi and G. Aravindan and Adoor Gopalakrishnan in Malayalam forged ahead on the trail blazed by the Bengali pioneers. Art cinema typically deals with rural narratives, often political in tone, and its themes treat India's social problems, destitution, and superstition realistically. It met with passionate opposition from the commercial industry, which accused it of cornering international prestige and winning awards by selling India's poverty to the West.

South Indian popular cinema—specifically in the Tamil and Telugu languages—offers one unique interface of dream factory with political reality. The states of Tamil Nadu and Andhra Pradesh have a relatively long history of electorates voting film stars into power because they have evidently been persuaded that the matinee idols they swoon over in "reel life" will repeat those heroics in real life. The reality that these screen saviors inevitably turned corrupt in office never led to much loss of faith among the populace. The most famous superstar-politicians include M. G. Ramachandran, J. Jayalalitha, and N. T. Rama Rao, all of whom became chief ministers. The star system exists, of course, in other regional cinemas—some notable icons with lengthy careers are Dilip Kumar, Nargis and Dev Anand (Hindi), Prem Nazir (Malayalam), and the romantic pairs of Uttam Kumar and Suchitra Sen (Bengali) and Rajkumar and Kalpana (Kannada)—but somehow their fans wisely refrained from encouraging them to run for office.

Commentators suggest that the art film and Indian cinema in general have been harmed by television's popularity. However, it is theater that has received the greatest battering from the TV-channel expansion. Admittedly, the sprouting of portable video shows across the country, often playing pirated copies of movies, has eaten into the film industry's legitimate receipts. In turn, the decline in audiences and fall in revenues has led to poor hall maintenance, so that the filmgoing experience is not the luxury it used to be. Nevertheless, hit movies continue to break previous records, and in the art circuit, the arrival of the film festival as cultural event and the growth of about 250 film societies indicates that Indian cinema is flourishing—and may even get better through healthy competition with television.

■ Television

Leaving aside cutting-edge (and expensive) computer and Internet technology, the latest vehicle for popular entertainment in India has the greatest potential for mass communication, owing to its convenience. Besides the book, the television is the one artistic medium that people can access in the comfort of their homes. True, they can play a music CD on their personal stereos or a cassette of a film on their living room VCRs, but connoisseurs consider these incomplete experiences compared to a live concert or a movie hall screening. Television, like literature, does away with the social formalities of attendance and allows direct artist-to-audience outreach. Its added advantage over the book is that it does not require literacy. Until the advent of cable TV very recently in India, it did not even demand money, apart from the initial investment of purchasing a set and the costs of running it on electricity. It was virtually free, in contrast to the transportation expenses and price of a ticket incurred to go to a performance of any kind or the cost of buying each individual book or tape. No wonder it caught on so fast in impoverished India.

Compared to most nations, though, television entered India rather late. For many years after its introduction in 1959, it remained a preserve of the capital, New Delhi. Only in 1972 did stations start operating elsewhere, all under the control of Doordarshan, the official state-owned network. Color programming and commercial advertising

Rama and Sita in one of the many mythological
serials on Indian television

arrived as late as 1982. But by 1984, the government claimed that two-thirds of India's population could watch Doordarshan. Policy dictated that rural education form the bulk of programs, but soon the need to generate more income forced the sale of half-hour slots to independent producers of serials sponsored by advertisers. The first such soap opera was telecast in 1984. The most successful, in terms of viewer ratings but not critical appreciation, were the kitschy megaserials based on the ancient classical epics *Ramayana* (1986–1988) and *Mahabharata* (1988–1990).[11] The late 1980s was Doordarshan's peak period of popularity as well as financial revenue. In 1992, its monopoly was broken by Hong Kong's STAR network, which began beaming its satellite signals at the subcontinent, and satellite dishes mushroomed all over the country. Now more than fifty channels, international and regional, are available on cable to subscribers. Caught by surprise, Doordarshan has yet to design a suitable programming strategy to fight back.

Aesthetically, the art of Indian television, whether private or public in funding, is at an abysmal low. Derivative soaps and sentimental tearjerkers, each nearly identical to the next; grossly vulgar sitcoms dependent on physical slapstick rather than wit; and technically ludicrous (because so literal) prime-time mythological serials that mark an academically interesting return to the days of mythological theater productions and clearly fill a demand for devotional material comprise the staple of "creative" scheduling. Equally troubling is the ad-generated consumerism imposed by multinational companies on India's villagers—noticed as far back as 1984 by a government-appointed committee on television software—and a tendency toward lowbrow homogeneity in cultural matters, conforming to a fashionably "modern" western image or a Hindi-centric "Indianness," respectively. Indian television is at present the spoiled brat among the arts—possessing all the money, utterly undisciplined, and lacking any of the finer graces that make a child endearing.

Not enough research has been conducted to study exhaustively the impact of TV on all layers of Indian society. Nevertheless, it is clear that both the medium and its viewers need to mature. One hopes, as happened in the United States after the initial fascination with cable was satiated or in other parts of the world after the proliferation of satellite channels stabilized, that Indians' present fixation on television as art form of choice will falter and their minds turn back to more edifying means of entertainment. Of course, should TV programming actually improve, nothing could be better.

■ Challenges for the Traditional Performing Arts

As a body, the performing arts suffer the most in contemporary India, since their audiences have deserted them for the allure and convenience of television. This phenomenon has particularly hurt the traditional village performer, who used to hold his or her community spellbound until the razzle-dazzle of the tube lured it away with magic from afar brought near. Now, many of these musicians, dancers, and actors, whose professional knowledge and experience was handed down from generation to generation, confront the death of their old learning.[12] The idealists among them bemoan the sorry state of affairs, and the pragmatists encourage their juniors to seek employment in more promising occupations. Most traditional Indian performance genres are endangered species, threatened with extinction as lifestyles change rapidly in the countryside.

The unique dimension of Indian performing arts in the present time may well be their continuing link with religion. Ever since the European Renaissance, western arts became secularized, losing their historical connection with propitiatory ritual and ceremony. In Asia, however, art's connection to devotion survived. Whether classical or folk,

Ainslie T. Embree

Itinerant actors in south India travel from village to village, performing scenes from the lives of Hindu deities

traditional Indian musicians, dancers, and actors still dedicate their performances as offerings to their personal deities or as an act of general faith. Often this takes the simple shape of touching the musical instrument and raising one's hands to God before starting a concert or touching the stage floor and literally placing the dust of the platform on one's forehead in obeisance. The community participates in this spiritual act as well by just being present. The sacredness of traditional Indian performance makes it a much more "serious" object of study, even though many modern artists have dispensed with these formalities as meaningless convention.

In the cities, the classical genres found fewer and fewer followers, as first cinema and then television and videocassettes seduced spectators. The cornering of the market for popular entertainment by film and TV, the literate readership's continuing support of literature, and the interest in art as an investment mean that these "fixed" forms retain a widespread and committed clientele, whereas live music, dance, and theater have become niche arts, patronized by progressively smaller, if dedicated, segments of the urban population. The situation may appear different if one thinks of packed stadiums for divas like Lata Mangeshkar or young pop singers, but let me emphasize that this fame is connected either to cinema (songs sell through their presence on soundtracks) or television (music videos promoting the latest releases). Indigenous genres not connected to these media do not stand much chance of either commercial success or uncommonly large audiences. I also believe that some of this new neglect of the performing arts is due to their essence as fluid forms, for modern society seems to prefer its art fixed—preserved in cold storage and ready at any time in definite viewable or readable shape.

■ Music

Indian music ranges from the rarefied reaches and acquired taste of northern Hindusthani and southern Karnatak (previous spelling, Carnatic) classical heritages, to diverse folk idioms in every local dialect, to contemporary styles encompassing both film hits and western-influenced homegrown rap or rock. Music's finest achievements, however, remain within the classical mainstream, which traces an unbroken lineage from ancient times, mingled, in the case of the Hindusthani and folk currents, with Islamic Sufi music during the Mughal period of medieval history. Indian music presents a paradigm of communal harmony and integration where the Muslim minority has made and still makes significant contributions to the development of the form.

Since independence, classical music has passed through many changes at an unprecedented rate. Conventionally dependent on royal courts for patronage, the musicians faced a bleak future when the republic of India did away with the princely states. Forced to earn their living as professionals, they have only recently gained some respite through corporate sponsorship of music festivals—and although these sponsorships may have brought back funding to classical music, they have also encouraged the star system, whereby luminaries demand and receive very high appearance fees regardless of their actual form. The dissolution of *durbar*s (royal courts) also meant the disbanding of the age-old *gharana*s, stylistic schools centered around places that were famous for specific classical idioms. Instead, one saw more mixing and individualism of style, though one can still recognize the different *gharana*s if one wishes.

Meanwhile, the limited audiences grew, as classical musicians began performing for a ticket-buying public and music education became more democratized. The leading stars played in newly built halls across urban India, gaining visibility and also resulting in some degree of interregional exchange not possible before. For example, musicians from Madras (now Chennai) were heard in cities like Delhi, Calcutta, and Bombay (now Mumbai), leading to greater understanding of Karnatak music in the north. From the 1960s onward, Indian music caught on in Europe and North America as well, after initial foreign visits by maestros on government-paid cultural junkets, much publicized in such high-profile encounters as Ravi Shankar's influence on the Beatles and George Harrison's decision to learn sitar as his disciple. India had considerable impact on British and U.S. rock and jazz, philosophically and instrumentally.

The desire to reach out to the western market combined with other factors to alter the performance conditions too. Orthodox expositions of single ragas can go on for hours, and overnight concerts used to be the norm, traditionally concluding with the dawn raga, Bhairavi, as the sun rose. (A raga is a musical mode, of notes in a fixed sequence on which the musician improvises, and associated with specific emotional, temporal, or seasonal qualities.) The custom of going to concerts after work in the evenings, in accordance with modern metropolitan habits, required that ragas intended for performance during the day or late at night had to be either dropped or accommodated within the audience's after-hours leisure period, both procedures violating the time-honored

theory and practice of the repertoire. The listener's need to go home by
10 P.M. also meant the curtailment of lengthy recitals and the fabrica-
tion of truncated "designer music," as some critics have called it.[13]

Purists decried the compromises made by classical musicians in
utilizing twentieth-century technology. At first, the invention of 78-rpm
records allowed the preservation of three-minute snatches of ragas—
obviously inadequate capsule renditions. Although the invention of
long-playing records and compact discs gave more elbowroom for
recordings of forty-five minutes to over one hour, the capacity
remained far short of ideal raga parameters. Meanwhile, as radio wilted
under the onslaught of TV, classical masters had to condense their ragas
to cope with the progressively shorter attention spans for and format of
TV. Of late, music companies have gone in for anthologies containing
several compact raga tracks on one cassette or CD, motivated by easy
marketability and packaging of the product. These compilations under
thematic titles such as "Seasons" or "Desert Music" may serve as intro-
ductory samplers for the uninitiated but by no means convey the depth
of Indian classical music.

It is always unkind to others to single out some personalities for
special mention, but any list of the classical maestros in recent decades
should include the following, renowned for new directions or experi-
mentation in improvisation—the test of Indian musical creativity:
Begum Akhtar, Amir Khan, Bhimsen Joshi, Bade Ghulam Ali Khan,
Mallikarjun Mansoor, Hirabai Barodekar, and the Dagar brothers (all
Hindusthani vocalists); Zia Mohiuddin Dagar (on *rudravina,* a much
older, larger, and deeper-sounding progenitor of the sitar); Annapurna
Devi (*surbahar,* a more resonant cousin of the sitar); Ravi Shankar,
Vilayat Khan, and Nikhil Banerjee (sitar); Ali Akbar Khan and Amjad
Ali Khan (*sarod*); Shakoor Khan (*sarangi,* a short-bowed instrument);
G. Joshi (violin); Bismillah Khan (*shehnai,* an Indian version of the
oboe); Pannalal Ghosh and Hari Prasad Chaurasia (flute); Ayodhya
Prasad (*pakhawaj,* an elongated double-headed drum played with the
hands); Ahmed Jan Thirakwa and Alla Rakha and his son Zakir Hussain
(*tablas,* the accompanying percussion instruments that have enjoyed a
tremendous rise in popular appeal over the last few decades); and Shiv-
kumar Sharma (*santoor,* a folk zither that he raised to classical status).

Among musicians of the Karnatak system from south India, one
must cite M. S. Subbalakshmi, S. R. Srinivasa Iyer, D. K. Pattammal,
and K. V. Narayanaswamy (vocalists); S. Balachander and Chitti Babu
(*vina*); B. Krishnamurthi Sastri (*gottuvadyam,* an ancient fretless *vina*
played with a slide); M. S. Gopalakrishnan and Lalgudi Jayaraman

(violin); T. R. Mahalingam (flute); A. K. C. Natarajan (clarinet); S. Chinna Moulana (*nagaswaram,* a very large and elongated double-reed horn); Palghat Mani Iyer (*mridangam,* a double-faced tuned drum like the *pakhawaj*); V. Shanmugasundaram Pillai (*thavil,* a double-ended barrel-shaped drum played with hand and stick); and T. H. Vinayakram (*ghatam,* or claypot).[14]

Semiclassical song has a devoted following too, for such genres as the Urdu *ghazal,* the Hindi *thumri,* the religious *kirtan* and *bhajan,* or the Bengali lyrics of Tagore, called Rabindrasangit. Large audiences listen to regional folk music, and some artists become critical successes like Purna Das Baul from Bengal (whose concerts brought to international stages the mystic devotional songs of the mendicant Baul minstrels) or commercial chart-toppers like Sachin Deb Burman from Tripura (whose versions of east Indian folk tunes won national attention via film soundtracks).

Hindi cinema itself has hugely encouraged the music industry: prolific playback singers (whose songs are lip-synched onscreen by the actors) like Lata Mangeshkar, Asha Bhonsle, Kishore Kumar, and Mohammad Rafi have broken all kinds of records, topped by Mangeshkar's attainment of having recorded the most number of songs (30,000) by anyone in the world. Of late, however, instead of plumbing Indian traditions, film-music composers resort to profligate borrowing—or, more legally speaking, plagiarism—from western pop music. Pop in regional languages may now contain rap vocals, funky disco rhythms, and western instrumentation, without any indigenous content whatsoever, apart from the lyrics. The largest cities also boast a tiny but knowledgeable coterie of rock and jazz bands and buffs, as well as loyal but even fewer aficionados of European classical music. Conductors like Zubin Mehta, rockers like Freddie Mercury, and jazzmen like Trilok Gurtu were born in India. It may be worth mentioning that many Indian classical musicians have collaborated with jazz greats since the 1960s. Much of this Indo-jazz fusion succeeded aesthetically because of the premium placed by both systems on improvisation.[15]

■ Dance

As in the West, dance in India commands arguably the smallest sector of arts audiences, even though, as with Indian music and theater, it includes many varieties within classical, folk, and modern styles. Besides, owing to the common ancient roots of Indian theater and dance, their shared connection to Bharata's classical theoretical treatise, the *Natya-sastra*, and their constant practical overlap, theater lays equal claim to some traditional genres of dance-drama, whether folk like Chhau from Orissa or classical like Kathakali from Kerala—the latter further confounding western scholars obsessed with categories, because the Indian dance establishment considers Kathakali classical, whereas theater regards it as folk.

The history of Indian dance in the twentieth century provides an example of repeated reclamation of different genres from obscurity and social ostracization to classical levels. A hundred years ago, female dancers bore the stigma of immorality from their occupation as *devadasis* ("maidservants of God," the sacred but exploitative tradition of women serving gods and priests as temple dancers) or their association with prostitution (the profane tradition of dancing entertainers or nautch girls [from *nāch*, "dance"] having to satisfy their customers). The renaissance of their art before independence gained support from public eminences like Tagore, who "discovered" the little-known "tribal" form of Manipuri and raised it to classical respectability; Rukmini Arundale, crusader for Bharatanatyam (a form of dance) in south India; the poet Vallathol Menon, patron of Kathakali; and Uday Shankar, who popularized dance via his choreography in cinema. Academic study of the *Natya-sastra* and scholarly excursions into *rasa* theory, as in V. Raghavan's essays, helped dance's resurrection in venerable incarnations.[16]

Consequently, by 1947, the four genres of Bharatanatyam, Manipuri, Kathakali, and Kathak had established themselves as classical. They received additional incentives from government aid and popular approval as dances worthy of practice, plus the efforts of single-minded institutions like the Manipur Dance Academy, Kerala Kalamandalam, and Kathak Kendra in Delhi. Bharatanatyam, in particular, under such noted teacher-exponents as T. Balasaraswati, managed to emerge from its southern birthplace and become truly *Bharatiya* (Indian), with schools and disciples all over the country. Since 1947, other genres have won the classical tag: Kuchipudi from Andhra Pradesh (the Siddhendra Kalakshetra institute in the village of Kuchipudi contributing much to its present status), Odissi from Orissa, and Mohiniattam from Kerala. Of these, Kuchipudi shares Kathakali's theatrical duality—its collective choreography qualifies it as dance-drama, enabling its acceptance by theater historians as a traditional form.

Individual dancer-gurus have also left their mark on the development of their specific genres in the last fifty years. One must mention

A female impersonator
in traditional/classical
Kathakali dance

Pronab Basu

the contributions of K. Krishnan Nair to Kathakali, Birju Maharaj to Kathak, Kelucharan Mohapatra to Odissi, Yamini Krishnamurthy to Bharatanatyam, Bipin Singh to Manipuri, and V. Satyanarayana Sarma to Kuchipudi. The return of Kalanidhi Narayanan to the stage after a self-imposed layoff restored the art of subtle *abhinaya* (acting) to Bharatanatyam: as in music, many dances now present the problem of too much technical virtuosity, which spoils the emotional nuances that lie at the heart of Indian aesthetics. Experimentation of various kinds has taken place, too. Kathak has incorporated group choreography; Kuchipudi has seen male roles played by women. A few progressives have introduced Hindusthani (northern) music to Bharatanatyam or created compositions with radical concepts such as the deaths of wives from nonpayment of dowry.

Indeed, the lack of obvious social relevance in classical dance and the preponderance of mythological characters with whom many performers cannot identify caused the evolution of modern and contemporary dance in India. Uday Shankar is generally credited with the invention of modern dance before independence. Afterward, women such as Mrinalini Sarabhai, Chandralekha, Maya Rao, Kumudini Lakhia, and Manjusri Chaki-Sircar—all with a strong classical foundation—used contemporary techniques for productions on feminist, political, and environmental issues. Others, like the Odissi specialist Sanjukta Panigrahi, actively collaborated with western performers (in her case, the theater company of Eugenio Barba, who was born in Italy but is based in Denmark), and yet others like Uttara Asha Coorlawalla settled abroad and concentrated exclusively on modern dance.

One must not forget India's folk dances of a myriad varieties (for instance, Bhangra in Punjab, Garba in Gujarat), still performed to celebrate harvesting and festive occasions in every rural district yet largely unresearched and undocumented. Nor should one ignore the subgenre of film dance, however hybridized and below academic dignity it may be, with influences as far-ranging as Indian classical dance and the Hollywood musical, and as modern as hip-hop break dancing and crude pelvic thrusts. If one leaves these populist inheritances out of the discussion, "art dance" faces serious difficulties nowadays, among them a severe paucity of male dancers and a dwindling of interest in the young generation. Fortunately, a few concerned bodies like the Society for the Promotion of Indian Classical Music and Culture Amongst Youth have taken it upon themselves to inculcate the young crowd with appreciation of the classical arts through lecture-demonstrations by renowned performers.

■ Theater

The complex linguistic circumstances of Indian literature obviously obtain for drama as well, so that no general survey of Indian theater can presume to speak for all parts of the country.[17] In addition, unlike printed literature but like performed music and dance, theater envelops countless traditional genres in Indian villages that have existed for several centuries but now—as explained earlier in this chapter—face the threat of extinction from increased competition with film and television. Most are open-air, stylized, lengthy performances with substantial musical and dance input. Theater historians have documented a few major forms among these, but many remain little-known and unrecorded. One example is the various puppet traditions in India, which contain some of the oldest shadow puppetry in the world and were progenitors of the better-publicized forms from Indonesia. They fight a losing battle for rural audiences and have been virtually forgotten in urban India.[18]

I distinguish four broad periods in the development of urban Indian drama since 1947, one of which involved appropriating the folk theater in a back-to-the-roots movement stemming from a desire to be more Indian. Although Tagore had incorporated such techniques in his plays in the early decades of the twentieth century, the folk-influenced city theater I refer to arose around 1970. The pioneers of this revival included the Kannada actor-dramatists Chandrasekhar Kambar and Girish Karnad; the Malayalam dramatist and director in Sanskrit, K. N. Panikkar; and the director B. V. Karanth, who works in several Indian languages. The trouble began later, when folk theater turned into a fad. Practitioners bent over backward to create "folk-based" plays in a self-conscious search for native idioms that merely betrayed their own poverty of imagination. More unethically, pseudo-rural productions cashed in on government-sponsored promotions of culture and did well abroad because of their colorful, exotic otherness. Many critics justifiably questioned the "Indianness" of these spectacles, compared to their village antecedents that, for a lack of money, now lie in their death throes.

Prior to the resurgence in folk theater, however, two urban dramatic trends had become distinctly visible since the 1950s: the poetical and the political. Both emerged in Bengal and subsequently influenced theater workers everywhere. The poetical theater, once again, drew inspiration from Tagore, as the actor-director Sombhu Mitra and his group Bohurupee proved the stageworthiness of Tagore's plays in one production after another, which toured the rest of the country to widespread acclaim. Heavily dependent on symbols and myth-making, they established the theatrical possibilities of modern antirealism. Important followers of this mode included Mohan Rakesh, who wrote symbolic plays in Hindi; Mohit Chattopadhyay, a Bengali dramatist among a host of Indians who emulated European absurdist models; and Mahesh Elkunchwar, perhaps the most literary yet subtextual of Marathi playwrights.

In contrast, the political theater was exclusively Marxist in agenda, idolizing if not imitating Bertolt Brecht and reflecting the abject conditions of India's low society realistically. The senior actor-manager-authors of this vanguard were Utpal Dutt in Bengali and Habib Tanvir

in Urdu. The eclectic Marathi playwright Vijay Tendulkar also had
political messages to convey, even if not in an ideologically partisan
manner. A significant offshoot of political theater consists of the "Third
Theatre," a term coined by Bengali dramatist-director Badal Sircar.
Rejecting the bourgeois auditorium, Third Theatre troupes perform at
street corners and in the villages with no sets, minimal props, and
everyday costumes. They do not charge any fee but solicit voluntary
donations at the end of every show to keep their protest movement
alive. That way, they argue, theater ceases to be a capitalistic commod-
ity that one buys or sells. Many such small, dedicated, if sadly short-
lived groups began operating in Sircar's footsteps throughout India in
the 1970s.

The main problem besetting urban art theater has been a lack of
professionalism. The commercial companies that until recently used to

Habib Tanvir
(standing) in one of
the biggest successes in
contemporary Indian
theater, *Charandas
Chor,* which he wrote
and directed

Pronab Basu

Arun Chattopadhyay

Writer and director
Badal Sircar

flourish in the cities catered to crowds wanting entertainment; once these viewers left for the glitter offered by cinema and television, the companies disappeared. In any case, more often than not, they pandered to popular tastes. The "serious" groups, however, could never make enough money from theater alone. Members earn their living in other professions during the day. Unlike most developed nations, but curiously like the United States, India has never granted much official subsidy to theater. With the defection of even their audiences to film and TV in recent years, the groups are also in bad shape. The other aspect of unprofessionalism is the paucity of theater education: only the National School of Drama in Delhi and a handful of universities impart training in theater; as a result, many of these financially amateur troupes look amateur on stage in terms of production values too, even though they possess great enthusiasm.

The paradox right now is that although much theater plays to empty halls after the TV boom, corporate sponsorship has boosted big-name actors and directors, so that the gap between the theatrical haves and have-nots has grown. Since 1980, festivals have multiplied both inside and outside India. Positively speaking, this trend has given considerable exposure to regional theaters elsewhere. Negatively, however, it seems that more or less the same faces and companies receive the benefits of such festival largesse. Industry funding has its own ironies, as when a multinational cigarette manufacturer hosts an avowedly left-wing theater outfit, which appears not to understand the built-in contradiction. Besides, the fact that mercantile patrons need guaranteed advertising mileage translates into support for big-name extravaganzas once again: a vicious circle. Small-group theater, Third Theater, or folk

and traditional genres continue to barely survive on the fringe, inade-
quately visible on the cultural stage.

As with Indian music, Indian theater has had a profound impact on
world theater in contemporary times. Directors of the stature of Jerzy
Grotowski and Peter Brook and many lesser mortals have turned to
India for both themes and techniques. Grotowski, for instance, applied
Kathakali in his actor-training methods and interpreted the classical
Sanskrit masterwork, *Sakuntala*. Brook uses yoga and dramatized the
ancient epic *Mahabharata*, which some commentators have termed the
theater event of the twentieth century. Apart from foreign artists inter-
facing with Indian theater, interculturalism has other features too:
Indian groups now tour internationally (sometimes playing to the large
Indian diaspora), and directors stage Indian texts abroad with foreign
casts. The globalization of the Indian artist has come to stay.

■ Notes

1. Sahitya Akademi has published the standard reference work on Indian
literatures, Datta 1987–1994.
2. For a fairly exhaustive and copiously illustrated catalogue, see Tuli
1997.
3. Walls of village huts serve as "canvas" in Madhubani, and cloth or
paper scrolls fill the same function in Patachitra.
4. Rabindranath Tagore (1861–1941), India's foremost twentieth-century
artistic personality, was a poet, novelist, dramatist, philosopher, educator,
painter, composer, choreographer, and actor. The extended Tagore family in
Calcutta occupied a central position in Indian culture for its significant contributions in every sphere.
5. *Patuya* means "*pat*-maker," a *pat* being a painting on paper.
6. Having made this qualification, however, one must praise the comprehensive and encyclopedic range of Das (1995), *A History of Indian Literature*. Two volumes have appeared, of which the second is relevant to postindependence literature.
7. Apart from the Sahitya Akademi publications already cited, the reader
interested in Indian literatures can look up George (1984–1985), *Comparative
Indian Literature*.
8. Hindi belongs to the Indo-Aryan family of languages, mothered by
Sanskrit, and Tamil is part of the unrelated Dravidian family.
9. See Rajadhyaksha and Willemen (1998), *Encyclopaedia of Indian
Cinema*, the most detailed compendium on the subject.
10. One recent controversial but best-selling song from a movie soundtrack, *Choli ke pichhe kya hai?,* means "What's behind the blouse?"
11. The centrality of the *Mahabharata* in Indian cultural discourse even
now, for instance, forms the theme of *Vyasa's "Mahabharata,"* edited by P. Lal

(1992). This compilation contains analyses of the teleserial and excerpts from its screenplay, discussions of Peter Brook's stage and film versions, and literary pieces inspired by the epic.

12. The checklist of *Fellows and Awardees* (1998) published by Sangeet Natak Akademi, India's national academy of performing arts, gives an indication of eminent individuals in different fields of music, dance, and theater over the past fifty years.

13. For a collection of critical essays on current debates in Indian music and dance, see Mukherjee and Kothari 1995.

14. The most reliable and readable guide in English to Karnatak music is Pesch 1999.

15. For an account of the influence of Indian music on and its interaction with rock and jazz, see my chapter, "Rock and Raga: The Indo-West Music Interface" (Lal 1995).

16. See Vatsyayan 1968 and Raghavan 1975.

17. Hence, in an anthology of essays I coedited on the subject, I commissioned scholars from each linguistic region to write on their respective regional theaters: see Dasgupta and Lal 1995.

18. For example, despite the title of Jacob's 1989 collection, *Contemporary Indian Theatre*, all the dramatists and directors included in it are urban. Nevertheless, this book, mainly comprising interviews, contains valuable primary material.

■ Bibliography

Das, Sisir Kumar. 1995. *A History of Indian Literature*. New Delhi: Sahitya Akademi.

Dasgupta, Chidananda, and Ananda Lal, eds. 1995. *Rasa: The Indian Performing Arts in the Last Twenty-five Years*. Vol. 2, *Theatre and Cinema*. Calcutta: Anamika Kala Sangam.

Datta, Amaresh, ed. 1987–1994. *Encyclopaedia of Indian Literature*. 6 vols. New Delhi: Sahitya Akademi.

Fellows and Awardees: 1952–97. 1998. New Delhi: Sangeet Natak Akademi.

George, K. M., ed. 1984–1985. *Comparative Indian Literature*. 2 vols. Madras: Macmillan.

Jacob, Paul, ed. 1989. *Contemporary Indian Theatre*. New Delhi: Sangeet Natak Akademi.

Lal, Ananda. 1995. "Rock and Raga: The Indo-West Music Interface." In *Rasa: The Indian Performing Arts in the Last Twenty-five Years*, Vol. 1, *Music and Dance*, Bimal Mukherjee and Sunil Kothari, eds. Calcutta: Anamika Kala Sangam.

Lal, P., ed. 1992. *Vyasa's "Mahabharata": Creative Insights*. Calcutta: Writers Workshop.

Mukherjee, Bimal, and Sunil Kothari, eds. 1995. *Rasa: The Indian Performing Arts in the Last Twenty-five Years*. Vol. 1, *Music and Dance*. Calcutta: Anamika Kala Sangam.

Pesch, Ludwig. 1999. *The Illustrated Companion to South Indian Classical Music.* New Delhi: Oxford University Press.

Raghavan, V. 1975. *The Number of Rasas.* 3rd ed. Madras: Adyar Library.

Rajadhyaksha, Ashish, and Paul Willemen. 1998. *Encyclopaedia of Indian Cinema.* 2nd ed. New Delhi: Oxford University Press.

Rushdie, Salman. 1997. "Damn, This Is the Oriental Scene for You!" *The New Yorker,* June 23–30, pp. 50–61.

Tuli, Neville. 1997. *The Flamed-Mosaic: Indian Contemporary Painting.* Ahmadabad: Heart-Mapin.

Vatsyayan, Kapila. 1968. *Classical Indian Dance in Literature and the Arts.* New Delhi: Sangeet Natak Akademi.

Trends and Prospects

Sumit Ganguly and Neil DeVotta

The previous chapters have it made amply clear that India has over-come severe odds since its independence in 1947. The country will face numerous opportunities and constraints as it moves into the twenty-first century and solidifies its position as a major power on the global stage, and this chapter is an attempt to divine what those oppor-tunities and constraints are likely to be. There is little doubt that India will play a major role militarily, politically, economically, and diplo-matically in the decades ahead. Indeed, with the country having jetti-soned its vaunted nonaligned policy, one might say that India is des-tined to pursue a more important role in international affairs. This noted, the problems that have plagued India since independence (i.e., accommodating and pacifying the diverse religious and regional com-munities, negotiating changing political dynamics, stemming environ-mental and population pressures, forging a more equitable society, and dealing with the threats to its territorial integrity) will continue to chal-lenge the country and determine domestic stability and its international influence in the decades ahead.

At the domestic level, India and its more than 1 billion people will have to determine whether to continue along the secular path their founding fathers envisioned or to allow ethnonationalist sentiments to undermine that secularism. The vast majority of Indians have justifi-ably taken great pride in their secular state, and the policies Mohandas Gandhi and Jawaharlal Nehru advocated certainly solidified such secu-larism. This legacy, however, has been challenged by Hindu nationalists, who demand that all Indians, including the country's Muslims and Christians, subscribe to a culturally Hindu ethos. The demagoguery these forces have unleashed has legitimized anti-Muslim and anti-Christian violence and, not surprisingly, undermined minority confidence in the state. The fact that the governing Bharatiya Janata Party (BJP) was at the forefront in advocating *Hindutva* (Hinduness) on its way to becoming a national party has only aggravated the minorities' concerns. By rioting against movies that are perceived as antithetical to Hindu ideals, protesting against foreign companies and practices that are likewise seen to undermine Hindu identity, demanding that certain Muslim preferences that were incorporated into the constitution be discarded, and sanctioning violence against Christian missionaries and their congregations, these extremist Hindu forces threaten the tolerance and conciliation that India's founding fathers worked hard to institute. For example, in 2001 Hindu extremists ran amuck destroying Valentine's Day products in Bombay, claiming that this western practice promoted unhealthy romantic tendencies among the impressionistic youth and was contrary to fundamental Hindu norms. A rumor claiming that McDonald's restaurants cooked their french fries in beef fat, a sacrilege to Hindus, who eschew beef products, likewise led to major protests. It is clear that Hindu fanatics grasp at every opportunity to create mayhem and thereby manipulate the country's political processes, and there is no denying that the communalism they have consequently advocated is greatly responsible for some of the anti-Muslim rioting and anti-Christian violence that have taken place in the recent past. How India's governing elites tame such extremism and instead encourage multireligious and multicultural tolerance will be important, not only for the country's stability but also for its international reputation as a major player on the global stage.

With regard to the political arena, gone are the days when the Congress Party dominated the Indian political scene as a single, nearly indispensable entity. Most India specialists now agree that the current milieu that has seen regional parties dominating politics will continue to make India a more federated polity. There are two fundamental reasons for this prognosis. The first is the belief that the present and future political dynamics are unlikely to see any single party dominate the national scene as the Congress Party did under Nehru. The second has to do with the fact that economic gains in a free market are better achieved when power has been transferred from the center to state entities. Consequently, national parties like the Congress and the BJP now seek election in most states as part of a coalition with regional parties.

If this trend has made regional parties more influential, it has also led to rather unstable coalition governments at the national level. Thus, India's last election, in September and October 1999, saw the BJP come to power leading a twenty-four-party coalition called the National Democratic Alliance (NDA). Being forced to govern by relying on twenty-three other regional entities has no doubt tamed the BJP's communalist rhetoric, though the party must be given credit for maintaining this complicated alliance. Indeed, the NDA is likely to be the model by which India will continue to be governed in the foreseeable future. The difficulties and tensions that inevitably arise from such coalition governments are balanced by the more democratic nature of the entire process: the more that regional entities call the shots at the national level, the more effectively they can prevent a prime minister from ruling in a roughshod manner; and the more influence that regional entities command at the center, the more likely that they will be willing to settle disputes through dialogue as opposed to destabilizing tactics.

In the main, settling disputes between the states and the center through political rather than violent means is now a well-instituted practice in India. It is partly due to successive governments' willingness to accommodate rebellious groups into the democratic mainstream, even while making it clear that any attempt to weaken or dismember the Indian union would be met with extraordinary force. The Indians have consequently shown that even intractable ethnic minorities can be coaxed into participating within a democratic polity, provided that serious attempts are made to accommodate them. This policy will continue, despite some questioning of its viability in Kashmir, where Islamic fundamentalists are determined to merge India-administered Kashmir with Pakistan, and in the northeast, where certain leftist groups seek separation from the Indian union. The Indian state's success at co-opting and coercing rebellious groups into the democratic process must be viewed as a significant achievement for its democracy. And as far as that goes, there can be no doubt that India's democracy will survive. Indeed, a strong and independent electoral commission that brooks no nonsense when it comes to holding free and fair elections, a judiciary that is now showing increasing independence and assertiveness, and an electorate that consistently has voted to replace parties at both the state and national levels clearly indicate that India's democracy is only likely to grow stronger.

Though Indians can take genuine pride in having created a consolidated democracy, ensuring equitable growth across that democracy remains a major challenge. Currently, India's southern states—Karnataka, Kerala, Tamil Nadu, and Andhra Pradesh—enjoy higher literacy rates and per capita incomes than most of their northern counterparts. The innovative strategies adopted by these states' elites, higher English-language standards, and the determination to ride the information technology wave have led to growing disparities between them and such northern states as Uttar Pradesh, Madhya Pradesh, and Bihar. For example, Bihar continues to wallow in caste politics and violence, so that even Indians are loath to invest within its boundaries, whereas Karnataka and Andhra Pradesh cater to U.S. and British companies seeking software programmers and call centers that advise and assist international customers. As the disparity between states such as Bihar and Karnataka increases, so will tensions stemming from resource allocation and decisionmaking at the national level, for a country that is relatively uniformly developed will most likely benefit collectively from economic decisions made at the center, but a country that is disproportionately developed will experience varied gains and losses. That not only makes fashioning policy in an exceedingly politicized arena more complicated, but it also facilitates stereotyping along caste, ethnic, and regional lines; contributes to jealousy and envy; and undermines national unity. Avoiding such dissension requires that the government somehow boost economic growth across the country. With 300 million Indians living in abject poverty, however, that is easier said than done.

Such poverty coupled with the country's growing population will also test India's resolve to move from a developing to a middle-income country. When campaigning for India's independence, Gandhi loved to quip that the British in India would drown if all Indians spat in unison. It is India's increasing population, however, that is likely to drown the socioeconomic gains that the country has thus far made and will continue to make over the next few decades—unless well-coordinated programs dealing with population and environmental control are instituted across the country. Other countries' experiences show that an increase in per capita income and education promotes slower population growth. Southern India's experience suggests that to be the case as well. Consequently, there is no reason why the gains the south has made cannot be replicated throughout the union. Doing so, however, would require immense investment by both central and state authorities. The Indian government, like all governments, constantly struggles to allocate resources to various programs. Inevitably, most funds are allocated based on political calculations geared toward immediate political gain. Given that protecting the environment and curbing the country's population growth do not command the same urgency as do the numerous mundane concerns facing many poverty-stricken electorates, successive governments have conveniently avoided seriously dealing with such issues. It is, however, imperative that the Indian government realize that the longer it postpones reversing the current population and economic forecasts, the more money the country will ultimately have to spend to manage the problem. The country will no doubt require major assistance from external donors if it is effectively to curb population growth and pollution. That noted, India in general and the northern regions in particular will first need to show a willingness to tackle these issues; and the country's degree of success in doing so will be significant in determining its future stability and viability.

In the global trading arena, the combination of multinational corporations seeking Indian markets and India's own economic reforms make it clear that the country will slowly but surely play a significant role. Some Indian software development companies have already led the way in proving that Indians can compete at the highest levels. Indeed, given the economic reforms that have already taken place in India, it will be difficult, if not impossible, for India to withdraw from its growing involvement in the world economy. Although India's contribution to world trade still remains relatively miniscule, the country has joined various trading regimes and clearly indicated its desire to participate within a global free market economy. This seriousness is evident, given that even a nationalist party like the BJP has sought to further the country's multilateral trading relationships. Nehruvian socialism, which was responsible for some spectacular successes, has no doubt created numerous pressure groups that are averse to embracing the new economic realities. Yet, the post–Cold War trading regime and India's own expanding and ambitious agenda will ensure that the country with the world's largest middle class (which some claim numbers more than 150 million people) plays a significant role in the global economy.

Despite the ongoing violence in Kashmir, India today remains more secure and more confident regarding its place in the world than was the case during its first twenty-five years as an independent country. India is already viewed as a regional superpower in South Asia, and the country's space program, nuclear capability, and domestic military production guarantee that it will also become a significant military power on the world stage in the near future. An increasingly unstable Pakistan and the Islamic fundamentalist influence stemming from Afghanistan and the central Asian republics will likely see India draw closer to the United States, even as it attempts to maintain stable relations with China. China, with the predominantly Muslim population in its Xinjiang province having ties to Islamic fundamentalists in Afghanistan, is now concerned about serious fissures developing within its territory, and it will consequently share common concerns with India, even as both compete on various issues and eye each other as regional rivals. Thus, for example, while India complains that cheap Chinese goods get dumped in its markets, trade between the two countries has gradually inched upward, and both seek an optimum opportunity to negotiate their disputed borders. At the same time, with the United States viewing China as a potential military competitor over the long run, there is ample opportunity for the world's most influential democracy and the world's largest democracy to develop binding ties. India's commitment to market reforms should also encourage closer India-U.S. ties.

Pakistan remains India's nemesis, and that is unlikely to change in the near future, especially since no Pakistani regime can command the people's support without demanding that India-administered Kashmir be merged with Pakistan, even as no Indian government can relinquish Kashmir for fear that it would create a precedent for dismembering the Indian union. This dilemma also means that the ongoing carnage in Kashmir will continue and that developments in that region may actually get worse before any settlement is reached.

Within the United Nations, a revamped Security Council may welcome India as a permanent member. Should this occur, India's diplomatic stock in the global community will attain new heights. India was a major voice for the nonaligned movement in the 1950s, 1960s, and 1970s, and the country currently contributes soldiers to a number of UN peacekeeping missions; it is well respected within the diplomatic community for both its democracy and its diplomatic finesse. There is little doubt that India's influence within the various international forums will only increase as it grows stronger economically and militarily. Indeed, there is ample reason to believe that if current trends hold and India is able to deal with its population and environmental pressures, the country and its teeming millions have every right to be optimistic.

Glossary

arya: "noble," related to the ancient Aryan migrants into India

bhakti: Hindu mysticism; complete devotion to a particular deity

caste: an endogamous status group, usually associated with an occupational category, occupying a specific position in a social hierarchy

communalism: creation of exclusionary communities based on ethnicity or religion

Dalits: members of the lowest caste (formerly known as Harijan or Untouchables)

Delhi Sultanate: 1206–1526

doctrine of lapse: a policy under which the British assumed direct control over native territory if local rulers were guilty of "misrule" or if they had no legitimate heir

dyarchy: an arrangement in which areas such as education, health, and agriculture became the responsibility of provincial legislatures, in which Indians had greater participation, while such important issues as revenue and law enforcement were reserved for the central British authority gross domestic product: the total dollar value of all goods and services produced in a country

gross national product: the total dollar value of all goods and services produced by a country's population within and without its borders. The measure was used for U.S. production between 1941 and 1991 until it was replaced by GDP.

Gupta Empire: 320 C.E. to ca. 497 C.E.

Harijan: literally, "children of God"; Mohandas Gandhi's term for Untouchables

Hinduism: "Hindu" was the term used by Persians for the people of the Indian subcontinent. "Hinduism" later came to be used by outsiders for the varied religious beliefs of the majority of the people.

Hyderabadi Treaty: laid the standards for all future agreements between the British and other South Asian rulers. Treaty stated that (1) Hyderabad would finance British-controlled military force for internal and external security purposes; (2) failure to make payments would result in lapse of territory to Britain; (3) all foreign affairs would be handled by the East India Company.

Islam: literally, "submission" (to God) in Arabic. Refers to the religion founded by the Prophet Muhammad.

Jain: an adherent of a very ancient Indian religious sect dating from at least the sixth century B.C.E. that stresses extreme nonviolence and asceticism. Jains became famous as bankers and merchants because these professions were regarded as nonviolent.

jajmani relations: relations of groups within the caste system

jati: subcaste

jhuggi: temporary structures made of mud, thatch, plastic, and other discarded objects

khalsa: "the pure," the order instituted for Sikhs by their guru, Gobind Singh, about 1699, that requires its members to identify themselves to both friends and enemies as true Sikhs, devoted to the protection of the faith, by always having five symbols. These were: leaving their beards and hair uncut, carrying a comb, wearing a sword, wearing a steel bracelet, and wearing knee-length shorts. Originally, the *khalsa* was a military group, under strict discipline.

Lok Sahba: "House of the People"; the popularly elected lower house of the Indian Parliament

Maratha Empire: 1600s–1818

Mauryan Empire: last decades of the 300s B.C.E. to 185 B.C.E.

nawab: a person (usually British) who became wealthy in India

Other Backward Castes: an open-ended category of affirmative action to accommodate those belonging to the Shudra *varna,* or lowest caste

panchayat: "council of five" village elders responsible for village governance

panchayati raj: a three-tier model of local government instituted by the central government in 1959

partition: the division of the subcontinent into India and Pakistan in 1947

Rajya Sabha: "Council of the States"; the upper house of the Indian Parliament, whose members are mostly elected by state legislatures, or Vidhan Sabhas

Rowlatt Acts: legislation that allowed the British to hold Indians without trial, 1919

sati: the burning of widows on the funeral pyres of their dead husbands

Scheduled Castes: term used to denote Dalits after untouchability was abolished by Indian Constitution

shuddhi: a movement aimed at reclaiming Hindus who had converted to Islam

Sikh: an adherent of the religious community that originated with Nanak (1469–1539) in Punjab, India, who preached a message of devotion to the divine name and of obedience to his teaching and his successors, known as "gurus." Their followers became famous as warriors, farmers, and entrepreneurs.

Sufi: a Muslim mystic

swadeshi: a boycott of goods manufactured in Britain and an emphasis on indigenous production

taluqs or *tehsils:* divisions of states, run by *taluqdar* or *tehsildar*

ulema: the Muslim religious scholarly community

Untouchables: a term previously used for Dalits

varnas: castes: Brahman, Kshatriya, Vaishya, and Shudra

Vedas, the: most ancient and most sacred collection of the religious texts regarded as of fundamental truth. In its narrower sense, *Veda* refers to the four collections, some of which may date from 1800 B.C.E. (the *Rig Veda, Sama Veda, Yajur Veda,* and *Atharva Veda*), but the term *Vedic literature* is used for an immense body of writings that trace their origin to one of these texts.

Vidhan Sabhas: state legislatures

The Contributors

John Adams is visiting scholar at the University of Virginia and a consultant to the Asian Development Bank. He is former chair of economics and professor emeritus at the University of Maryland and Northeastern University. He has written extensively on economic development policies in South Asia. His books include *Corporate Governance in Nepal; India: The Search for Unity, Democracy, and Progress;* and *Pakistan: Exports, Politics, and Economic Development.*

Manu Bhagavan is assistant professor in the Department of History and Political Science at Manchester College. He has previously taught at Carleton and St. Olaf Colleges, the University of Texas at Austin, and Yale University. He has published a variety of articles and essays on South Asian history and is the author of *Sovereign Spheres: Princes, Education, and Empire in Colonial India* (forthcoming 2003).

Barbara Crossette taught journalism in India as a Fulbright visiting professor in 1980–1981 and was the *New York Times* correspondent for South Asia, based in New Delhi, 1988–1991. She is the author of *So Close to Heaven: The Vanishing Buddhist Kingdoms of the Himalayas, The Great Hill Stations of Asia,* and *India: Old Civilization in a New World.*

Neil DeVotta is visiting assistant professor of political science at James Madison College, Michigan State University. His articles have appeared in numerous journals, including the *Journal of Democracy*, *Pacific Affairs*, and *Commonwealth and Comparative Politics*.

Ashok K. Dutt is professor of geography, planning, and urban studies at the University of Akron. Though he specializes in urban geography and planning, his research interests also encompass cultural and medical geography. He has published in major journals of the world and has written several books including *The Asian City* and *Atlas of South Asia*: *Cultural Patterns of India.*

Ainslie T. Embree, professor emeritus of history at Columbia University, has served as chairman of the History Department, director of the Southern Asian Institute, and associate dean of the School of International and Public Affairs at Columbia. He has served as president of the American Institute of Indian Studies and of the Association of Asian Studies. From 1978 to 1980, he was counselor for cultural affairs at the U.S. Embassy in Delhi and from 1994 to 1995 he was special consultant to the U.S. ambassador. His books include *India's Search for National Identity, Imagining India: Essays on Indian History,* and *Utopias in Conflict: Religion and Nationalism in India.*

Sumit Ganguly is a professor of Asian studies and government at the University of Texas at Austin. His numerous publications include *The Crisis in Kashmir: Portents of War, Hopes of Peace* and *Conflict Unending: India-Pakistan Tensions Since 1947.*

Ananda Lal is professor of English at Jadavpur University, Calcutta, and a theater director. His works include *Rabindranath Tagore: Three Plays*, *The Voice of Rabindranath Tagore,* and *Shakespeare on the Calcutta Stage.* He is currently editing the *Oxford Companion to Indian Theatre.*

Pratap Bhanu Mehta is professor of philosophy and of law and governance, Jawaharlal Nehru University, New Delhi. He was previously associate professor of government and social studies at Harvard. He is widely published in political theory, intellectual history, and politics in India. His book *Facing Democracy* is forthcoming in 2003.

Vibha Pinglé is a governance fellow at the Institute of Development Studies in Sussex, UK, and is on leave from the University of Notre Dame, where she is an assistant professor of sociology. Her research has examined how institutions and identities shape development in India and Africa. Her recent work on India focuses on culture, democracy, and Dalit identity. Her recent publications include *Rethinking the Developmental State: India's Industry in Comparative Perspective.*

Shalendra D. Sharma is associate professor of political science at the University of San Francisco (USF). He is the author of *Democracy and Development in India,* which won the Choice Outstanding Academic Title for 1999, and editor of *Asia in the New Millennium: Geopolitics, Security and Foreign Policy.* His most recent book, *From Crisis, Reform and Recovery: A Political Economy of the Asian Financial Crisis and the New International Financial Architecture* is forthcoming in 2003. He was the recipient of USF's Distinguished Teaching Award in 1996–1997.

Holly Sims is associate professor at the School of Public Affairs at the State University of New York, Albany. She is also North American editor of *Public Adminstration and Development.* She is one of a few scholars with comparative research experience in both India and Pakistan.

Index

About the Book

Understanding Contemporary India is an interdisciplinary book designed for use both as a core text for "Introduction to India" and "Introduction to South Asia" courses and as a supplement in a variety of discipline-oriented curriculums.

There are few books for classroom use that introduce students to India as a whole rather than focusing on a specific discipline. *Understanding Contemporary India* fills this gap. The twelve authors, writing with clarity and precision, address a range of crucial issues facing India as it moves into the twenty-first century; there are chapters on history, politics, economics, international relations, the status of women, religion, caste, population growth and the environment, and the arts and popular culture. Each chapter provides an up-to-date—and engaging— description and analysis, along with bibliographies. Maps and photographs enhance the text.

Sumit Ganguly is a professor of Asian studies and government at the University of Texas at Austin. His numerous publications include *The Crisis in Kashmir: Portraits of War, Hopes of Peace* and *The Origins of War in South Asia*. **Neil DeVotta** is a visiting assistant professor of political science at James Madison College, Michigan State University.